JONATHAN DEWHURST

JONATHAN DEWHURST

The Lancashire Tragedian

Philip & Susan Taylor

To Candida
with our best wishes
Phil + Sue

The Book Guild Ltd
Sussex, England

Sept. 2006

First published in Great Britain in 2001 by
The Book Guild Ltd
25 High Street,
Lewes, East Sussex
BN7 2LU

Typesetting in Bembo by
Keyboard Services, Luton, Bedfordshire

Printed in Great Britain by
Bookcraft (Bath) Ltd, Avon

A catalogue record for this book is
available from The British Library

ISBN 1 85776 524 9

CONTENTS

LIST OF ILLUSTRATIONS

The authors are grateful to the following sources for their kind permission to reproduce the following illustrations:

Wigan Heritage Services, illustrations 1, 2, 4 and 16.

Manchester Central Library, Arts Library Theatre Collection, illustrations 6, 7, 9 and 10.

Birmingham Library Services Shakespeare Library, illustrations 11 and 17.

The V & A Picture Library, illustrations 14, 28 and 43.

The Illustrated London News Picture Library, jacket illustration and illustrations 15 and 26.

National Maritime Museum, London, illustration 20.

National Library of Australia, illustration 23.

The Raymond Mander and Joe Mitchenson Theatre Collection, illustration 51.

Illustration 54 was reproduced from Theatre World Magazine (May 1936) and illustration 55 from the Theatre World Annual No. 9.

The remaining items are from the authors' personal collection. They wish to apologise, however, if despite their efforts to trace sources from which permission for reproduction is required, they have been unable to obtain such permission.

FOREWORD

This book is an act of recovery and a glimpse of what might have been. It is also a combination of family and theatrical history. Philip Taylor is the great-great nephew of Jonathan Dewhurst, and the narrative records snippets of family 'memory', containing, as such memories do, a measure of hearsay beside a measure of probability. Most of all, though, it is the outcome of dogged research, fuelled by a personal quest. In whatever mysterious way, Jonathan Dewhurst is present in the authors, and they have been unravelling the mystery. Dewhurst is one among many actors, powerful in his time but until now lost in history. To that extent, he may be seen as representative of many nineteenth-century performers. But his story is also a very particular one. There was a point – and the authors are almost sure that they can identify it – when he might have grasped fame on the London stage. Their admission of uncertainties is one of the charms of this narrative. Why, then, did he return to his Lancashire roots, and comparative obscurity? He served for eighteen years as manager of the Theatre Royal in Leigh, before Rugby League on television alerted sports followers to the existence of such a place. Not many London managers lasted as long, but it is only recently that the achievements of provincial managers have begun to be widely recognised. And the extraordinary fact that emerges from Dewhurst's story is that this strenuous period of management was a coda to a glittering career that brought him into close contact with the Calverts, Irving, Adelaide Neilson and Wilson Barrett and included a star-billed tour of Australia and a homeward stopover in India, where he acted his favourite Shakespearian roles and was feted in Calcutta and Simla.

From what this book has taught me, I would suppose that Dewhurst's approach to character was in the Kemble-Macready line, rather than the roguish line of Edmund Kean, Irving and Beerbohm Tree. His Hamlet, Othello, Shylock and Macbeth were studied portraits, and he boasted always of the theatre's capacity to improve the manners and morals of its audience. Given some of the conditions in which he had to perform, though, he must have had a sense of humour and a healthy tolerance. And I like the gamut from grocer's assistant to Drury Lane star, to provincial manager, to landlord of the Royal Oak in Chorley. It has a satisfying completeness, though I doubt whether that would have been Dewhurst's own retrospect. There is the rawness of a scarred sensitivity in the man who emerges through this narrative. He knew what he might have been, and the knowledge hurt. That, at least, is how I read his discourse with *the local press*. I have italicised those last three words with a purpose. The prime subject of this book is certainly Jonathan Dewhurst, but the Taylors have depended on newspapers (from Wigan to Ballarat via London) in order to carry out their act of recovery. They have unearthed a peculiar (very peculiar!) talent in the dramatic critic of the *Sydney Bulletin*, but they have also given us enough quotations to furnish material for a study of the prose style of minor nineteenth-century dramatic criticism: so earnest, so florid, so school-of-George Eliot. We have a few (winsomely autobiographical for the most part) accounts of nineteenth-century provincial players, but Dewhurst was a star, and he is here placed in his firmament. The actor and his world (cotton, freemasonry and steamships): a social biography and a cautionary tale.

Peter Thomson
Professor of Drama
Exeter University

ACKNOWLEDGEMENTS

Inevitably, the production of a book such as this with all the attendant research could not be completed with any degree of success were it not for the help, support and encouragement of many people. We are delighted to express our gratitude to:

Tony Ashcroft, Local History Officer at Leigh Library. Were it not for his enthusiasm in showing us various papers from his archives, our work would never have started.

Professor Peter Thomson of Exeter University who throughout has given us unfailing support and guidance.

Many who have helped with our research, providing information, suggestions and material, notably:

Wendy Baker, Alex Bisset, Jennie Bisset, Nicholas Butler, Norman Fenner of the Richmond Theatre, John Foster, Dr Richard Foulkes of the Society for Theatre Research, Elaine Hart of the *Illustrated London News*, Mike and Kim Lewis, John Steward and the late Bert Worsley.

The ladies and gentlemen of the theatre whose reminiscences have helped to bring to life several of the characters in our story:

Colin Bean, Nicholas Brent, Wyn Calvin MBE, the late Raymond Graham, Peter Green, Patrick Macnee, Paul Scofield CH, Keith Short, Dame Dorothy Tutin, Veronica Twidle and Hubert Warren

We feel we must also make special mention of contributions, albeit unintended, from two long-departed gentlemen of the stage. We have found many newspaper references to Jonathan Dewhurst's acting, but the thoughts of the late Ben Iden Payne (quoted in Chapter 15) and 'an old actor' (Chapter 18) spoke of Dewhurst the man. They both touched us deeply.

Our thanks also to the staff of the following libraries and museums for their invaluable and friendly help with our constant enquiries:

Birmingham Central Library
The British Library
The British Library, Newspaper Library, Colindale
Bodleian Library, University of Oxford
Bolton Central Library
Brighton Library
Edinburgh Central Library
Leigh Library
Liverpool Central Library
Manchester Central Library
Mitchell Library, Glasgow
National Maritime Museum
Newcastle City Library
Norfolk Studies Library
Nottinghamshire Local Studies Library
Oldham Local Studies Library
Oxford Central Library
Redcar Reference Library
Sheffield Central Library
Southend Library
Stowmarket Library
The Theatre Museum
The Victoria and Albert Museum
West Yorkshire Archive Service, Bradford
Wigan Heritage Services

and Richard Mangan, Administrator, The Raymond Mander and Joe Mitchenson Theatre Collection

Australia:

Central Highlands Regional Library, Ballarat
John Oxley Library, State Library of Queensland, Brisbane
La Trobe Library, State Library of Victoria, Melbourne
Mitchell Library, State Library of New South Wales, Sydney
National Library of Australia, Canberra
Performing Arts Museum, Melbourne
The State Library of South Australia, Adelaide
The State Library of Tasmania, Hobart

Finally to Carol Biss and her colleagues at The Book Guild. Throughout our association with them we have been impressed by their professionalism and grateful for their enthusiasm. Without their considerable efforts our work would not have seen the light of day in this form.

INTRODUCTION

My great-great uncle was Jonathan Dewhurst and for most of my life all I knew about him was that he was an actor who, at the turn of the twentieth century, had managed the Theatre Royal in Leigh, an industrial town in Lancashire. Curiosity does not seem to have persuaded me to seek more information about Dewhurst until July 1993 when my wife, Susan, and I visited Leigh and, on impulse, visited the local library to see if Dewhurst figured in their archives. To our surprise we found that Tony Ashcroft, the Local History Officer, was keenly interested in the theatre and in Dewhurst, and was able to provide us with something that was to affect our lives significantly for some time to come – the report of an interview given by Dewhurst to the *Leigh Chronicle* in 1888, when he took over the local theatre. In this interview he gave a detailed résumé of his career and outlined his plans for the future. Within an hour we progressed from mild interest to a pitch of fevered excitement. This 'local actor' had proved to be a serious tragedian of substance, one who had shared the boards with some of the legends of the stage, who himself enjoyed an international career, and who ran his own 'powerful legitimate company'.

But despite his achievements, what is known of him today? Virtually nothing. A few – a very small few – achieved such prominence on the stage that their lives and careers are well-documented. Others remedied any possible omission by publishing their autobiographies. Some biographers have been assisted by copious correspondence or by their subjects being committed diarists, but over the vast majority of past generations of our actors the waters closed, leaving them virtually without trace. We knew then that we had to unearth as much information as possible about his life and career, and for over six years that is what we have done. This initially represented research into my family history, and our intention was to write Dewhurst's story in the form in which we would have wanted to read it if another member of the family had written it. It was somewhat later, when many words had been committed to print, that we thought – and hoped – that our book might have a wider relevance: the story of Jonathan Dewhurst set against the backdrop of the world in which he lived and the theatre which he loved and served so well. Our book is therefore a tribute to Jonathan Dewhurst and to all those other unsung heroes of the stage without whose contributions our theatrical heritage would be far less colourful.

Our research and the book have been a joint effort throughout, although there are occasional references to 'my' family where the context so requires. In 'searching for Dewhurst' we have inevitably become involved with what might be regarded as incidental detail, information which, while not directly relevant, helps our understanding of the times in which he pursued his career. Much of it is interesting in its own right and we have decided to include some of this detail. The text has no annotations although references are included where appropriate. A list of sources is given at the end.

PT

1

Jonathan – Family Background

Jonathan Dewhurst first saw the light of day on 28 April 1837, the year in which the young Queen Victoria acceded to the throne. He was the fourth child of John and Mary Dewhurst, a working-class couple living in Lancashire. John and Mary had both been born in Wigan – in 1790 and 1795 respectively. They had lived through the Napoleonic Wars and through some of the most dramatic changes Great Britain had seen. When they were born the Industrial Revolution had already started, and although agriculture was still the biggest single industry, they would have witnessed the substantial movement of workers from the country to the town to provide the labour force needed for the expansion of our major industries – coal, cotton, construction, mining and engineering.

Britain was the world's leading industrial nation, with an empire to match, and exuded confidence – at least on the surface. John and Mary would have been aware of the immense pride in national achievements in many different fields. They would have seen the success and profitability of industrialisation, but perhaps they would not have been so aware of the fears of the upper classes that the revolution and civil unrest experienced on the Continent might be repeated here. But why should such fears exist? Despite the overall prosperity, poverty was still the lot of the vast majority of the labouring poor. New and efficient working methods had depressed wages and increased unemployment. The workers were more aware of the prosperity that somehow continued to elude them and of the widening gulf between the 'haves' and the 'have nots'. They were becoming less inclined to accept the role that fate – or the upper classes – seemed to have designed for them. In rural and urban areas housing conditions were generally poor and many houses had no indoor sanitation, water tap or ventilation. The growth in population and its migration to the towns – unprecedented in any earlier age – compounded the problems. Cheap housing was supplied by jerry-builders to meet the needs of the incoming workers – or rather the needs of the industrialists – and, as little was spent on building, repairs or amenities, the slums of the future were created. Although rural slums could be as bad as those in the towns, the worst were in the cities. For the majority of working people there was little or no hope of improving their lot and it is hardly surprising that the upper and middle classes feared the ways in which natural resentment might manifest itself.

John, however, would have been more concerned that he was employed and that he, Mary and their children should be housed and fed. The evidence we have shows that despite the times through which he lived he was always in work, although he did not appear to remain long in any one job. He and Mary were married on 5 August 1828 at All Saints Church, Wigan, the Parish Church. Both John and his brother Jonathan (after whom, no doubt, 'our' Jonathan was named) were baptised and the family had at least nominal church connections. Although it is tempting to read into this some deeper religious conviction, it is more likely that it reflects the almost superstitious desire of most people that there should be religious involvement in their births, marriages and deaths. In a few years the Religious Census of 1851 would confirm what many feared – that the working class was largely absent from the churches and viewed them as middle-class institutions and rites-of-passage organisations. John was to a large extent fortunate to live in Wigan. Through the Industrial Revolution it had established itself as a forward-looking town of some importance.

The coal and cotton industries were at the forefront of industrial progress and Wigan, in common with several other Lancashire towns, had both. Not only did it produce coal, but iron as well with varied engineering and manufacturing businesses. It was at the centre of the Lancashire cotton industry, spinning the thread and weaving, with manufacture of clothing and the silk industry in support. A thriving town, typical of many which were to contribute to the coming mid-Victorian economic boom. But Wigan also enjoyed an excellent strategic position. It was on the main route from the industrial East Midlands to Cumbria and beyond, and was also on the east/west route between the towns on the foothills of the Pennines and the port of Liverpool.

This strategic importance ensured that Wigan figured prominently in the growth of the railway system and in 1838 Wallgate Station was built, with the lines of three major railway companies shortly to pass through the town. The trend was emphasised with the subsequent rise of Southport as a seaside resort, with Wigan the halfway stage between that town and the City of Manchester. With all this economic activity it is hardly surprising that work was available for those who were willing and able to do it. As with virtually all other urban areas, however, there was also much poverty.

John and Mary had been married previously and there were children from both earlier marriages. However, it is from the details of the births of John and Mary's children that a fascinating picture emerges of the varied working life of their father. At a time when unemployment was high he always managed to find work and showed a high degree of fortitude, resilience and imagination in keeping his family housed and fed. John was a provision dealer in Millgate, a street in the town centre, when their first son, John, was born on 9 September 1829. Young John was by all accounts a bright boy and by his mid-30s was the Chief Engineer at the Atlas Works of Sharp, Stewart & Co. in Manchester, a connection that was later to assume some importance in the life of Jonathan himself.

When their second child, Lucy, was born on 20 September 1831, John was described as a victualler of Wallgate in Wigan. Perhaps victualling did not provide enough excitement, for in 1833 when their third child, Henry, was born, John had become a police officer living again in Millgate. At this time the counties were not enabled by law to raise and equip police forces – that did not come about until 1839 – and it was not until 1856 that it was made obligatory. The provincial police force, such as it might have been, was in 1833 a purely parochial affair. In 1829, however, Robert Peel's Metropolitan Police Act had been passed, providing the basis for what was the start of proper policing in London, and although the populace did not wholeheartedly applaud this move, the criminal fraternity certainly found it an impediment to their activities, with the result that large numbers of them moved their business to the provinces, and provincial towns and cities found their crime rates rising rapidly. By 1837 it was estimated that in Liverpool, for example, one in 45 of the population were 'known bad characters', and in Newcastle the ratio increased to one in 27! In 1836 the good harvests previously enjoyed came to an end, unemployment reached new heights, and the population was larger than ever before. The year 1837 – in which Jonathan was born – marked the beginning of a five-year depression, which was probably the grimmest period in the nineteenth century.

By this time, a major change had occurred for the Dewhursts. The family had moved from Wigan to Lowton, a township some six miles from Wigan and rather nearer to the townships of Pennington, Westleigh and Bedford, which later amalgamated to form the town of Leigh. Jonathan was born in Stone Cross Lane, Lowton, and his father was described as a 'jail turnkey'. This presents us with something of a problem – there is no record of Lowton having a jail. Wigan certainly had one, but it was six miles away

– why move to Lowton if you still work in Wigan? So Wigan jail can probably be discounted. The 'Leigh' townships may have had a jail but the same objection arises, albeit to a lesser extent, although we have to remember that walking several miles to work was for many a normal requirement of being employed. There was a workhouse in Lowton, just round the corner from one end of Stone Cross Lane, and it is probable that John was employed there. The great fear of the working man was unemployment – through redundancy, sickness, injury and, ultimately, old age. Any work, however menial and badly paid, was preferable to the alternative – the workhouse and the pauper's funeral. Conditions in the jails had scarcely improved in 100 years and the workhouse (particularly under the system introduced in 1834 by the New Poor Law) was a place to be avoided at all costs.

However, in 1838 we know that John and his family were in the workhouse! In that year he moved back to Wigan, where he was appointed Governor of Wigan Workhouse in Frog Lane, with Mary as Matron. One of the qualifications for a man to be appointed as governor of a workhouse was that he was married, and that his wife would assume the duties of mistress or matron at the workhouse. They took with them three of their children, Lucy, Henry and Jonathan, and had to pay the workhouse authorities five shillings a week to support the children. John, the eldest child, by then nine years of age, is not mentioned and was presumably staying with relatives elsewhere. On 16 October 1839, their youngest child, Rebecca, my great-grandmother, was born. For almost six years the family stayed at Wigan Workhouse. The 1841 Census shows that on 6 June that year there were 17 people living there – seven adults, including John and Mary Dewhurst, with Mary's daughter Ann Weedall who lived there as a servant, and 10 children including the four young Dewhurst children.

But then in 1844 came the Great Workhouse Scandal. The minutes of the Workhouse Committee record that:

'On Sunday 14th April 1844 one of the inmates, Nicholas McKnight, aged 72, was attacked by paralysis and lost the use of one side of his body. Although Mr Dewhurst knew the man was seriously ill, he did not send for the Medical Officer or a clergyman until Tuesday afternoon when required by McKnight's daughter and on the 18th April refused admission to McKnight's sister and daughter. McKnight died on 22nd April. Mr Dewhurst's conduct towards McKnight was questionable and he was culpable for not calling the Medical Officer sooner. Mr Dewhurst was severely reprimanded and was dismissed on 7th June 1844.'

4

With the aim of keeping able-bodied men of working age in work, and therefore self-supporting, the authorities aimed to make life in the workhouse a particularly unattractive option. Thus the needs of others living there – the old, the children and the infirm – were frequently overlooked. John Dewhurst's apparent lack of concern for McKnight seems to be an example of this indifference. On 11 August 1854 the *Wigan Examiner* reported a proposal that a new workhouse should be built, as the old workhouse 'was not a workhouse properly speaking but a mere asylum and [the writer] did not think it fit even for an asylum'. The old workhouse was eventually demolished and rebuilt in 1857. Presumably, for those in charge, life in the workhouse would be more tolerable and Jonathan at least appears to have developed a very robust attitude towards it. In later life he often joked about being brought up in the workhouse.

John Dewhurst seemed to face his misfortune with his usual resilience. The family remained in Wigan and in 1855 John was again a provision dealer. However, in the next four years they moved back to Lowton, where, in his late 60s, he became innkeeper at the Hare and Hounds in Stone Cross Lane. It is interesting to note that only some seven years ago the interior of the Hare and Hounds was modernised and the original flagstone floor replaced. When the work was being carried out, two original wells were

1   The Hare and Hounds at Lowton. John Dewhurst was the publican here from the late 1850s to the mid-1860s.

discovered within the structure of the inn, which would have been in use when the Dewhurst family lived there. To some extent the move to Lowton was auspicious, for it was there that both Jonathan and Rebecca met their future spouses. The last reference we have to Mary is in 1861, when at the date of the Census she was visiting her widowed son Thomas and his family in Wigan. In 1878, at the age of 88, John Dewhurst had at last retired, being then described as 'a gentleman'. Lucy became a nurse and in 1851 was living with her step-sister Mary and her husband Richard Greenleas (a tea dealer and grocer) in Market Place, Wigan. In 1855 she married Richard Smith, a boiler maker, and their son James reappears in the story some 43 years later as the business manager of the Theatre Royal in Leigh, when Jonathan is lessee and manager. Of Henry nothing more is heard.

The 1830s, '40s and '50s were decades of great change, with magnificent technical achievements, though at the cost of considerable economic and social upheaval. People moved geographically, they changed occupations, the occupations themselves changed, there was increased acquisition of property and some amassed great wealth. There were also significant religious and cultural changes. As in any developing society there were myriad movements and pressure groups aimed at radical and social reform, among them the Chartists, the Anti-Poor Law Movement, the Anti-Corn Law League, the Trade Union Movement, the Friendly Benefit Societies, the Cooperative Movement and the Temperance Movement. But despite the strong impetus for reforms, after 1830 there were still far more people who endorsed (through satisfaction or apathy?) the institutions and values of the status quo. And thereby stability and law and order were maintained.

2

Jonathan – Early Life

If indeed 'the child is father of the man', what does the fuller figure of later years add to our knowledge of the boy Jonathan? He was physically robust and intelligent, with a strong feeling for the English language. He had a phenomenal memory and a strong liking for the theatre. Where this came from it is hard to say, as neither of his parents appears to have had any cultural leanings, and in those days 'the stage' was something to be frowned upon rather than encouraged. Jonathan Dewhurst seems without doubt to have been a man of strong principles and one who sought to achieve and present high standards in everything he did.

The family, at least nominally, was Anglican, but it does not seem that Jonathan's regard for principle included a very strong religious attachment. He was baptised in the Anglican church and married, firstly in the Roman Catholic church, secondly in the Anglican church and, thirdly, in a register office. As a child there was always a roof over his head and his father was rarely, if ever, out of work. In later life he referred to his happy childhood (for the first seven years of which he lived at the workhouse) and while this may reflect the roseate hue bestowed by the passage of time, it may more credibly reflect the resilience and strength of character that was much in evidence in his maturity.

For the lower-middle and working classes – the major part of the population – educational provision was inadequate, but it was starting to improve. There were private day schools, which in the main offered poor instruction for a few pence a week, Sunday schools, which offered religious education and occasionally basic instruction in other subjects. They were, however, handicapped by the part-time basis of their operation. Following the 1833 Factory Act, there were also the schools which the factories were required to provide. Few working-class children remained in education beyond the age of ten, and many attended school for only two or three years. Facilities were limited and, as a consequence, educational aspirations for the vast majority remained low. However, in 1833 the Government provided a small grant (initially £20,000 per annum) for the two voluntary religious school societies, which assisted in the building of a network of elementary schools across the country. Thus a system of public elementary education was established.

We have no record of the schools attended by his brothers and sisters, but Jonathan left some detail of his own schooling. His first school was a 'Miss Cartwright's', a Dame School at Mab's Cross on the northern edge of the town. From the workhouse, his journey – some one and a half miles – would take him down Frog Lane, under the railway bridge, alongside the rectory, then either (in bad weather) down Hallgate Street to the Market Place and along Standishgate to Mab's Cross, or (in good weather) along the edge of the Mesnes (open fields, now Mesnes Park), joining Standishgate nearer to Mab's Cross. One of his young schoolfellows at Miss Cartwright's

2 Mab's Cross, Standishgate, Wigan, along which the young Jonathan walked to his first school.

was C.B. Holmes, who later became an alderman of Wigan and was referred to as 'that doyen of legislators'. Before long, however, it was decided that Jonathan's talents were not being sufficiently stretched at Miss Cartwright's and he was moved to Mr Spry's school in Rodney Street in the centre of Wigan – a 'school of more academic pretensions'. We can only surmise that at Mr Spry's the love of literature, drama and, in particular, Shakespeare, was first nurtured. It was while he was at this school that he made his first stage appearance, aged eight, at the old Theatre Royal in Wigan. Alas, we have no details of the production or of young Jonathan's part in it. Was the introduction to the theatre the work of Mr Spry? Did he perhaps recognise in Jonathan the early signs of his later talent? Certainly this appearance on the stage made its mark on the boy and, possibly for the first time, his imagination was swept aloft by the romance of the theatre. Perhaps this initial, wonderful experience sowed in him the seeds that would ultimately flourish so proudly. He had breathed the theatre, it was now in his blood, and he would not be satisfied until he made it his life.

Jonathan referred later to completing his education in Manchester, but he makes no mention of the school. Why is this, when he specifically mentions Miss Cartwright's and Mr Spry's and, being a proud man, surely he would have named the grammar school in Manchester if indeed he attended one? But there were also grammar schools in Wigan – why did he not attend a local school? Although it is perhaps unthinkable that a boy of his abilities did not attend a grammar school, we have to remember that the educational system reflected the class system – for the aristocracy, gentry and wealthy middle class there were the public schools, and for most of the rest of the middle class there were the grammar schools. There were also private academies, where standards varied considerably, and the mechanics' institutes, which had originally existed to offer science to artisans. They were open to all and offered a wide range of educational and even cultural studies, with a strong appeal to the young person from the lower-middle class home who sought self-improvement. The possible answer to our question is that Jonathan went to live with his brother, John, in Manchester and attended a mechanics' institute.

Jonathan found it difficult to decide on a career, but his interest in language and words appears to have prompted him to try journalism, for, on leaving school in 1852 at the age of 15, he went to work in the editorial offices of the *Leigh Chronicle* which had been founded that year, having progressed to that august title from the smaller monthly *Leigh Advertiser*. How long he worked there is not known, but within the next few years he left and returned to Manchester to live again with his brother John, and to work at the Atlas Works of the engineering company Sharp, Stewart & Co., of which John was then Chief Engineer.

Engineers and mechanics were the elite of the Industrial Revolution. The industrialists – the owners – relied on them totally, for they were the ones who ensured that the machines, and hence the factories, were able to function. They were better paid and generally more intelligent than other workers and were noted for taking a lead in educational movements. Sharp, Stewart & Co. was a product of the Industrial Revolution and, historically, its engineering base was the manufacture of machine tools and equipment for the textile industry. With the growth of the railways it switched to the manufacture of railway locomotives and was established in 1833 under its present name, moving to the Atlas Works in 1843. By the end of the century it had moved to Glasgow and had amalgamated with two other companies to form the North British Locomotive Co. John was elected a member of the Institution of Mechanical Engineers in 1864, indicating that he was recognised as a significant member of his profession and, in the next few years, he held a succession of important positions in engineering companies in Lancashire and Yorkshire.

Jonathan however was not destined to become an engineer, but his stay in Manchester – or at least one event during his stay – was to have a profound effect on him and on the rest of his life. His brother John took him to the Theatre Royal and there he saw the renowned actor Barry Sullivan. Barry Sullivan (1821–91) was an Irish actor and a Shakespearian of the old school. His acting has been described as majestic, flamboyant and passionate, and Sullivan needed only the boards from which he would seize the part and the audience by the throat. Subtlety was not his forte – his vigorous and dynamic delivery was far removed from the more contemplative style of acting that was soon to become fashionable. His London debut was as Hamlet at the Haymarket in 1853, but he was not a great success in London where the more sophisticated audiences were looking for something more refined. Sullivan, however, was idolised by George Bernard Shaw and in the provinces, where he kept alive the old traditions of Shakespearian acting.

His style was well-suited to tragedy rather than comedy or romance, which he seldom played. He toured America and Australia and in 1879 appeared as Benedick to Helen Faucit's Beatrice in *Much Ado About Nothing* in the inaugural performance at the first Shakespeare Memorial Theatre in Stratford-Upon-Avon. Jonathan may well have made frequent visits to the theatre with John, but he had never seen anything like Sullivan. The Royal in Manchester was a far cry from Wigan and at that moment Jonathan knew without any shadow of doubt where his future lay. It would however be a

MR BARRY SULLIVAN AS HAMLET.

HAMLET. "Slanders, sir: for the satirical rogue says here, that old men have grey beards; that their faces are wrinkled; their eyes purging thick amber and plum tree gum; and that they have a plentiful lack of wit, together with most weak hams. All of which, sir, though I most powerfully and potently believe, yet I hold it not honesty to have it thus set down; for you yourself, sir, should be as old as I am, if, like a crab, you could go backward." *HAMLET* *Act 2, Sc 2.*

Engraved by J. Moore, from a Daguerreotype by Mayall.

JOHN TALLIS & COMPANY, LONDON & NEW YORK.

3　It was seeing Barry Sullivan in Manchester that inspired Jonathan to choose the stage as his career.

few years before his stage career began – and before that he was to leave engineering and become a grocer's assistant! The grocer's shop occupied a corner site on the western side of Market Street, Leigh, subsequently occupied by a Mr Thomas Danby (a grocer and draper) and later demolished as part of the present town hall development.

Many years later Jonathan commented that 'when studying for the stage' he followed the trade of grocer's assistant. What did 'studying for the stage' entail? Certainly not attending drama school. At the time he was well-versed in Shakespeare's plays, an accomplished reciter with a prodigious memory and a vast repertoire of poetic offerings. Perhaps it involved reading, learning and attending the theatre whenever possible. In 1863 a temporary booth for drama had been erected in Leigh by a Mr Wardhaugh on the site where the Sems (Assembly Rooms) subsequently stood, and this was just round the corner from the grocer's shop. There was also in Leigh one of the oldest dramatic societies in the country – the St Joseph's Players. Basically an amateur society, they included from time to time professional actors. The Players presented their first major play *Fabiola* at the old town hall in Leigh in 1860, the same year that the new St Joseph's Church was built, enabling the society to use the old church as their theatre. As the only players for miles around, St Joseph's attracted people from the surrounding villages. Dewhurst attended their early productions as part of his 'theatrical exposure' and may well have taken part in some productions, although there is no record that this was the case. What is recorded is that some years later:

'A well-known visitor to the old chapel was the famous Shakespearean actor Jonathan Dewhurst, who prompted various members to form a Shakespearean group.'

While earning a living in more mundane ways, Dewhurst took the opportunity whenever possible to appear before the public, and his sense of drama, excellent memory and clear diction found their outlet in poetic recitations. He travelled throughout Lancashire to give these entertainments, which were always well-received and for which he acquired a growing reputation. Reciting poetry was something he enjoyed very much, and something which he would continue to do for the rest of his life.

But life for Jonathan did not consist solely of studying for the stage or assisting the grocer. He had met a young lady, Margaret Mary Taylor, a dressmaker from Lowton, and there was a strong mutual attraction. What made it all the more satisfactory was that Jonathan's sister, Rebecca, was courting Joseph Taylor, Margaret's brother, who by trade was a cobbler. Did Jonathan's

4 The shops in Market Square, Leigh, which were demolished to make way for the new Town Hall at the turn of the century. The left-hand corner shop was occupied by the grocer for whom Jonathan worked before starting his stage career.

romantic leanings towards the stage come to the fore in his personal life? Was he the romantic lover in real life – a Romeo to Margaret Taylor's Juliet? He was a good-looking young man – talkative, enthusiastic and good company – and perhaps we may be forgiven for making the assumption that he swept young Margaret off her feet. Romance bloomed and on the 13 August 1859 Jonathan, aged 22, and Margaret, aged 20, were married at St Patrick's, a Roman Catholic church in Wigan. At this time his father John was keeping the Hare and Hounds in Lowton, and Margaret's father is shown on their marriage certificate as William Taylor (deceased), a provision dealer. The witnesses were my great-grandparents, Joseph Taylor and Rebecca Dewhurst, who were themselves married on 5 September 1861.

Margaret Mary had married a grocer with theatrical ambitions. Did she take them seriously or did she think, 'Yes, all very well, but one day with a bit of luck we'll be running our own grocer's shop'? As the years went by she no doubt decided that the stage was but one of Jonathan's romantic and fanciful ideas, for six years of their married life were to elapse before their lives changed – dramatically. What had their life together been like? We have no record of any children, and presumably Margaret continued with her

13

5   Rebecca (Jonathan's sister) with her husband, Joseph Taylor, and two of their daughters, Edith and Ada.

dressmaking. Despite his mundane job as a grocer's assistant, was Jonathan still the life and soul of the party, the family favourite? Certainly nothing before or since indicates that circumstances subdued him for very long. No doubt he still dreamed – and studied for the stage – and perhaps those dreams, those optimistic, confident day-dreams helped him through the daily monotonous routine of the shop. We don't know, but in 1865 came the dramatic change in their circumstances. Many years later when Jonathan was reminiscing to friends about his early career, he often told the following story, which provides an explanation (possibly apocryphal) and contains at least an element of dramatic licence. A friend recounted that:

'He was by trade a grocer, but his soul was on the Prince's boards, and forgetful of his work he struck such attitudes and recited so much of the play he was at the time interested in, that his employer believed he was as Dewhurst put it, "off his onion". One day he was sent into the cellar store with a large treacle can and instructions to fill it from a puncheon. Whilst waiting for his jug to fill his infirmity overcame him and assuming what he considered the right posture he recited with

14

fervour Romeo's love address to Juliet in the balcony scene. When he had finished spouting he bethought him of his treacle errand and essayed to see if his can was filled. But he couldn't lift his feet without difficulty, for the treacle had long overflowed the jug and the syrup had covered his part of the cellar to several inches in depth. For that he was discharged, but his employer, when his temper had lowered to equilibrium, and knowing Dewhurst's passion for the stage, gave him a note to Mr Calvert, with whom he had some influence, and he got a walking job. He soon rose in the profession and became one of Mr Calvert's principals.'

Whatever the explanation, Jonathan left the grocer's in 1865 and on 5 April that year he appeared on the professional stage at the relatively new Prince's Theatre, Manchester, under the direction of Mr Charles Calvert.

3

Starting on the Boards

Although the initial 'potted biography' we had obtained from the Leigh Library gave us a promising start, we were short of meat to put on the admittedly substantial skeleton. We were able to plot a rough chronological schedule of his movements, but far more than this was needed. Dewhurst, we knew, had an excellent memory and we felt that we could rely to a large extent on the accuracy of the events he had detailed. So the long search began. Using our skeleton, we wrote to the libraries of all the towns and cities mentioned, asking whether their archives offered anything relevant. But our first break – and a source of much excitement to us – was with the *Illustrated London News*.

Dewhurst had mentioned that the *News* had reviewed the production of *Rebecca* at Drury Lane, in which he had appeared with Adelaide Neilson in 1871, and to our delight they were able to supply us with a review and an illustration. And then suddenly, so it seemed, we had him in our hands and for the first time saw Jonathan Dewhurst in his acting prime – a fine figure of a man in the chain-mail of Sir Brian de Bois Guilbert – in the dramatic scene with the Jewess Rebecca (Adelaide Neilson), where she threatens to throw herself from the castle window rather than yield to his Norman advances. At this moment we felt very close to Dewhurst.

Not all our enquiries produced such positive results and many proved to be dead ends. But little by little more information would arrive, accompanied sometimes by a copy playbill or programme. Our visits to the Bodleian Library in Oxford produced nothing of Dewhurst's visits to that city, but we were delighted to find the programme for *Rebecca* at Drury Lane, and several programmes recording performances there of Henry Rivers and his daughter Fanny, Jonathan's third wife. It was our visit to Manchester Central Library that provided us with the detailed information of Jonathan's first year at the Prince's Theatre under the direction of Mr Charles Calvert, and that was the next stage of our journey of discovery.

In the mid-1860s, theatre in Britain was experiencing a further period of change. Drury Lane, Covent Garden and the Haymarket still held pride of place in London, but the new prosperity and confidence in the country at large was starting to lead to the building of new theatres in the West End. In the provinces virtually all the important cities of early Victorian Britain had their theatre royals, and the theatres in cities such as Edinburgh, Liverpool, Manchester, Hull, Newcastle and Birmingham led the way. They ran their own stock companies and earlier in the century had been the centres for circuits – the arrangement by which a company from the central theatre would take a production on tour to the surrounding towns in its circuit.

By 1865 the circuit system had virtually disappeared and the expanding number of important provincial theatres provided a home for their own stock companies and a stage for the occasional visiting star actor. Although smaller provincial theatres could succeed, generally their numbers declined as audiences could see better shows at bigger theatres. The financial difficulty experienced by the theatre earlier in the century had led to a popularisation of the repertoire and, in London and the provinces, audiences were offered a bill of fare consisting of drama, melodrama, farce, pantomime and Shakespeare, with spectacle a very important ingredient. Quite apart from financial difficulties, a major problem faced by the theatre at large was the attitude of the religious establishment. The Victorian Era was a period of strong evangelical fervour and revival, and the prevailing attitude was that the theatre was immoral and consequently no true Christian would enter a theatre. This puritan attitude had existed for centuries and seemed to be aimed at the theatre building itself rather than the play, but the result was the same. It was only towards the end of the century that attitudes would change, and plays such as Wilson Barrett's *Sign of the Cross* would convert many in the church to a different way of thinking.

Jonathan Dewhurst could hardly have had a better start. The Prince's Theatre in Oxford Street, which had opened in 1864, was run by Manchester's most celebrated actor-manager, Charles Calvert. It was in direct competition with the Theatre Royal and the Queen's Theatre, both of which were well-established. But Charles Calvert had an excellent company and his productions were considered the equal of those in London. Unlike his wife Adelaide, Calvert had not come from a theatrical background. As a young man he had been articled to a solicitor and had then gone into 'business', working for a silk merchant. But he had strong if somewhat unfocused religious feelings and on one occasion discussed his future with

6   The Prince's Theatre, Manchester, where Dewhurst's professional career began.

7   The interior of the Prince's Theatre, Manchester, as it was when
Dewhurst started there.

Samuel Wilberforce, the Bishop of Oxford, who suggested that he might consider missionary work. Perhaps, fortunately for the theatre, he decided against taking this advice.

In his teens Calvert had visited the professional theatre for the first time and had seen Samuel Phelps as Macbeth. The experience affected him in much the same way as seeing Barry Sullivan had inspired Dewhurst and, although he did not become an actor until he was 24, from the moment he saw Phelps his fate was sealed. Calvert's theatrical career started in the South of England and, while appearing at Southampton, he shared the stage with Adelaide Biddles, who later became his wife. Northern tours followed and then he joined John Knowles's company at the Theatre Royal, Manchester, as leading man and stage manager. Despite Knowles's reputation the Royal was in the doldrums, but Calvert's appearance made an immediate impact, both through his acting and his work as stage manager. It was here that he met and befriended the young Henry Irving, who was trying to establish himself in the theatre. Calvert acquired a reputation for his acting, stage spectacle, costume, make-up and attention to detail but he found it increasingly difficult to work with Knowles. He needed his own theatre to show what he could do, and his opportunity came in 1864 with the opening of the new Prince's Theatre, a comfortable, more intimate theatre on a smaller scale than the Royal.

Calvert went to the Prince's on a three-year contract and immediately made his mark. He opened with *The Tempest* and this set the tone for the future – Shakespeare, melodrama, pantomime, with occasional visiting stars and companies. In fact the pattern generally adopted by the major provincial theatres. Calvert's reputation for spectacle and for revivals of Shakespeare was immense. His objective was to attain a very high standard in the entertainment he presented and he did not spare himself. He had the ability to spot talent in young actors but was under too much pressure himself to do much to further their development. What he did was to create an ideal environment in which actors with talent could gain the experience to provide the springboard for their future. Jonathan Dewhurst could not have had a better start to his theatrical career.

Dewhurst was 27 years of age when he joined Charles Calvert's company in April 1865. Calvert was already successful, building on the reputation he had earned at the Royal and he had attracted a capable and talented group of actors to support his wife and himself. But whereas Dewhurst might have expected to begin with minor roles, this proved not to be the case and, in only his first season, he was given several substantial roles. In the Victorian theatre there was no 'director' or 'producer' as such. The actor was responsible for knowing his lines and he would be given his stage entrances and exits by the stage manager, or someone fulfilling that role. Thus there was no one to coach the actor in his role, nor was there the time for such niceties. The actor decided how best to develop his part (if he thought about it at all) and for much of the time worked out his own moves on stage. The job of those lower down the acting hierarchy was to support those higher up – whether resident leading actors or visiting stars. The 'training' – and the benefit of belonging to a good company – lay in being able to observe experienced and talented actors at close hand and to learn from them. Dewhurst's professional debut on 5 April 1865 was in *Louis XI* and, apart from experienced players such as Henry Haynes, James L. Cathcart, John Hudspeth and Florence Haydon, the cast included Henry Irving who had come from the Royal to make his debut at the Prince's.

To the present-day reader the name of Henry Irving is synonymous with

MR. PHELPS, AS MACBETH.

I go, and it is done; the bell invites me.
Hear it not Duncan; for it is a knell.
That summons thee to heaven or to hell.

ACT 2. SCENE 1.

8   It was seeing Samuel Phelps that inspired both Charles Calvert and Henry Irving
to take up the stage.

THE PRINCE'S THEATRE,

OXFORD STREET, MANCHESTER

PROPRIETORS - - THE MANCHESTER PUBLIC ENTERTAINMENTS COMPANY LIMITED.

Henry Barry Peacock, Stretford, near Manchester.

Under the Direction of MR. CHARLES CALVERT.

WEDNESDAY, APRIL 5th, 1865,

MR. FREDERIC

MACCABE

HAS THE HONOUR TO ANNOUNCE HIS

FIRST BENEFIT,

ON WHICH OCCASION

MR. HENRY IRVING

(From the Theatre Royal) will sustain the character of Duc de Nemours.

MR. CHAS. CALVERT

Will appear as Louis XI.

The performance will commence with an Historical Drama, in five Acts, by W. R. Markwell, Esq., entitled

LOUIS XI.

WITH APPROPRIATE SCENERY, DRESSES, AND NEW APPOINTMENTS.

Louis XI. was of a character purely selfish—guiltless of entertaining any purpose unconnected with his ambition—covetous and desirous of self enjoyment. The cruelties, the perjuries, the suspicions of this Prince were rendered more detestable by the gross and debasing superstition which he practised. To a total want of scruple, or, it would appear, of any sense of moral obligation, Louis XI. added great natural firmness and sagacity of character.—*Sir Walter Scott.*

Louis XI	Mr. CHAS. CALVERT.
The Dauphin	Miss ALICE DODD.
Duc de Nemours	Mr. HENRY IRVING.
Philip de Cominie	Mr. DEWHIRST.
Coiter (the King's Physician)	Mr. HENRY HAYNES.
Francois de Paule	Mr. J. L. CATHCART.
Oliver le Daime	Mr. EDWIN DIXON.
Tristau le Hermite	Mr. J. WAINWRIGHT.
Count de Dreux	Mr. J. BRADLEY.
Crauford	Mr. PEARSON.
Marcel	Mr. RUSSELL.
Richard } Peasants	Mr. BARRIER.
Didier	Mr. JONES.
Officer	Mr. O'MALLEY.
Marie de Cominie	Miss FLORENCE HAYDON
Martha	Miss ROSE MASSEY.
Julie	Miss HELEN MASSEY.

Pages, Heralds, Soldiers, Peasants, Courtiers, Knights, &c., &c.

ACT I.—THE CHATEAU OF PLESSIS LES TOURS—DAYBREAK.
ACT II.—TAPESTRY CHAMBER IN THE CHATEAU.
ACT III.—THE WOODLAND CHAPEL.
ACT IV.—THE KING'S BEDCHAMBER.
ACT V.—THE GRAND HALL IN THE CHATEAU OF PLESSIS LES TOURS.

After which, Mr. MACCABE will appear in a selection from his popular Entertainment, including his famous Song, "EARLY IN THE MORNING," and will Recite (in Character) the Poem of "SHAMUS O'BRIEN."

TO CONCLUDE WITH

THE LOAN OF A LOVER

A FARCE IN ONE ACT.

Captain Amersfort	Mr. PHILIP DAY.
Peter Spyk	Mr. FRED. MACCABE.
Swyzel	Mr. J. HUDSPETH.
Delve	Mr. EDWIN DIXON.
Gertrude (with songs)	Miss ALICE DODD.
Ernestine Rosendale	Miss EDITH CHALLIS.

Musical Director - Mr. FERDINAND WALLERSTEIN.

Doors Open at Half-past Six, Performance to Commence at SEVEN

Treasurer, MR. M. COOKE, to whom all applications respecting bills and advertisements must be addressed.

Prices of Admission: Orchestra Stalls (Reservable) 4s.; Lower Circle (Reservable) 3s.; Upper Circle, 2s.; Pit, 1s.
Gallery, 6d. Private Boxes, £1. 1s. and £2. 2s. No Half-price to any part of the house.
Gallery entrance in the rear of the Theatre in Bale Street. Children in arms not admitted to any part of the house. No Money returned.
Pass-out Checks not Transferable. Box Office open from Eleven to Two.

A. IRELAND AND CO., PRINTERS, PALL MALL COURT, MANCHESTER.

9 *Louis XI*, in which Dewhurst mde his professional debut on 5 April 1865.

22

complete theatrical success, capped by his being created the theatre's first knight. A giant of the stage. But it had not always been so, and it was not like that in April 1865. Irving, a few months younger than Dewhurst, was born John Henry Brodribb. He, too, did not come from a theatrical background, indeed his family were against his going on the stage. At the age of twelve he shared an experience of both Calvert and Dewhurst – he was taken to see a professional performance which inspired him and which showed him clearly where his future must lie. Like Calvert, his hero was Samuel Phelps, who on this occasion appeared as Hamlet. By 1865 he had been on the stage for ten years and had changed his name to Henry Irving. At that point he had achieved no real success, but despite disappointments and shortage of money he never doubted his vocation, nor that he would one day be successful. Charles and Adelaide Calvert had befriended him at the Royal, but John Knowles did not regard him highly and after a disagreement with his manager, over what Irving felt was a matter of principle, he left. The episode that led to Irving's departure from the Royal does bear repeating and underlines his strong character and beliefs.

As students of the Victorian Era will be aware, there was at that time great interest in spiritualism, mesmerism and the occult, thus providing an audience or market for the serious investigator and the charlatan alike. Two men, the Davenport Brothers, had come to England from America and toured the country presenting a pseudo-spiritualist act, which claimed to be entirely genuine. In this they were assisted by a fake clergyman, the Reverend Dr Ferguson, who added a touch of false religiosity, introducing the act and providing a running commentary. They had enjoyed complete success – until they appeared in Manchester, when Irving with two fellow actors, Philip Day and Fred Maccabe, went to see the exhibition. No doubt it was Irving's Methodist background that caused him to be outraged by what he saw. A performance by a stage conjuror was one thing; the pretence of involving the spirit world was blasphemy and quite a different matter. Maccabe was an amateur magician of some note, and the three actors were soon able to work out how the tricks were achieved. A sum of £100 had been offered to anyone who could perform the Davenport Brothers' feats, and the three actors decided to take up the challenge and expose the deception.

On 5 February 1865 they appeared before a full house at the Library Hall of the Manchester Athenaeum. Maccabe and Day assumed the roles of the Davenport Brothers, while Irving, suitably disguised, took the part of the reverend doctor. The act was performed without aid from the spirits and Irving's introduction and commentary, a witty parody of Ferguson, was received with loud applause and laughter. The local press was ecstatic in its praise for the way in which Irving and his two friends had performed, and the clever way in which they had exposed the fraud. The exposé was repeated at the Free Trade Hall and was so successful that John Knowles, appreciating its money-making possibilities, tried to persuade Irving to continue with his act at the Royal. But Irving, sensitive to the dignity of the theatre, and having achieved his objective of exposing the Davenport Brothers, refused. Knowles and his management were furious and dispensed with his services.

The Calverts were more than happy to give their young friend work, and so it was that by their different routes Jonathan Dewhurst and Henry Irving appeared at the Prince's in *Louis XI*, the version by W.R. Markwell, not the better known play by Dion Boucicault. The occasion was the farewell benefit of the comedian Frederick Maccabe, who appeared in the supporting farce *The Loan of a Lover*. In the principal play Charles Calvert took the leading role of Louis, with Florence Haydon as Marie. Irving played the second lead, the Duc de Nemours, and Dewhurst appeared as Philip de Cominie.

Calvert's greatest successes were his Shakespeare revivals and, if Dewhurst had felt even the slightest disappointment that he had not made his debut in Shakespeare, he would have been delighted with his next role. Calvert's presentation of *The Tempest* drew nothing but praise from the Manchester critics, who commented without exception on the beautiful and artistic effects and the dramatic spectacle. The *Manchester Guardian* opined that, 'In all respects the play is uniformly excellent, music, dresses, scenery, acting, declamation – all are first class'. The playbill tells us that the music 'with the exception of Purcell's and Dr Arne's songs will be that composed by Mr A. Sullivan'. Dewhurst played Gonzalo, Calvert naturally taking the role of Prospero, with Florence Haydon as Miranda. As was usual at that time, there was a supporting feature, the five acts of *The Tempest* not being considered a sufficient evening's entertainment! The support was Buckstone's one-act comic drama *The Maid With The Milking Pail*, Dewhurst getting further exposure as Lord Philander and Fred Maccabe playing Diccon. *Othello* followed with Dewhurst playing Lodovico, and then came the play which, despite his love of Shakespeare, provided Dewhurst in the years to come with his favourite role – *Richelieu*, the romantic drama by Edward Bulwer-Lytton. His part in this production was Baradas, the king's favourite, but who can doubt that watching Calvert as the Cardinal, Dewhurst sensed that Richelieu was the right vehicle for his own acting ambitions.

Dewhurst's fine physical presence was frequently noted by critics and it is evident that in build and voice he offered maturity and gravitas. This is reflected in the parts he played in his first season, which included the Duke

24

PRINCE'S THEATRE

OXFORD STREET,   MANCHESTER.

PROPRIETORS ...... THE MANCHESTER PUBLIC ENTERTAINMENTS COMPANY LIMITED.

Under the Direction of Mr. CHARLES CALVERT.

LAST NIGHTS OF THE SEASON.

WHIT-MONDAY, JUNE 5th,

FOR THE BENEFIT

OF MR.

CHAS. CALVERT.

The performance will commence with Shakspere's Tragedy, in Five Acts,

KING LEAR.

Lear, King of Britain	Mr. CHARLES CALVERT
King of France	Mr. RUSSELL
Duke of Burgundy	Mr. W. PEARSON
Duke of Cornwall	Mr. WAINWRIGHT
Duke of Albany	Mr. PHILIP DAY
Earl of Kent	Mr. J L. CATHCART
Earl of Gloster	Mr. J. DEWHURST
Edgar (Son of Gloster)	Mr. HENRY BAYNES
Edmund (Bastard Son of Gloster)	Mr. HENRY IRVING
Curan (a Courtier) Mr. JOHNSON Physician	Mr. MORRIS
Oswald (Steward to Goneril)	Mr. J. HUDSPETH
Fool	Miss BRENNAN
Knight Mr. JONES Gentleman Mr SIMMONDS Herald	Mr. WILLIAMS
Old Man (Tenant to Gloster) Mr. BARRIER Messenger	Mr. BRADLEY
Goneril	Miss REINHARDT
Regan } The Three Daughters of Lear {	Miss EDITH CHALLIS
Cordelia	Miss FLORENCE HAYDON
Lords, Knights, Attendants, &c., &c.	

ANCIENT BRITISH INTERIOR.   HALL IN THE EARL OF GLOSTER'S CASTLE.
EXTERIOR OF THE DUKE OF ALBANY'S PALACE.
EXTERIOR OF THE EARL OF GLOSTER'S CASTLE.
THE HEATH.   A TENT.   THE HEIGHTS OF DOVER

In the course of the Evening, Mr. CALVERT will have the honour of Addressing
the Patrons of the Prince's Theatre.

Concluding with the Laughable Farce of

MY WIFE'S DENTIST.

Sir John Beauville	Mr. P. DAY.
General Squadron	Mr. J. HUDSPETH.
Dick Hazard	Mr. H. IRVING.
David	Mr. J. DIXON.
Lady Beauville	Miss MAUD HAYDON.
Cicely Squadron	Miss EDITH CHALLIS.
Rhoda	Miss R. MASSEY.

To-Morrow (Tuesday) - - -	Lady of Lyons
Wednesday - - - - - - -	King Lear
Thursday - - - - - - -	Extremes

CONCLUDING EACH NIGHT WITH MY WIFE'S DENTIST

Musical Director - Mr. FERDINAND WALLERSTEIN.

Doors open at Seven, Performance to Commence at Half-past Seven.

Treasurer, Mr. M. COOKE, to whom all applications respecting bills and advertisements must be addressed.

Prices of Admission : Orchestra Stalls (Reservable), 4s. ; Lower Circle (Reservable), 3s. ; Upper Circle, 2s. ; Pit, 1s. ;
Gallery, 6d.   Private Boxes, £1. 1s. and £2. 2s.   No Half-price to any part of the house.

Gallery entrance in the rear of the Theatre in Bale Street.   Children in arms not admitted to any part of the house.   No money returned.
Pass-out Checks not Transferable.   Box Office open from Eleven to Two.

A. IRELAND AND CO. PRINTERS, PALL MALL COURT, MANCHESTER.

10   By June, in his first year at Manchester, Dewhurst was playing leading roles.

MR. CHARLES CALVERT,

AS

KING LEAR.

11   Charles Calvert as Lear.

of Venice in *The Merchant of Venice* and the Friar in *Much Ado About Nothing*. Shakespeare was produced in tandem with melodrama, the most notable offerings being *Money* and *The Lady of Lyons* both by Bulwer-Lytton. There were numerous supporting plays and, at Christmas, the pantomime *Little Bo Peep*! Pantomime and some of the supports may not have been to Dewhurst's taste, but it was all experience. Irving had left the Prince's briefly, but now returned and repeated his villainous role of Robert Macaire in the melodrama of that name. The season finished with what was probably its highlight – *King Lear* with Calvert as Lear, Irving as Edmund, Dewhurst as Gloster, Henry Haynes as Edgar and Florence Haydon as Cordelia. Dewhurst's first season had been one of considerable success – he had acted in all the main plays and in most of the supports; he had sustained increasingly major roles and he had acquired a growing reputation.

The next season opened in July with the Shakespeare revivals exciting the most attention. Irving had again left, as had Florence Haydon, but among the actresses who joined the company was the young Maria B. Jones. During the season there were three notable Shakespeare productions – *A Midsummer Night's Dream*, *Macbeth* and *Hamlet*.

A Midsummer Night's Dream was an amazing success and critical comment focused on the spectacle:

> 'Nothing can excel the excellence with which the play has been presented to the public.
>
> (*City News*)

> '(the play) in simple truth surpasses all the previous efforts of this establishment.
>
> (*Manchester Weekly Times*)

> '...we confess that for appropriateness of detail, richness of dress, beauty of scenery and a general completeness not often realised in metropolitan theatres, we have seen nothing to exceed this exposition of Shakespeare's wondrous *Dream*.'
>
> (*Manchester Examiner and Times*)

The incidental music called for special comment. As we might expect, it featured Mendlessohn as well as Weber, Henry Bishop and Thomas Cooke. Dewhurst played Egeus, Rose Massey and Maria B. Jones played Hermia and Helena, while Teresa Furtado was expressly engaged to play Puck. It is a sad thought that these three young actresses were all to die young – Maria B.

Jones aged 27 and Miss Furtado and Miss Massey both aged 32. By now James Cathcart had died, aged 65, and John Hudspeth had only a few months to live. Life in the theatre was not easy, but for many others in Victorian times life was far from comfortable.

In *Macbeth* Dewhurst played Rosse, and in *Hamlet* the Ghost, clearly indicating the position he had established in the company. He could reasonably have decided to stay at the Prince's at least for another season, but ambition persuaded him that he was now ready for leading roles. He reasoned that, although Charles Calvert had only one year of his three-year contract to complete, it would nevertheless be a year in which the leading roles would be occupied by Calvert and there was every possibility that Calvert's contract would be renewed. As things transpired Calvert left the Prince's shortly before the expiration of his contract – but Dewhurst could not have anticipated that move.

12   Teresa Furtado joined Calvert's company for *A Midsummer Night's Dream*.

4

The Leading Man

Although the stage was very much a changing scene, many actors formed connections and stayed with a single company, pursuing their line of business in established surroundings. This limited their opportunities, but doubtless for many who took this path the opportunities were in any event limited by their talents, and they accepted the reality while at the same time enjoying the benefit of a more settled home life. But others, driven by ambition, recognised the need for mobility and no doubt found excitement in never being quite sure what lay round the next theatrical corner. They might have echoed with Shakespeare that 'there is a tide in the affairs of men, which, taken at the flood, leads on to fortune'.

Jonathan Dewhurst's theatrical career had taken off, but what of his domestic life with Margaret Mary? Frustratingly much of this remains unknown. They had been married for seven years, but had they no children? It seems hardly likely, but Dewhurst makes no mention of any children of the marriage. My grandmother's Birthday Book records a Lizzie Dewhurst born 18 March 1867 – she would have been the right age, but was she their child? Eventually we traced her birth – no, not Jonathan's daughter but his brother John Dewhurst's daughter.

Margaret Mary was a seamstress and would have continued to work, probably from home, to supplement her husband's earnings from the grocer's or the stage. In the early years of their married life they lived in Lowton, but did they remain there when Jonathan started at the Prince's and if so did he commute or did he live in digs during the week, returning home only at the weekends? Our efforts to throw more light on their domestic arrangements have gone unrewarded.

When Dewhurst left the Prince's he was invited by Clifford Cooper to join his company at the Victoria Theatre in Oxford for an eight-week season. Oxford was not a leading theatrical centre and the Victoria could not compare with the Prince's in Manchester, but the move would undoubtedly broaden Jonathan's experience and Cooper had assembled a talented company including G.F. Sinclair, Samuel Phelps's son Edmund, the comedian Edward Righton, Jane Hudspeth and Maud Haydon, the sister of Florence Haydon. The fare offered to the Oxford public was the usual blend of Shakespeare, drama and melodrama. Dewhurst started in supporting roles and quickly established himself with the audiences and the press. Of his Baradas in *Richelieu*, the *Era* commented:

> 'Mr Dewhurst, a stranger to Oxford, personated most effectively the part of Count Baradas; his voice, actions and appearance are remarkably good and he cannot fail to become a favourite.'

He played Rosse in *Macbeth*, Mr Gibson in *The Ticket-of-Leave Man*, Antonio in *The Merchant of Venice* and, as Lavarennes in *Belphegor The Mountebank*, 'showed his capability for heavy business'. Then, towards the end of the season, he had a stroke of luck – both Sinclair and Phelps left the company and Dewhurst was offered the leading parts previously assumed by Sinclair. Within two years of his professional debut he was playing Hamlet and Macbeth. He did not let false modesty cloud his view of the progress he had achieved:

> 'As a different piece was generally produced each evening, the studying and the getting up of the parts was no light task but I succeeded wonderfully well and my reputation was growing apace.'

East Lynne was performed in Oxford for the first time, Lady Isabel being played by Miss Ida Russelle, who had just joined the company, with Dewhurst as Mr Carlyle. The *Era* reported:

> 'If the feelings of the audience be any proof of acting, then must that of the newcomers be superlative, for the emotion betrayed during the progress of the piece was everywhere visible... As Mr Carlyle, Mr Dewhurst was faultless, his natural and gentlemanly bearing eminently fitting him for the character.'

And of *The Lady of Lyons* the *Era* commented:

> 'On Friday that charming actress Miss Jane Rignold took her benefit and as Pauline Deschappelles in *The Lady of Lyons* displayed an unusual

degree of grace and talent. Mr Dewhurst as Claud Melnotte, to award him the highest praise, excelled himself and in the cottage scene the united efforts of these two great and deserved favourites received a roar of approbation. *The Stranger* was given the night previously and the conception of the chief character by Mr Dewhurst stamps him at once as an actor of uncommon ability. The last night was devoted to the benefit of Mr Dewhurst.'

His reputation was indeed growing and, on the recommendation of Charles Calvert, he was engaged by E.D. Davies to play the leading parts at the Theatre Royal, Newcastle for the entire season.

With the departure of Charles Calvert, the Prince's Theatre in Manchester was under the management of Henry Haynes, who had been one of the leading men in Dewhurst's first season. Dewhurst was specially engaged by Haynes to play Lord Dalgarno in Andrew Halliday's *King O' Scots*. While Dewhurst was at the Prince's, it was agreed that *Othello* should be presented as a single performance for the benefit of Robert Cooke – a member of the company – and Dewhurst was highly delighted to be asked to play the lead role. He had not played Othello before and it was now apparent that his ambitions were being fulfilled – that he was regarded as a clear choice, not only for leading roles in melodrama, but more importantly to him for the major roles in the Shakespearian tragedies. The performance was intended for one night only, but as Dewhurst later recalled:

'As the theatre was crowded to overflowing the performance was repeated on a second night to a very big house.'

Long before he had gone into the theatre Dewhurst had shown a keen interest in poetic recitation and he continued to supplement his stage roles with these 'dramatic recitals' for the rest of his life. The poetry now was augmented by selections from Shakespeare and suitable melodramatic offerings. The visit to the Prince's presented the opportunity to give a recital at the Free Trade Hall billed as 'Dramatic Recitals From Memory', and the *Manchester Courier* commented:

'To a good presence and a fine voice Mr Dewhurst brings to his task a wonderful memory and a careful and critical study of the authors with whose works he deals.'

Following his Manchester appearances Dewhurst joined E.D. Davies's company from Newcastle for their summer season at Carlisle, after which he returned briefly to Oxford.

It seems, however, that his heart was in the north and in 1869 he returned to Lancashire. In considering how his stage career developed it can be seen that, apart from his London appearances (and, of course, his visits to Australia and India), virtually all his stage work took place north of Watford. He was a northerner and very happy to work in the north, but many years later he admitted that perhaps it had not been a good career move – perhaps at the significant moment in his life he should have stayed in London. But in 1869 that was still in the future and it did give him the immediate benefit of being able to run his domestic life more easily than if he had toured in the South of England. For the next two years he took leading roles at the theatres of the north – Oldham, Rochdale, Manchester, Bradford, etc. supported by their stock companies, and at the same time fitting in his dramatic recitals whenever he could. He records that for his *A Night With The Poets* he would often take over £70 – a not inconsiderable sum in those days. The syndicate running the Theatre Royal at Oldham was known as the Twelve Apostles and, although Dewhurst was more than happy to accept an engagement with them, he was less than enamoured of the dramatic fare offered to the Oldham public. In his words:

'At Oldham, I speedily became a great favourite, but as the common melodramatic plays were the only things produced I eventually prevailed upon the directors, or the "Twelve Apostles", to introduce some good Shakespearean pieces to the public. We arranged for *Macbeth*, which I played for four weeks, and this was followed by *The Tempest* for six weeks, in which I played Prospero. We also had a run of *Faust and Marguerite* in which I played Mephistopheles for four weeks. Having completed my engagement there I took my benefit in *Richard III* on the night of which I had to fight my way up Horsedge Street to the theatre. The house was crowded to suffocation whilst outside thousands were fighting to get in. The performance was a big success and I had a most enthusiastic reception.'

Although there may be an element of exaggeration in his account, it does underline his strong belief (which never deserted him) that theatre-goers should be offered first-class drama performed to the limit of the players' abilities. He was a man of his times and to him first-class drama was not only Shakespeare (although that must be the bedrock) but good modern drama or melodrama as well. So while he turned up his nose at *Jack Long of Texas*, in which he performed at the start of his Oldham engagement, he was very happy with plays such as Tom Taylor's *Still Waters Run Deep*, Bulwer-Lytton's *Richelieu*, and the historical romances of Andrew Halliday. Fortunately these plays were also very popular with the audiences. Dewhurst also believed strongly in production values – in accurate costume presented attractively, in good make-up and not least in spectacular scenic effects. One may not always succeed, but no stone should be left unturned to present each performance as a memorable experience for the audience.

Henry Haynes had not proved to be a successful manager at the Prince's, Manchester, and the theatre's artistic and financial fortunes had declined. A company was formed to take over the theatre, and in May 1868 the new proprietors persuaded Charles Calvert to return on more favourable terms. Thus, when Dewhurst returned to the Prince's to play in Andrew Halliday's *King O' Scots*, he was able to renew his acquaintance with his old friend. His eight-week engagement at the Theatre Royal, Bradford, was particularly successful, and on leaving Bradford Dewhurst recalls that he was:

'... presented with an illuminated address together with a beautiful ring engraved with the Borough Coat of Arms. The address, surmounted by the Borough Coat of Arms with the motto "*Labor omnia vincit*", was as follows:- "To Mr Jonathan Dewhurst, tragedian of the Theatre Royal, Bradford, Yorkshire. Sir – We, the undersigned, having witnessed your display of talent as an *artiste* at the Theatre Royal in Bradford, and your gentlemanly conduct during your stay of eight weeks, and hearing with regret that your engagement with Mr Rice has been fulfilled, are anxious of showing the respect we entertain for you as an actor and gentleman, by tendering to you the small present which accompanies this testimonial and which we hope you will accept. We sincerely wish you every prosperity in life, and hope you may again return amongst us ere long. We are, yours most respectfully." Then followed about a score of signatories.'

Apart from 'acceptable' melodrama, Dewhurst had added more Shakespearian roles to his repertoire – Romeo, Prospero, Petruchio and Richard III. His reputation was now firmly established with the northern theatres.

5

London at Last

Up to around 1870 the common practice had been for each theatre to have its own stock or resident company. Each member of the company would have his or her own line of business and the plays performed would be cast accordingly. Smaller provincial theatres might not have their own companies, but would receive visits from the company resident at the major theatre in their 'circuit'. Star actors, perhaps two or three of them, would tour but would be supported by the stock companies of the theatres they visited.

From around 1870 this started to change and full-scale productions, mainly from London, would arrange provincial tours, taking everything they needed with them. The productions were generally of a higher standard than those presented by the stock companies, and the growth of interest in the theatre can be gauged from the fact that a visiting company could fill a theatre for a week with one play, whereas even with a nightly change of programme stock companies often played to half-full houses. The growth in the railway system was instrumental in this change and there grew up a chain of large, well-equipped provincial theatres capable of housing the touring productions.

In his book *Sixty Years of the Theater*, the theatre-goer and critic J.R. Towse offers an interesting view of the stock companies and the developing 'star system' of this time and, writing in 1910, adds his opinion of the comparative merits of the stars of 'yesterday and today'. His comments might well be repeated in the present day.

'The fresh enthusiasm of youth is utterly subversive of sound judgment, and I shall not pretend to speak authoritatively concerning performances which I saw before my twentieth year. That is not a judicious age, but by that time I had served a pretty long apprenticeship in theatergoing and had acquired some small power of discrimination.

34

Already theatrical conditions were changing. Only four or five of the old stock organizations in London survived. Chief among them was the company at the Haymarket Theater, under J.B. Buckstone, the recognised home of the higher comedy for many years; the Adelphi, largely devoted to melodrama under the management of Benjamin Webster, and Sadler's Wells, where the mantle of the illustrious Samuel Phelps – of whom more hereafter – had descended to Miss Marriott and others.

'Of lesser note were the companies headed by Sarah Lane at the huge Victoria Theater, in Hoxton – where fried fish was served in the boxes as a relish to dramatic art – and the Surrey Theater, under the direction of Creswick and Shepherd. These two were reckoned among the transpontine houses, and catered to enormous audiences of the poorest kind drawn from the working classes, small tradesfolk, mechanics, costers and others. The entertainments in them, naturally, were as a rule of a popular kind, consisting of spectacles, screaming farce, sentimental domestic plays and highly colored melodramas, but the actors, especially the low comedians, were thoroughly capable, and Shakespearean tragedies and comedies and other standard pieces were not infrequently the principal dishes in a theatrical menu of great variety and abundance.

'In those days it was not uncommon to find a tragedy, a comedy and a couple of farces upon the same programme, and the spectators sat with unflagging satisfaction through them all. And the representations, if seldom brilliant, were as seldom slovenly or incomplete. Actors had to work for their living then, many of them appearing in three or four widely contrasted parts in a single evening. Sometimes the cast was headed by a visiting player of the first rank – the beginning of the star system which has since been so prodigiously and mischievously developed – who was generally assured of satisfactory support. Unless I am mistaken, Macready himself acted at the Surrey; Phelps certainly did. Mrs Lane and Messrs Shepherd and Creswick were all sound interpreters of Shakespearean character.

'I have not included the company which for several years supported Charles Kean at the Princess's Theater among the regular stock companies, because he organised it for his own special purpose, and added to it or subtracted from it as occasion required. But nevertheless it was the stock system which produced the accomplished players who helped to make his management at that house so memorable. This was the case also at other prominent West End theaters, where eminent performers were supported by scratch companies engaged for a season or a run. All the best subordinate performers owed their capacity to their long

35

training in the 'stock', either in London or in the old established provincial theaters. The day was yet to come when the public should be asked to welcome the representation of ancient or modern master-pieces – productions of the latter kind, unfortunately, are few and far between – by a star and a bundle of sticks. Now, alas, the star himself – or herself – shines only with a fictitious glitter, the reflection of flaming and mendacious advertisement. Most of our contemporary theatrical valuations are ridiculously extravagant, and the stage itself, perhaps, is suffering quite as much from the false glamor with which the box-office and the daily press have conspired to invest it as from any other particular condition.

'It is the fashion to describe our second- or third-rate mummers in terms which would be flattering to a Siddons or a Garrick and to record their petty sayings and doings as if these were actually matters of public importance and interest. How many of the names of existing stage luminaries which now confront us on the street posters and in the newspapers will be remembered in the next generation? The question is easily answered.'

But to continue our story. While Dewhurst was at Bradford, he received an offer from Edward Saker of the Alexandra Theatre, Liverpool, to appear there with Adelaide Neilson in *Amy Robsart*, Andrew Halliday's adaptation of Sir Walter Scott's *Kenilworth*. The play had opened successfully at Drury Lane and was now making its appearance at leading provincial theatres. However, it was not a tour of the Drury Lane production, but a visit by leading performers specially engaged for the play – Adelaide Neilson repeating her Drury Lane role of Amy and Jonathan Dewhurst playing the villainous Varney for the first time. They were supported by the resident Alexandra company and the play was under the personal direction of Andrew Halliday. Dewhurst recalls that he gladly accepted Saker's offer and the opportunity of playing opposite Adelaide Neilson.

In 1871 the young Adelaide Neilson was one of the most popular, and arguably one of the most talented, actresses on the national or the international stage. Born in 1846, the illegitimate daughter of a strolling player, she had not enjoyed a happy childhood and in her teens ran away from home to seek her fortune in London. She loved reading and reciting, had an excellent memory and showed a capacity and a determination to learn. She had great natural beauty, with an expressive face, a fine speaking voice and the ability to communicate with any audience. In 1865 she played her first leading role at Margate, but was soon in demand in London and the major

13   A young Adelaide Neilson at the start of her career.

provincial theatres and rapidly acquired an enviable reputation in Shakespeare and the popular plays of the day. She subsequently made two tours of America, where she was, if anything, more popular than in England. Sadly she came to be numbered among those talented actresses who died young – she was only 34. There have been many glowing tributes paid to her, but perhaps this extract from the *Daily Gazette* (25 September 1877) can appropriately speak for them all:

'Wonderfully gifted by nature, with a face very lovely, and, what is better, remarkably expressive and capable of registering and reflecting the emotions of the mind, and with a degree of intelligence and talent which fairly passes the indefinable borderline that separates mere cleverness from real genius, she has by assiduous cultivation of the details of her art succeeded in attaining the very front rank in the highest walk of her profession.'

The production of *Amy Robsart* was a great success. The *Porcupine's* review (11 March 1871) complimented Halliday on his adaptation, which in its

37

view possessed 'the supreme merit of being perfectly intelligible and interesting even to those who have had no previous acquaintance with the novel... An adaptation of this character almost rises to the dignity of a work of invention'. Halliday had 'made a play in which the interest is sustained without break or pause from the opening to the conclusion'. And, continued the *Porcupine*, 'The achievement is all the more creditable when we remember the numerous temptations to discursive prolixity presented by such a work as *Kenilworth* – temptations which in previous instances Mr Halliday has shown but feeble inclination to resist'. However, the *Porcupine* regarded Adelaide Neilson's performance as the major reason for the success of the production and praised her for the way in which she took full advantage of the role presented by the author:

'It is an advantage that everyone can appreciate to have for such a part as Amy Robsart an actress who, like Miss Neilson, looks the character; and this advantage is immensely increased when she is able, as Miss Neilson is, to act it with the bright tenderness of girlhood added to the force, passion, and intensity rarely found except in the ripe maturity of experience.'

Dewhurst, a forceful actor by nature:

'...deserves praise for a rendering of Varney which was all the more effective from its quietude, and the absence of anything like demonstrative villainy.'

Edward Saker's wife, the actress Marie O'Berne, 'was much too graceful for the brusque and imperious Elizabeth but displayed no lack of energy when her part demanded it'. Saker was congratulated on the mounting of the piece, 'that constitutes an attraction in itself'.

The play had been a great success for Dewhurst. In his words:

'At the Alexandra, in company with Miss Neilson, I had the good fortune to make a decided hit. On the first night of my appearance, Mr Andrew Halliday came round behind the scenes and offered me an engagement for next season at Drury Lane, London. Mr Saker also made me an offer, but the national theatre had a greater attraction for me. The Liverpool Press were unanimous in my praise, one of the papers saying that my acting reminded them very strongly of the sterling actor Mr John Ryder when at his best. I afterwards went on tour, playing Varney with Miss Neilson at Birmingham and other places.'

The future looked bright indeed, touring *Amy Robsart* with Adelaide Neilson and with the prospect of Drury Lane for the following season. His appearance at the Prince of Wales, Birmingham, was Dewhurst's first visit to the city. The theatre was managed by James Rodgers, whose wife Katherine was a Drury Lane actress. Rodgers was intent on mounting a splendid production. The new and magnificent scenery was based on the model of Drury Lane; the costumes specially made by Mr Vokes, costumier of Drury Lane; the Revels at Kenilworth Castle were arranged by Miss Alice Attewill, ballet mistress of the Alexandra Theatre, Liverpool, who had been specially engaged, and the piece was produced under the personal direction of Andrew Halliday. Miss Neilson was the star attraction and Jonathan Dewhurst was specially engaged for the part of Master Richard Varney. The *Birmingham Post* reported that Miss Neilson, its original exponent, played the part of Amy:

'...with wonderful grace, tenderness and dignity. In point of conception and appearance, indeed, it would be difficult to improve on this assumption, which combines in a rare degree all those qualities of mind and person which tradition has assigned to the beautiful and unfortunate Amy Robsart.'

The review continued:

'Next to Miss Neilson's acting the most histrionic performance of the evening was the Varney of Mr Dewhurst. In the character itself there is not much to call forth an actor's powers for Varney is a commonplace villain, but Mr Dewhurst invests the character with a picturesqueness and individuality which, though nowhere overstrained or outstepping the modesty of nature, is productive of a most powerful and incisive effect. His cool, quiet, self-contained manner, careful avoidance of exaggeration, invariable readiness and thorough ease and finish, combined with his excellent presence impart a completeness and freshness to his assumption, very unusual in parts of so conventional an order.'

By the end of April Adelaide Neilson had moved on, but *Amy Robsart* continued its success in the provinces and when it appeared at the Theatre Royal, Sheffield, Miss Katherine Rodgers had been engaged by Mr Halliday to play the title role, with Dewhurst continuing as Varney. They were supported by a talented company, ballet and 100 supernumeraries! The *Sheffield and Rotherham Independent* reported:

'Mr J. Dewhurst, an old Sheffield favourite, appears in the character of Varney. His reception was of a most flattering description, the house testifying its welcome by applause which was sustained for some time. His Varney was all that could be desired.'

At the end of May, Dewhurst and Miss Rodgers (billed now as Mrs James Rodgers) appeared with the play at her husband's theatre, the Prince of Wales in Birmingham. She was, of course, a great local favourite and the play was greeted by crowded and enthusiastic audiences. Mrs Rodgers was rewarded with critical comment, which was, if anything, even more adulatory than that bestowed a few weeks earlier on Miss Neilson, and:

'As the villain, Varney, Mr Dewhurst played all through with consummate art, never forgetting who he was and never allowing his audience to see the person underneath the "part" he played. In face, in voice, in walk, in action, he made a most effective realisation of Varney and well deserved the applause which he received.'

Following the success of *Amy Robsart*, Dewhurst found himself travelling to Scotland. To celebrate the Scott Centenary, the proprietors of the Theatre Royal, Glasgow had arranged to put on *The Lady of the Lake*, a dramatised version by Charles Webb of Sir Walter Scott's 'Greatest Work'. Again no expense was to be spared and the resident company was strengthened by no fewer than eight specially selected actors including Mr Charles Webb, the author. Mr H. Loraine (the Eminent Tragedian) was cast as Roderick Dhu, Miss Louise Pereira as Ellen, the Lady of the Lake, with Dewhurst appearing as James FitzJames, the King of Scotland. The *Glasgow Herald's* first night review was very brief, blaming the brevity on the length of the play itself, but commented that 'apart from the literary merits and the quality of the acting, it was the most brilliant success we have perhaps ever seen even in the Royal'. It did go to some length to suggest that Roderick should test the strength of his sword, as in his duel with FitzJames it 'had snapped in two, reducing the doughty chief to the ridiculous necessity of pausing in the combat to procure a fresh weapon from behind the scenes'.

The *Herald's* full review two days later, which ran to 21 column inches, concentrated firstly on praising the production's success as a spectacle, and

THEATRE ROYAL,

DRURY LANE

Sole Lessee and Manager   ....   Mr F. B. CHATTERTON.

MONDAY, December 4th, 1871, & Every Evening during the Week,

Her Majesty's Servants will perform the Laughable Sketch by JOHN OXENFORD, entitled the

WRONG MAN IN THE RIGHT PLACE

In which the Members of the CELEBRATED VOKES FAMILY WILL APPEAR.

After which, at a Quarter to Eight, will be produced, a New Romantic and Spectacular Drama, entitled

REBECCA

Founded on Sir Walter Scott's celebrated Novel of "IVANHOE."

BY ANDREW HALLIDAY,

ILLUSTRATED WITH CHARACTERISTIC SCENERY, BY

WILLIAM BEVERLY.

The Overture, Vocal and Incidental Music, including Selections from Familiar and Favourite Airs of the Period, the Processions, Marches, Airs de Ballet, are Composed especially for this Drama, by Mr W. C. LEVEY. The Dances and Groupings arranged by Mr J. CORMACK. Costumes by Mr VOKES and Mrs LAWLER, from Authentic Authorities (by an Eminent Artist.) The Decorations and Properties by Mr BRUNTON. Machinery by Mr J. TUCKER. The whole produced under the Direction of Mr EDWARD STIRLING.

Richard Cœur de Lion - -	Mr E. ROSENTHAL
Prince John - - -	Mr S. DYNELEY
Cedric of Rotherwood - -	Mr DOLMAN
Wilfred of Ivanhoe - -	Mr J. B. HOWARD
Athelstane - -	Mr BRUTON
Brian de Bois Gulibert - -	Mr DEWHURST
Front de Bœuf - - -	Mr B. EGAN
Lucas de Beaumanoir -	Mr MILTON
De Bracy & Fitzurse (Knights)	Messrs. WOOD & THOMPSON
Isaac of York - - -	Mr PHELPS
Robin Hood - -	Mr W. TERRISS
Friar Tuck Mr ERSSER JONES	Oswald Mr DOUGLAS
Gurth - Mr McINTYRE	Wamba - Mr J. FRANCIS
Bertrand - Mr NAYLOR	Gaoler - Mr HARCOURT
Rebecca - -	Miss NEILSON
Lady Rowena - -	Miss MATTIE REINHARDT
Ulrica - -	Miss FANNY ADDISON
Elgitha - -	Miss KATHLEEN RYAN

14   Dewhurst's London debut, playing opposite Adelaide Neilson in
Andrew Halliday's *Rebecca*.

15   Scene from *Rebecca* at Drury Lane.
Dewhurst as Sir Brian de Bois Guilbert and Adelaide Neilson as Rebecca.

secondly in adverse criticism of the quality of the dramatist's efforts. The review gave only five inches to the acting, which it felt was on the whole 'fair'. Mr Dewhurst made an excellent FitzJames; Mr Loraine's 'fine physique and vigorous – at times too vigorous – acting specially suited his part' and Miss Pereira made a graceful Ellen. However, Miss Irwin was 'painfully over-weight' and Mr Slater was not physically suited to the part of the stalwart Douglas. The *Herald*'s final thought was that, with a considerable amount of judicious pruning and rearrangement, it would make a really splendid success. These comments must have made some impact, for the play ran successfully for over six weeks.

And so, after six years as an actor, Jonathan Dewhurst appeared in London, on the stage of Drury Lane. The play was *Rebecca*, Andrew Halliday's adaptation of Scott's *Ivanhoe*. The *Illustrated London News* complained that the national theatre (Drury Lane) should have more regard for what they put on, that 'the abundance of original dramas of the highest merit lying on their author's hands awaiting performance' were overlooked yet again for sordid commercial reasons. The theatre management had found it very profitable to stage a dramatic adaptation of one of Scott's romances and was clearly intent on giving its audiences more of what they wanted. We are tempted to ask whether anything has really changed. *Rebecca* relied on narrative power, excitement, strong playing and spectacle – and was hugely successful. Halliday had assembled a strong cast: J.B. Howard as Wilfred of Ivanhoe, Samuel Phelps as Isaac of York and the young William Terriss as Robin Hood; Adelaide Neilson played Rebecca, the central character in the adaptation, and Lady Rowena was played by Mattie Reinhardt. Dewhurst was Sir Brian de Bois Guilbert, the Knight Templar.

The play opened in September 1871 and the early and somewhat dyspeptic review by the *Illustrated London News* seems to have been coloured by its dislike of historical adaptations in general and its disapproval of the Drury Lane management in particular. It recorded that:

'...the mere "playwright", as Mr Halliday modestly dubs himself, is called in to arrange the materials for the boards in such a way as, with the aid of spectacle and scenery, may prove attractive to the modern playgoer. And in accordance with this design an adaptation (by the way of the very poorest kind) of Scott's grand romance was produced on Saturday to a crowded house. Meanwhile original drama is supplanted for the purpose of making room for an arrangement of scenes in which there is no novelty and the utilisation of stage accessories in which there is no merit; and thus a fair trial for the dramatic genius of the country is fatally postponed, and its productions are sacrificed to the supposed commercial interests of incompetent speculators.'

It went on to 'speak well of Mr Dolman who supported Cedric of Rotherwood with judicious emphasis and Mr E. Rosenthal whose Richard Coeur de Lion was respectable. He sang a song in character which is likely we think to become popular'. Mr Dewhurst and Mr Egan 'had rather more than they could well sustain', Mr McIntyre was 'ambitious in vain as Gurth', and Mr J. Francis as Wamba was 'totally inefficient'. Mr Phelps 'exhibited some forceful acting', and Miss Neilson, 'in the scene with the Templar threw as much energy into the situation as she could command. It was evidently beyond her powers, but she was in earnest'. Not an encouraging review, but it ended by recording that 'at the conclusion the general applause outweighed the cries of a few dissentients, whose opinions were not in accordance with the interests of the management'. It is evident that the public at large did not share the views of the *News* – the play ran well into December to full houses – and neither did the drama critics of other newspapers. The *Court Circular* singled out Dewhurst with the comments:

'The most noteworthy impersonation was the Sir Brian de Bois Guilbert of Mr Dewhurst, an actor new to London, who at once made his mark.'

The Times commented that:

'Mr Dewhurst has a fine and manly presence and looked the bold Templar to the life.'

The *News* did not subsequently change its views, but in October it printed a short notice accompanied by an illustration of the scene on the battlements, where Rebecca defies de Bois Guilbert, and commented that '(the play) appears to suit the present state of the public taste. It is acted with earnestness and accordingly is very successful with the audience. As an opportunity for ambitious acting it merits praise and all parties are to be congratulated on the result'. The illustration gives us a good impression of Dewhurst's physique which was much admired throughout his career, and no doubt provided the strength and vitality to enable him to combat the rigours of life on the Victorian stage.

During the run of *Rebecca*, the comedian Harry Boleno, a great national favourite, retired from the stage and on the morning of Saturday, 25 November, a Farewell Benefit was given for him at Drury Lane. There were twelve items of entertainment and the programme contained the caveat that, should it prove to be too long, Mr Boleno craved the indulgence of his patrons if he was compelled to omit part of it, 'the Theatre having to be got ready for the Evening Entertainment'. Several members of the cast of *Rebecca* took part, in addition to whom there were over 50 other performers drawn from all branches of the theatre. The entertainment commenced with Mr

A.S. Spiller, 'the celebrated Russian Skater (Champion of the World)' and included scenes from *Romeo and Juliet* (Adelaide Neilson and J.B. Howard), *Othello* (Dewhurst as Othello), dramatic excerpts featuring Messrs Phelps and Terriss and Miss Teresa Furtado, and concluded with a pantomime sketch in which Harry Boleno put on his 'motley suit' for the last time!

When the run of *Rebecca* ended in mid-December, Dewhurst was very happy to be re-engaged for the following season but did not stay for the pantomime. This cannot have been a coincidence and it is evident that he had decided that his unavoidable involvement with *Little Bo Peep* in his first season at Manchester would be his last. In the event he spent the winter season in the north with the Pitney Weston Company, taking the leads in legitimate drama, mainly in Shakespearian roles. Mr J. Pitney Weston had recently converted, at considerable expense, the Star Theatre of Varieties in Wigan to the new Weston's Royal Amphitheatre. For the Grand Opening Performance he had invited the:

'Two Greatest Tragedians in the World

MR CHARLES DILLON

The acknowledged Premier Actor of the Stage; and

MR J. DEWHURST

The future Star Artist of London, and who has, since
his last appearance here, in his native town, stamped
himself to rank one of our leading London Actors.'

Dillon appeared on the first two nights in what were two of his greatest roles, Belphegor and King Lear, and Dewhurst followed those performances with Macbeth and Hamlet, after which the theatre was to be turned over to pantomime.

Charles Dillon was indeed a stalwart of the theatre and had played most of the leading dramatic roles, generally to great critical acclaim. The impact he made can be judged from Westland Marston's report on him as a young actor, taking the part of Aubri in *The Dog of Montargis*:

'The hero of the night ... was enacted by an abnormally ugly young
man whose name did not appear on the bill. This gentleman had
a huge, cavernous mouth, with protruding and irregular teeth, a

corrugated nose, snake-like, glittering eyes, a head of long, lank black hair, growing very low down on a broad but receding forehead... But when Aubri had been on the stage five minutes, I'd lost sight of his plebeian appearance in my admiration of his ability. He moved with ease, grace and distinction. In his one great, indeed his only, scene – the scene of the murder – his sword-play was magnificent; his pathos and his passion were alike admirable. Such was my first impression of Charles Dillon.'

Marston saw him as an actor of great emotional rather than intellectual gifts, most successful when portraying feeling, which he did with power, force and delicacy.

But Pitney Weston's plans had to be changed. The opening performances had been so successful that the pantomime was delayed, and Dewhurst took his farewell benefit on the Friday with *Othello* (Weston playing Iago) and *Katherine and Petruchio*, and ended on the Saturday with *Richard III*. Shakespeare and melodrama continued to be presented on the northern circuit and Dewhurst (and others) must have felt that their audiences could happily accept the intellectual challenge of Shakespeare – or at least be thrilled by bravura acting and stage spectacle. Having returned to Drury Lane, Dewhurst found himself once more playing de Bois Guilbert in *Rebecca*. The play moved to the Olympic Theatre, where Maria B. Jones, Dewhurst's colleague from his Manchester days, played the part of Rebecca. Still under the personal direction of Halliday, the production then embarked on a tour of the major provincial theatres.

The version of *The Lady of the Lake* by Charles Webb, which had been so poorly received by the Glasgow critics, seems to have disappeared from the public gaze. The Drury Lane management, looking for a follow-up to *Rebecca*, knew that they could not fail with the partnership of Sir Walter Scott and Andrew Halliday, and at their request Halliday produced for them his version of *The Lady of the Lake*. *The Times* (23 September 1872) reported that the play 'has proved as great a success as any of Mr Halliday's previous adaptations and he is entitled to great commendation'. The *Illustrated London News*, in what seems to have been a happier frame of mind, said, 'It has indeed been already dramatised as opera and burlesque; but never so carefully and picturesquely interpreted as by Mr Halliday'. The highest praise however was reserved for William Beverley, who, said the *Echo*, 'has supplied scenery certainly not surpassed by anything yet seen on the London stage' and went into raptures over the magnificent effects. To a large extent the popular success of historical romances, such as those supplied by Mr Halliday, relied on the scenic effect, but this was the era of the major theatres show-ing what could be done to give their audiences breathtaking spectacle – it was just that Drury Lane did it more spectacularly and successfully than any-one else. A strong, fast-moving narrative helped and music culled from the well-known tunes of the popular composers of the day kept the audience on the edge of its seat. One might be tempted to think that the acting was rela-tively unimportant, but this was not so. Dramas – or melodramas – of this kind needed strong, sympathetic playing to give them conviction.

Andrew Halliday had assembled a strong cast with James Fernandez as FitzJames, Dewhurst as Douglas and Henry Sinclair as Roderick Dhu. William Terriss and George Rignold appeared in supporting roles. Maria B. Jones, as the leading lady at Drury Lane, took the part of the heroine. The leading players were all reviewed favourably, the *Echo* awarding the greatest praise to Miss Jones for her 'command of pathos ... and graceful tender-ness'. The *Evening Standard* pronounced Jonathan Dewhurst, 'the most noble of Douglas's' and the *Standard* commented that 'The best piece of acting, however, falls to the share of Mr Dewhurst, whose Douglas was one of those spirited performances too rare to pass by unacknowledged'. The *Echo* said that 'Mr Dewhurst in appearance, speech and action satisfied the require-ments of the role of Douglas, his spirited interposition in the quarrel of the rivals Roderick and FitzJames eliciting a well-merited cheer'.

Having established himself on the London stage – at the national theatre – Dewhurst now decided to look elsewhere. It could not have been solely to play more Shakespeare, which one might have expected. He largely spent the next few years touring with leading actresses who invited him to play their leading man, mainly in melodramas. Later in his life he expressed some regret for this decision, but in 1872 his future seemed completely assured.

6

On Tour

At the time of his first Drury Lane appearance, Jonathan Dewhurst probably assumed that he would stay in London for some time. He and Margaret had moved from Lancashire to 14 Trevor Square, Knightsbridge, London. What Margaret did with her time can only be a matter for speculation – she may have continued with her needlework or she may have devoted her time to looking after the children. But both possibilities seem unlikely. We have traced no record of any children of the marriage and Jonathan's stage career seems to have brought in enough money for them to live in Knightsbridge – not the cheapest district in the capital. Margaret was doubtless thrilled by the move to London, by the excitement and by her involvement (in whatever way) in her husband's burgeoning career.

Dewhurst tells us that 'At the close of this season I was engaged as leading actor by Mlle Beatrice and toured the provinces with her company for about three years'. Mlle Beatrice was a young French actress who, to judge by press comment on the performance of *Nos Intimes* in London, exhibited grace, earnestness and intelligence. Her performance in the central role was much praised and the influence she had exercised on her company – which was helped by keeping the same players together – showed in the entire performance, where there was not one weakness. The *Observer* felt that London actors would have to look to their laurels and the *Illustrated London News* that 'Her company is unrivalled and ought to read [as] a lesson to our London managers'. She was 33 at the time, a successful actress and manager, but six years later she, too, had died. Dewhurst continues to present us with a problem. We know that he joined her company, the 'London Comedy – Drama Company', and toured the provinces with her production of *Nos Intimes*, taking the leading part of Dr Tholosan. We also know, from press comment, that the production had toured the provinces for over two years before being presented at the Olympic in May 1872. The programme for the visit to the

Theatre Royal, Birmingham (June 1873) indicates that this was the 170th week and the 1,020th night of the tour, which dates the opening to February 1870. It also states that the cast, including Dewhurst, was 'the entire Original Cast as played in London'. But does this mean the original cast (from February 1870) or the cast that originally played in London? Or is the programme mistaken in the claim that Dewhurst was in the original cast?

We have three possibilities:

- Dewhurst was in the original cast in February 1870 but omitted to mention it. It could have been fitted in while he was touring in the north.
- He joined the company in May 1872 for the London opening, between the tour of *Rebecca* and *The Lady of the Lake* at Drury Lane. However, in press reports of this performance he is not mentioned as being in the cast.
- He joined the production only when the play went on provincial tour in May/June 1873. If this is the case it would have been impossible for him to have toured with Mlle Beatrice 'for about three years'.

Our best guess must be that he had acted in earlier performances of the play as far as his other commitments allowed, but that in his recollections he covered the involvement with a generalisation. Dewhurst stayed with Mlle Beatrice's company until well into 1874, playing all the leading roles. But when they returned to the Haymarket he received another attractive offer – to accompany the leading Australian actress, Mrs Mary Gladstane, on her tour of the provinces.

Mary Gladstane had built a considerable reputation in her own country and in America, particularly in tragic roles. Her plan was to appear in 'all the leading cities of the Empire' and she now embarked on the English stage of the tour, the repertoire consisting mainly of drama, melodrama and historical romance. Dewhurst was pleased to receive the invitation from Mrs Gladstane, and also pleased that before he needed to take it up there was time for a visit to his northern roots and the opportunity to get back to Shakespeare.

Melodrama was all very well and he could not complain about being in constant demand, but although there were one or two non-Shakespearian roles which he would play throughout his career, it was the work of the Bard that meant most to him. In June 1874 he appeared at the Theatre Royal, Wigan, and for Charles Duval at Chorley in a round of Shakespearian plays, supported by the resident companies. Appropriately fortified, he was ready to join Mrs Gladstane. The role with which she was principally identified

PROGRAMME

Royal Court Theatre

WIGAN

THEATRE ROYAL COURT

CIRCLE

OPEN
EVERY EVENING
AT 6·30
SATURDAY
AT 6·15
TELEPHONE 0394

Proprietor & Manager
JOHN WORSWICK

THE GEM THEATRE of LANCASHIRE

16   The Royal Court Theatre, Wigan, depicted on its ornate programme.

was the Queen in the historical romance *Elizabeth, Queen of England* and her portrayal had received ecstatic reviews in Australia and America. The play was the focal point of the tour for the sole reason that it offered her the opportunity to show off her dramatic talents to the full. The press was not impressed by the play itself as this quote from the *Birmingham Daily Post* suggests:

'Undramatic in construction, clumsy and careless in dialogue, destitute of any series of good scenes, and sadly deficient in the dignity and impressiveness of true dramatic art... Still it affords, by some rather reckless grouping of historic incidents, room enough for the development of a fine character and for the display of very high histrionic powers.'

The *Midland Counties Herald* felt that Mrs Gladstane's 'realisation of the character of Elizabeth is, however, so powerful, so perfect, as to leave all faults of the piece to be forgotten'. The opportunity for bravura playing was seized by all concerned and the *Post* reported that, 'As the Earl of Essex, Mr J. Dewhurst was powerful, almost more so than required in the presence of the Queen'. The play continued to draw excellent audiences, but Mrs Gladstane was not content with maintaining her current repertoire.

In 1874 there had appeared yet another stage version of *East Lynne*, Mrs Henry Wood's successful novel, and Mary Gladstane saw a splendid opportunity for herself in the tragic role of Isabel. The play was added to the repertoire with Mrs Gladstane as Isabel Carlyle and Jonathan Dewhurst as her wronged husband, Archibald. Two months later the company returned to Birmingham's Theatre Royal to present the same programme of plays. The *Birmingham Post* found space only to record this fact and that *East Lynne* passed off smoothly and had been well-received by a large audience. The reason for the shortage of space was the review devoted to a visit by Mr and Mrs Kendal to the Prince of Wales Theatre, the *Post*'s critic panning their production of *Romeo and Juliet* for a variety of reasons, not least the mangled version of the last act which ruined the play.

But there was a dark cloud on the horizon. Margaret had not been well for some time and her condition now became decidedly worse. Jonathan interrupted his tour with Mary Gladstane to be with her, but on 3 October 1874 she died. The tuberculosis that killed her accounted for a high proportion of deaths in the Victorian Era, numbering amongst its victims several young actresses with whom Dewhurst had shared the stage. He returned to work with Mrs Gladstane and, after completing his engagement with her, was asked by John Douglass to join Miss Teresa Furtado to create the leading roles in the new play *Rank and Fame* at the Standard Theatre, Shoreditch. He stayed for the complete run of the play and then joined Mrs Gladstane again, this time for only a short period. *Elizabeth* was performed with Mrs Gladstane at the Standard Theatre, the *Illustrated Sporting and Dramatic News* commenting that Dewhurst, 'who was specially engaged for the part of the chivalrous "Essex", added one more to the many successes that have placed his name high in the list of our best leading actors'.

Despite his physical strength and fitness, Dewhurst had to accept that he needed a rest. Reaction to the death of his wife was perhaps delayed; the theatre, adrenalin and the belief that 'the show must go on' having disguised his need to slow down, but now he recognised the inevitable. Giving up his home in Knightsbridge, he returned to Lancashire and took up residence in Southport. The man of action, however, found it virtually impossible to do nothing. He recalled later:

> 'I went there principally in order to get a little rest and only played occasionally. Whilst there, however, I produced *Antigone*, and also gave a recital from memory of *Macbeth*. These were so successful that I endeavoured to persuade the directors of the Winter Gardens to obtain a dramatic licence so as to allow me to produce Shakespearean plays. The so-called religious scruples, however, proved too strong for anything of the kind just then. Nothing daunted, however, I secured a licence on my own hook for the Cambridge Hall, and having had it open for a week to crowded audiences, the directors of the Winter Gardens began to see their mistake and they were now induced to apply themselves for a dramatic licence, and from that time to the present, dramatic performances have contributed very largely to the success of the Winter Gardens. My production of *Antigone* proved a great attraction. Mrs Charles Calvert appeared in the title role, and Mendelssohn's music was excellently rendered by the Liverpool Choral Union. My own character was that of Creon.'

Dewhurst also gave a number of benefit performances and recitals for local charities. He raised over £50 for the Southport Infirmary, which entitled him to be a life governor of that institution, and in similar fashion raised money for the Chorley Dispensary and the Wigan Infirmary. He was always ready to help others and happily volunteered his services free of charge to appear at the Theatre Royal, Newcastle, on 21 February 1876. The occasion was the first performance in Newcastle of Sophocles' *Antigone*, the play being given for the benefit of Mr Henry Egerton, the popular stage manager of the theatre, with Dewhurst and Miss Phyllis Glover (who also gave her services) taking the principal roles. Dewhurst later recalled that 'poor Henry Egerton ... got burned to death in a fire at the Theatre Royal, Dublin'. The performance of *Antigone* was 'a grand success' and he was afterwards presented with a marked copy of the play as a memento of the occasion. But *Antigone* and Dewhurst's charitable inclinations were not the only reason for the visit to Newcastle. His work in Southport had had a beneficial and therapeutic effect, but he 'had been induced to lay out a lot of money for the production of high-class dramatic pieces' and while it had been artistically satisfying, it had not been a financial success. It was time to resume his proper role.

The two performances of *Antigone* at Newcastle's Theatre Royal were followed by a two-week run of Charles Webb's version of *The Lady of the Lake* which, despite earlier criticism, was still considered a good vehicle for stage spectacle. Dewhurst ('the well-known tragedian from the Theatre Royal, Drury Lane') was specially engaged to play Fitzjames, Miss Katherine Compton took the title role, with Miss Phyllis Glover as Blanche of Devon, and Mr A.D. McNeill, from the Princess's Theatre, Edinburgh, played Rhoderick Dhu. The *Newcastle Daily Journal* welcomed the production as 'the most rich and brilliant spectacular display that has ever been presented on a Newcastle stage ... enriched by gorgeous costumes and appointments and by some of the best efforts of the highest scenic art' and praised the ability of all the cast and their careful preparation leading to a resounding success. Dewhurst and McNeill, the two principal actors who had been specially engaged, were given benefits. Dewhurst took his on the final performance of *The Lady of the Lake*, but the following night McNeill took his benefit as Macbeth, with Dewhurst as Macduff and Phyllis Glover as Lady Macbeth. Not to be outdone, on the Saturday night *Macbeth* was repeated with Dewhurst now taking the lead opposite Phyllis Glover and McNeill playing Macduff.

In September Dewhurst accepted an invitation to play Leontes in Edward Saker's magnificent new production of *The Winter's Tale* at the Alexandra Theatre, Liverpool. Saker's wife, Marie O'Berne, was to play Hermione, and Saker himself was Autolycus, a part 'in which his peculiar powers are seen to great advantage'. Mrs Saker was a great favourite in Liverpool and as well as being an accomplished actress was a woman of determination and character. The production was a great success:

17 Dewhurst as Leontes and Mrs Saker as Hermione in Edward Saker's
magnificent production of *The Winter's Tale* at the Royal Alexandra Theatre, Liverpool
in September 1876.

'Mr Saker's splendid revival of *The Winter's Tale* at the above-named
theatre, vying in magnificence, as it does, with the best productions of
the kind with which the late Charles Kean's name is associated – to say
nothing of Mr Charles Calvert's equally noteworthy Manchester revivals
– has won the enthusiastic approval of the Liverpool play-goers, and the
applause of the entire Liverpudlian press.'

The acting was more than equal to the demands made on it – Mrs Saker
showed 'a thorough grasp of the character of Hermione... and the speeches
are delivered with telling effect'. Dewhurst gave 'an intelligent and effective
realisation of the cruel, jealous Leontes, but at times he is rather too noisy
and demonstrative'. But what the press found most deserving of its superlatives were the scenic effects, the description of the trial scene representing
the peak of Saker's achievement:

'The greatest scene of the whole piece is the open-air theatre of
Syracuse – of Coliseum form of course – in which Queen Hermione is
tried for her infidelity to her lord. In the foreground sits the king on high,

while the queen pleads from below in the splendid "not guilty" speech... Extending right and left and far out into the background stretched the noble theatre, with its circular benches crowded in front and for some distance back with real persons, while in the rear, with great skill, these thronged benches melted into painted tiers on tiers, equally crowded and looking not less real. The effect to be produced by this, however, was only dimly foreshadowed by the prospect which it presented in the full light as the trial of Hermione commenced and proceeded. It was when the oracle had vindicated her chastity and King Leontes had daringly defied the oracle that the great effect of the play took place.

'On the instant, darkness fell upon the body of the theatre, while a thunderbolt glanced swiftly across it in a diagonal direction, illuminating the scene with a baleful, angry projectile of gleaming light. At the same moment, while the crowd in the centre started up in every attitude of alarm, there darted upon the upper tiers, and settled there, a pale steel-blue radiance, in whose ghastly but intense light the figures on those distant benches were seen in similar poses of terror. The thunderbolt was momentary, but this thrilling effect of the nether darkness and the distant weird light coming from the point whence the thunderbolt had emanated lasted throughout the scene, and gave peculiar power to the awful situation in which Leontes finds himself when, having added defiance of the heavenly powers to the ruthless impiety of unfounded marital suspicion, he is suddenly rebuked in the sight of his horror-stricken people for his double sin.'

The local press was unanimous in its enthusiasm, even to the extent that some newspapers quoted from the reviews of their competitors, but the extent to which they applauded the spectacle indicates how important was this aspect of production and how successfully the major theatres, both in London and the provinces, recognised the fact. Jonathan Dewhurst had reached the top of his profession. He was always in work and to a large extent could choose where he worked and for whom. He played leading roles, generally in plays he thought worthy of his talents. But to some small extent there existed a feeling of dissatisfaction, a feeling that it was time to move on. He was a leading man, but was frequently 'invited' by leading ladies who were running the show; he could (and could afford to) say no, but working meant inevitably that he did not choose the play, nor the cast; and in this situation he responded to outside influences rather than directing the course of the future himself. There was only one way to go from here and that was to create his own company.

7

Jonathan Dewhurst's 'Powerful Legitimate Company'

Despite the attractions of running his own company, Jonathan Dewhurst took some time to get this initiative off the ground. He was a man of action, but he wanted to plan for success. His personal life had also taken a fresh turn. While appearing at Wigan he had chanced to meet Elizabeth Ingram, a young widow twelve years his junior. We do not know how they met, but perhaps the most plausible explanation is that the widowed Mrs Ingram supplemented her income by taking in boarders and that, when playing at Wigan, Jonathan Dewhurst stayed with her.

Jonathan and Elizabeth were married by special licence on 4 February 1878 at the Parish Church of Wigan. The marriage certificate gives Elizabeth's father as John Fairhurst, a colliery manager, and, as previously noted, Jonathan's father John, now in his late 80s, had retired and acquired the description of 'gentleman'. Elizabeth was 28 years of age and Jonathan 40, although the register gives his age as 39. A desire perhaps to cling to the 30s rather than embrace the next decade? Jonathan was still living in Southport and this is where, five months later, their daughter Amy Elizabeth was born, perhaps providing the reason for their marriage. Sadly the baby died in infancy. The sad and traumatic loss of a child was something only too common in Victorian Britain. Sanitary conditions and public health in lower-class urban and rural areas were poor and, although by 1878 standards were improving, there was a long way to go. The Dewhursts enjoyed a good standard of living, but even that would not protect them against all eventualities. In 1875 the death rate in England and Wales was 22.7 deaths per 1,000 persons and in the larger cities it was much higher – 27.5 in Liverpool, better in Manchester, but rather worse in some of the Yorkshire woollen towns. Inevitably very young children were most at risk.

The Dewhurst theatrical career continued to flourish. *Richelieu*, the historical drama by Edward Bulwer-Lytton, was strong theatre and offered in the central role of the great cardinal a part which appealed to all the leading actors of the period – Barry Sullivan, Samuel Phelps, Macready and Irving had all assumed the role to varying degrees of critical approbation. Early in his career Dewhurst had played Baradas to the Richelieus of Charles Calvert and G.F. Sinclair, and in August 1878 came the opportunity to play Richelieu himself in London. The press reported that:

'The most enthusiastic applause broke forth after Mr Dewhurst's delivery of each of the striking declamatory passages with which the Play is studded – while rarely has the tenderness for Julie, pity for De Mauprat and enmity towards Baradas been more clearly and artistically depicted. Mr Dewhurst's commanding height and really fine presence enable him to impersonate the Statesman Priest with graceful dignity; his assumption of age was very accurate and indeed his performance is at all points one of even excellence.'

Dewhurst had become a Freemason, joining the Liverpool Dramatic Lodge 1609 and, later that year, the Lodge gave a special performance in aid of the Masonic Hall Fund. The play was *Still Waters Run Deep* by Tom Taylor and was performed under the patronage of the Mayor of Liverpool, the Rt Hon Lord Skelmersdale. Brother J. Dewhurst took the leading part of John Mildmay, a 'Manchester Man'. Dewhurst's pleasure at his recognition by the higher levels of business and civic authority, as opposed to the theatrical world, was evident and perhaps indicates an ambition not only to rise above his humble beginnings but also in the future to become more the businessman. Whatever his religious beliefs, or lack of them, the Victorian work ethic and his belief in self-improvement burned strongly in Jonathan Dewhurst. During this period he had toured with Mrs Calvert in the North of England, but he recognised that the time had come for him to form his 'powerful legitimate company'. 'Powerful' was a subjective assessment of their ability; 'legitimate' implied the presentation of 'proper' dramas, tragedies or comedies without music.

In January 1880, when they appeared at Leigh, the town could not boast a purpose-built theatre and public performances took place at the Assembly Rooms. Dewhurst's company included some seasoned professionals and some young actors in the early stages of their careers. It also included the names of several who were to make their marks later in the annals of the theatre. The company opened with *Hamlet*, Dewhurst playing the Prince to the Ophelia of the popular and talented Ellen Cranston, who took all the leading female roles. The Ghost was the 23-year-old Edmund Tearle of the

18　Edmund Tearle, a member of Dewhurst's 'powerful legitimate company'.

Tearle theatrical dynasty, cousin of Osmond, the father of Sir Godfrey Tearle. Osric was played by the young Kate Clinton, who later married Edmund Tearle, and together they would run their own company with Edmund and Kate playing the leading roles.

Rosencrantz and the Second Gravedigger were played by the young Leonard Calvert, the son of Charles and Adelaide Calvert. Charles had given Jonathan his chance 15 years earlier and Jonathan was now returning the favour. The First Gravedigger was F.A. Scudamore who achieved success as actor and dramatist but not, perhaps, quite the success of his grandson, Michael Redgrave. In a few years Scudamore would be running his own 'powerful company'.

As we have already noted, production values were important to Dewhurst and the newspaper advertisements for the week's performances underlined this point:

'NOTICE – In presenting the immortal works of Shakespeare and others of the Great Masters, strict attention to costume, period and

58

detail has been observed, each Member of the Company having been carefully selected for the parts they are entrusted with, whilst the Plays have been carefully rehearsed and produced under the personal direction of Mr DEWHURST, who has the pleasure of submitting to the Public the Strongest Legitimate DRAMATIC COMBINATION Travelling.

'The Wardrobe and Dresses, specially manufactured for this Tour (from authentic sketches of the period), by Mr James Carr, Liverpool.'

Six different plays were presented during the week and on four of the evenings there was a supporting feature. Dewhurst's roles are shown in brackets:

Monday	*Hamlet*	(Hamlet)
Tuesday	*The Lady of Lyons* plus *The Lottery Ticket*	(Claude Melnotte)
Wednesday	*Othello*	(Othello)
Thursday	*The Merchant of Venice* plus *Intrigue*	(Shylock)
Friday	*Still Waters Run Deep* plus *The Taming of the Shrew*	(John Mildmay) (Petruchio)
Saturday	*Richard III* plus *The Sailor of France*	(Richard)

The local newspapers, the *Chronicle* and the *Journal*, contained glowing reports of Dewhurst's performances and those of Ellen Cranston. As was common practice at the time, the reports concentrated their attention on the star performer and to a much lesser extent on his leading lady or the other players. In *Hamlet*, 'Mr Dewhurst's acting of the difficult part of the Prince was throughout a conscientious and painstaking study. The true poetry of Shakespeare was never better realised in Leigh than by Mr Dewhurst'. His make-up as Othello was 'excellent and his part was rendered with good taste and fine dramatic point' and 'Mr Dewhurst as Othello confirmed the justice of the unusual praise he has received from dramatic critics'. Audiences were good, but for *Hamlet*, 'the gentry were conspicuous by their absence', although on Friday things had improved – 'there was almost a fashionable audience, the front seats being comfortably patronized'. Jonathan Dewhurst was a very popular performer in the north, but the success of his own company was a source of real pleasure to him. At the end of the week the *Leigh Chronicle* commented that:

'Mr Dewhurst met with a very hearty reception, and we trust that the recognition given to his undoubted abilities as an actor in the town of his youth will induce Mr Dewhurst to come again among us.'

In March the company appeared at the Theatre Royal, Oldham, and by then *The Lady of Lyons*, *Richelieu* and *Robert Macaire* had been added to the repertoire. Unfortunately the week coincided with the general election. As the *Oldham Chronicle* commented:

'A great treat has been afforded during the week to the lovers of the legitimate drama. The name of Mr J. Dewhurst has now become a household word and, although owing to the excitement attendant on the election, the "houses" have not been so crowded as they would have been, those who did go to the "Royal" can bear testimony to Mr Dewhurst's sterling ability as a tragedian.'

It may seem odd to us today that a general election should adversely affect theatre attendances, and in 1880 the vast majority of adults were not in any event concerned with going to the polls. Only something over one-half of adult males had the vote and women were entirely without the franchise – so it was not attendance at the poll booth that kept them away. Even without the vote, however, the 1880 election had seized the imagination of the public and we can only surmise that the theatre-going public had its mind on more pressing matters than entertainment. Benjamin Disraeli, despite (or perhaps because of) a widespread programme of social reform, had finally lost the support of the electorate and was swept from power by the Liberal, William Gladstone, who concentrated his attack on Disraeli's foreign policy. Dewhurst had the vote, but whether he found time to exercise it is another matter.

The *Sheffield Daily Telegraph* commented that his impersonation of the avaricious Shylock was marked by much power and force and considered it to be one of his many best characters. When the company went to Southport, the *Southport Visitor* pronounced his Shylock 'splendid', and that as Hamlet, 'he knows no equal in this particular role – his impersonation is original, unique, graceful and pathetic'. In the view of the *Visitor*, 'he was a far better Hamlet than Fechter'. If we can accept the truth of this comment, then it is praise indeed. Fechter's Hamlet had been very well-regarded by the critics – it was an intellectual reading of the part, as was Dewhurst's, and it is interesting that the drama critic of the *Visitor* recognised this similarity in approach. When they played at Oldham, Dewhurst had included *The Taming of the Shrew* as a second feature, as indeed he had at Leigh and throughout his tour. This was not the whole of Shakespeare's play but rather an adaptation of parts of the play by David Garrick, usually presented under the title of *Katherine and Petruchio*. In November 1880, when the company returned to Leigh, the adaptation was presented under its correct title. The programme offered at Leigh was the standard for the company – Shakespeare and Bulwer-Lytton – *Hamlet*, *The Merchant of Venice*, *Much Ado About Nothing*, *Richard III* with *Richelieu* and *The Lady of Lyons*. A second feature was offered with every play except *Hamlet*, the advertisement in the local press somewhat apologetically explaining, 'Owing to the length of the Tragedy, Hamlet will constitute the entire evening's entertainment'.

Dewhurst saw himself mainly in dramatic and tragic roles, but occasionally he did play comedy and with success. In December 1880 he joined Miss Ellen Wallis in Manchester playing Benedick to her Beatrice in *Much Ado About Nothing*. The *Manchester Guardian* commented:

'In Mr J. Dewhurst she had an admirable Benedick to give her the reply. His voice had a fulness and contagious gaiety in it which exactly

19   Ellen Wallis who played Beatrice to Dewhurst's Benedick
in *Much Ado About Nothing*.

suited the part. There was something fresh and alert in his playing which won him all suffrages. If it be true that to like an actor or actress means not merely to take an intellectual pleasure in their performance, but to feel a certain sympathy for their personality, Mr Dewhurst is admirably calculated to be popular. He has that unaffected brightness and openness of manner, which are exactly the qualities that Frenchmen ignorantly deny to all Englishmen, and which Englishmen certainly appreciate if they do not always possess. Last night he carried through his conception of the part, not with a "rush", there was too much science in the performance for that to be the right word, but with an easy mastery and abounding high spirit which made his performance a real success.'

Jonathan Dewhurst had achieved his goal. He had his own company and, by all accounts, a very capable one. He was able to present his choice of plays to a high standard and he took all the leading parts – parts which suited his talents and which he enjoyed playing. Perhaps, best of all, he and his company were always in demand. What more could he want? Perhaps it was his involvement with foreign actresses such as Mlle Beatrice and Mrs Gladstane, perhaps it was the knowledge that actors from England were already touring the Empire, perhaps it was just time to move on to different pastures. Whatever the reason, Jonathan Dewhurst decided that his next career move should be in the direction of Australia. How he broke the news to Elizabeth, and how she received it, we shall never know.

8

On the High Seas

Once Jonathan Dewhurst had made a decision, his resolve to carry it out was total. However, he and Elizabeth could not go immediately. In 1880 they had another daughter, named Elizabeth after her mother, and anxious though he was to try his luck in Australia, Jonathan recognised that a long sea voyage was no place for a new baby. Biding his time was not too difficult for, as we have seen, work for him was always plentiful and in the meantime he needed to plan the enterprise. Although some actors toured abroad with their own companies, far more went alone and relied on support from the stock companies of the theatres they visited. The standard might not be as good as with their own company, but planning and logistics were much simplified and in any event this was the method generally accepted by most leading actors. The star would play the lead part as he might wish and the supporting cast would do the best it could.

In researching the theatre – perhaps in researching any subject – interesting snippets of information can be found, items which, while not strictly relevant to the subject in hand, might throw an amusing and illuminating light on the broader picture. Had we not been looking through the *Era Almanack* of 1878, it would not have occurred to us that there was interest in (and quite a trade in) the autographs of famous people at that time. The *Era* gives estimates of the price of some of those connected with the arts. For those too young to remember 'old money', the new equivalents are given in brackets:

David Garrick £2.12.6d (£2.62½); Edmund Kean £3.3s (£3.15); John Philip Kemble 7/6d (37½p); Mendelssohn £1.10s (£1.50); Hector Berlioz 5/- (25p); Joseph Haydn £5.5s (£5.25) and the darling of Victorian England, George Frederick Handel – £42!!

By 1881, luxury travel at sea was well-established. Sail had remained predominant on the Australia run for far longer than on the North Atlantic, but by the 1880s steam was the prime means of propulsion, with sail used in an auxiliary capacity. The route to Australia was via the Cape and, while sailing ships could take 65–75 days, steam enabled the voyage to be completed in well under 50 days. The discovery of gold in Australia in the early 1850s had led to a great increase in passenger trade and a demand for faster voyages. The paddle used extensively in early steamers had given way to the screw-driven mechanism, which was more efficient but unsuitable for wooden ships because of the strains imposed on the hull. The picture was transformed, firstly through the large-scale production of iron (and later, steel) and the ability to cast large plates which made the iron vessel possible. The other technological advance was the development of the compound engine, which was able to deliver more power from less coal. These great advances meant that travel to the ends of the earth (or at least to places served by the shipping companies) was a realistic proposition for all those who could afford it. Journeys were accomplished in far less time than before and, if all ships were not the height of luxury, they were at least comfortable.

On 25 May 1881, the Dewhursts – Jonathan, Elizabeth and the one-year-old Elizabeth – presented themselves at the London Docks, boarded the *Cotopaxi* and set sail for Australia, bound for Adelaide, Melbourne and Sydney. The *Cotopaxi* was built in 1873 for the Pacific Steam Navigation Company and transferred to Orient Line management in 1879, for use on

20   The *Cotopaxi*, on which the Dewhursts sailed to Australia in 1881.

the Australia run. She had a single screw, a compound engine which produced 600 HP, and auxiliary sail. She was 4,022 tons, 122.58 metres in length, 13.6 metres wide and had two decks, which meant that passengers were better protected from the elements. The dining saloon ran the full width of the ship and from it, fore and aft, were the cabins. There was some electric lighting, although gas lighting was still used, and forced-draught ventilation provided some control over the temperature in the cabins and fresh air for the steerage passengers. Although the voyage was expected to take half the time, the *Cotopaxi* carried provisions for 90 days – perhaps an indication that natural elements might interfere substantially with man's best-laid plans. Apart from the crew, the ship carried 300 passengers – 245 adults, 45 children between the ages of one and twelve, and ten infants. The passenger list shows that the Dewhursts had a cabin – it also shows Jonathan's age as 40, when it was actually 44, and Elizabeth's age as 39, when in fact she was only 31! Whatever his other accomplishments, Jonathan's accuracy over ages seems to have caused him something of a problem.

There is no record of anything untoward on the voyage, indeed there appears now to be no record of the voyage at all. Presumably it passed in much the same way as voyages do today, but perhaps we can assume that a theatrical extravert such as Jonathan Dewhurst would have seized the opportunity to entertain his fellow passengers. However, the passenger list does give us a further piece of information. Ten infants, including Elizabeth, embarked on the ship. Only nine disembarked when it reached its destination. When we add that to the knowledge that there is no mention of the young Elizabeth in Australia and that she did not eventually accompany her parents when they left Australia, we can only come to the sad conclusion that on this trip Mrs Elizabeth Dewhurst lost her second daughter. Whatever Elizabeth's feelings may have been about the proposed Australian venture, she must by now have been quite distraught, wishing that they had never left England.

It is of some interest, though not directly connected with the Dewhursts' story, to see what fate ultimately befell the *Cotopaxi*. Some time after the Dewhursts' voyage, she was taken off the Australia run and put on the Valparaiso service. In his book *Steam Conquers the Pacific*, Arthur C. Wardle gives a graphic account of what sea travel could be like in the late 1880s:

'On March 6th, 1889, the iron screw-steamer *Cotopaxi* sailed from the Mersey, under command of Captain H.W. Hayes. She made an uneventful voyage until approaching the Straits of Magellan, when the weather became thick. Calling at Punta Arenas, she steamed westwards through the Straits, and at 8 p.m. on April 8th was approaching Cape Forward, when the captain left the bridge, after giving instructions that he should be called if anything were sighted. Three hours later came a noise of rending iron. Both captain and second officer rushed to the bridge, to find that the German steamer *Olympia* had struck the *Cotopaxi* on her starboard side. The liner listed heavily, while the *Olympia* had her bows badly damaged. Quick decision became necessary. Without hesitation, Captain Hayes ordered full speed ahead, turning the *Cotopaxi* for the land and steering her for the only break in the towering cliffs which afforded any possibility of beaching her. So great was the inrush of water into the engine-room, the fires were kept going only with the greatest difficulty, the engineers working to their waists in water.

'When almost on the point of sinking, the bow of the *Cotopaxi* touched ground, and immediate danger was removed. Daylight revealed a rent extending 12 feet by 6 feet, with several smaller holes, in the hull of the ship. All hands, passengers and crew, were promptly employed in shifting cargo, so that the worst part of the damage could be brought above the surface of the water – a task rendered more difficult by the listing of the ship as the cargo-shifting proceeded. Eventually she was careened to such an angle as permitted an attempt at repairs. It was here that the traditional ingenuity of the Company's sea-going staff asserted itself. Among the cargo, the ship carried a considerable number of boiler plates. These were hove up, and the engineers, with assistance from some Liverpool boiler-makers who were on board as passengers, drilled and secured the plates over the holes torn in the hull. This work was completed by the afternoon of April 11th. Stern anchors were run out, but the vessel did not move until a quantity of cargo had been jettisoned and all hands kept employed running from side to side of the ship in an attempt to shake her off the bed she had made. It was a triumphant moment when at last the ship floated and proceeded on her voyage. The captain brought her to anchor at the entrance of the notorious Smyth's Channel, considering that in her crippled condition it was inadvisable to reach the Pacific by way of Cape Pillar. At daylight, the *Cotopaxi* proceeded slowly through the Channel, anchoring at night-time, while the engineers worked continuously to complete repair of the internal damage. On April 15th, she entered the Messier Channel, which was supposedly unobstructed, and a speed of 13 knots was worked up in an effort to reach the Pacific Ocean by nightfall. All seemed to be going well until 2.28 p.m., when the vessel struck an unknown rock. It then at once became apparent that she had not long to remain afloat. Fortunately, the boats had been kept swung out ever since collision with the *Olympia*, and all hands were ordered to lower them. On board the *Cotopaxi* were 202 people, but within eight minutes they had all left the ship, and two minutes later she sank stern first. Only the calmest of competence and discipline could have rendered such a feat possible, and it is the more remarkable because among the passengers were two paralytics, whom one of the crew, Charles Dalton, carried to safety within the few minutes the ship remained afloat. The boats were headed for Wellington Island. There they were turned bottom upwards to shelter the women and children. Driftwood was collected and fires were kept going. They had plenty of water, but the only food available was mutton tallow which drifted ashore from the wreck. Two days later, the party rowed to the mainland, and next morning were picked up by the steamer *Setos*, of the Kosmos Line. The incident ranks as an epic of the sea, and both commander and crew afterwards received many marks of appreciation and gratitude from the passengers.'

Nothing so dramatic befell the passengers and crew of the *Cotopaxi* in 1881, and so on 8 July in that year, after a voyage of 44 days, Jonathan and Elizabeth arrived in Melbourne, the principal city of Victoria and indeed of Australia.

9

Australia – 1881

Like many cities of the Empire, Melbourne had developed from humble beginnings. In 1837, the year of Jonathan Dewhurst's birth, the settlement had become a township and was named after Lord Melbourne, the British Prime Minister. It grew rapidly in size and importance and when the Dewhursts arrived in 1881 it was very much a typical Victorian – and in some ways a very British – city. It was also the focal point for people from all over Victoria, attractive for its shops and impressive buildings, including a university. It was also able to offer entertainment and boasted four theatres – the Royal, the Opera House, the Bijou and the Princess's.

The Dewhursts rented rooms in MacKenzie Street and, while Elizabeth could take time to become acclimatised, for Jonathan there was no such luxury. The serious business of his theatrical career and the equally serious business of earning the wherewithal to support his wife and himself could not be delayed. They had disembarked on Friday 8 July. On Saturday 16 July Jonathan appeared on the stage of the Theatre Royal, Melbourne, in *Othello*, supported by the theatre's resident company. Whether he took a little time to acclimatise to Australia in general and Melbourne Theatre Royal in particular, or whether after a lengthy sea voyage and the loss of a child he was off form, it is impossible to tell, but to his immense irritation his *Othello* was not well-received by the critics. The Melbourne newspapers had welcomed him, referring to his extensive repertoire, the 'flattering notices' he had received from the provincial press in England and the praise accorded his Drury Lane performances. The *Age* thought his love scenes 'lukewarm and cold' and his performance 'lacking in energy', although his stage presence was commended and he was judged a 'very able actor' – faint praise indeed. *Othello* was repeated on the following night, the *Age* commenting that there 'was a marked improvement in the acting all round, especially in that of Mr Dewhurst [who] was far more successful in displaying the jealous passion of

"They are comynge toe ye Playe, gette you a place."—HAMLET, PRYNCE OF DENMARKE.

oe alle Peple of everie degree whoe doe loven yᵉ goode olde Stage Playes—Greetynge.

HEARAS **MAISTER J. DEWHURST,** a Tragedyane and Comedyane of yᵉ olde countrie, havynge croffed atte fome perile untoe hymfelfe yᵉ ftormie feas, and ben tempefte-toffed thereon, but now beynge fafely landed on thefe hofpitable fhores, willen enaҫte divers Playes writ by one **WM. SHAKESPEARE,** of Stratforde, on yᵉ fayre River Avon, and other fkylfulle and cunnynge craftefmen of yᵉ penne. Yᵉ fame Playes ben of goode repute, and have oftimes ben gyven to yᵉ diverfione, yᵉ profite, and yᵉ greate contente of yᵉ publick. It ben hopen by Maifter J. DEWHURST that hys ftage crafte willen enable him to aҫte yᵉ faide Playes inne a manner which willen ben pleafynge and acceptable untoe yᵉ citizens and peples of alle degrees inne yᵉ vafte and comelie countrie of

~~~~~~~~~ AUSTRALASIA. ~~~~~~~~~

"Nowe there willen ben a crye of 'Hats offe,' downe inne ye fronte."—Extraҫte from yᵉ "Critick," writ by oone Maifter R. BRYNSLEY SHERYDENE.

Yᴱ

21   The front page of Dewhurst's Australian hand-out reflecting the attraction
in that country of 'Olde Englyshe'.

69

the Moor'. Despite adverse critical comment, Dewhurst always seemed to be popular with the audience and the *Age* records that he received several recalls. Critical comment was not entirely consistent. The *Melbourne Bulletin* thought:

'Mr Dewhurst made his acquaintance with a Melbourne audience on Saturday night last in the character of Othello, and to speak of his introduction in terms anything short of success would scarcely be doing an intelligent and scholarly actor justice.'

But went on to say:

'If there is any drawback to his performance it is perhaps the impression that his voice does not correspond with his tall and commanding presence. In a man of smaller stature this would not perhaps be noticed, but from one powerfully built the absence of deep, rounded tones is at once apparent. Otherwise, Mr Dewhurst's impersonation is highly commendable.'

'Mr F.C. Appleton played Iago "fairly well" and Miss Alice Deorwyn's Desdemona was "an agreeable surprise to many"!'

It was not a good start and was disappointing to any actor, but the next play to be presented was *Richelieu*, by now Dewhurst's favourite role. If this could not redress the balance, what could? The *Age* reported that:

'Mr Dewhurst on Wednesday night made his first appearance at the Theatre Royal in Lytton's clever and effective, but melodramatic and historically inaccurate, play of *Richelieu*. Of Mr Dewhurst's performance we are able to speak in terms of almost unqualified praise. Though laboring under the serious defect of hoarseness, he gave a most excellent rendering of the part, and succeeded in thoroughly rivetting the attention of his audience from the beginning of the play to its close. Mr Dewhurst's elocution was clear and forcible, his action neither tame nor overstrained, and last, but not least, his make-up and appearance were most appropriate. He looked every inch the crafty and yet magnanimous cardinal who, though conscious of his power and of his importance to the State, yet considered himself above all the servant and guardian of France. While fully recognising that Lord Lytton's conception of the great man who overthrew the power of the French nobility and firmly fixed the foundation of the French monarchy is in many points most improbable and unreal, we cannot help admitting that Mr Dewhurst gave a most sympathetic and intelligent rendering of the character.'

The *Tasmanian Mail* reported that:

'A contemporary speaking of his assumption of the French Cardinal says the character was eminently suited to him and that his whole performance was marked by force and dignity.'

It does seem, however, that it was not just a case of 'settling down'. Dewhurst presented eleven different plays in a four-week season and some were well-received while others were rather less successful. On *Much Ado About Nothing*, the *Age* commented that:

'His performance will not add very materially to his reputation, though there were points in his Benedick worthy of commendation. The advantage of physique in the first place made him look the part and one could understand Shakespeare's Beatrice, which ideal certainly was not realised by Miss Anstead, being captivated by the manly graces of his person, no less than by the charm of his wit, but there was wanting the eloquent persuasiveness of tone in the softer passages. He appeared to more advantage in the fourth act, where he challenges Claudio in obedience to the behest of Beatrice. Mr Dewhurst was recalled several times during the progress of the comedy.'

Dogberry was played by Bland Holt, later to become a leading figure in Australian theatre. The greatest opprobrium was, however, reserved for Dewhurst's Richard III:

'Anything more commonplace, extravagantly melodramatic and stagey has not been witnessed in Melbourne for some time. However disposed we might be to make allowance for various and unmistakable drawbacks with which this gentleman has had to contend during the season, there is no gainsaying the fact that his representation of the wicked Gloster was only worthy of a very minor theatre. It is difficult to explain why Mr Dewhurst's Richard should have proved so disappointing when we take into consideration the remarkable histrionic ability he displayed in his representation of Hamlet and Richelieu.'

(*Tasmanian Mail* 26 August 1881)

'Mr Dewhurst played Richard III on Saturday and Monday nights, and he dressed the character splendidly, but he failed to impress his audience with any favourable view of his effort. It was a tame Richard

– without fire, and lacking that evidence of energy of action with which the ambitious King is usually painted.'

(Melbourne Bulletin 12 August 1881)

However, the *Melbourne Bulletin* also reported that Mr Dewhurst, 'who is held in great esteem by the members of the Theatre Royal Company and stage-hands, was presented last evening with a testimonial, subscribed by the people connected with the theatre'. On the plus side his Claude Melnotte (*The Lady of Lyons*) was 'played with considerable success' (the *Age*) and he 'gave an excellent rendering of the part' (*Weekly Times*). Of *Still Waters Run Deep*, the *Age* commented:

'...[the play] gave Mr Dewhurst an opportunity of undertaking a part peculiarly suited to him. John Mildmay, the quiet self-contained Lancashire man has been performed by some of the best actors that have appeared in Australia, but Mr Dewhurst's delineation fell short only of the very best. He gave an excellent representation of the character. Mr Dewhurst's performance was genuine and unaffected, and wherever there was an opportunity of making a powerful impression he rose to the occasion. A strong, simple, earnest character such as John Mildmay seems better suited to this actor's powers than a more emotional part, and this will certainly rank among his best performances.'

The Merchant of Venice was performed with *Katherine and Petruchio* (the shortened version of *The Taming of the Shrew*) as a supporting feature. The *Melbourne Bulletin* praised Dewhurst's 'undoubted versatility' in appearing in these two quite dissimilar roles on the same evening and went on to say:

'Mr Dewhurst's interpretation of Shylock is very far ahead of many we have lately seen. We must however admit that after seeing his Richelieu we could not appreciate it to the extent perhaps that it deserved. On another occasion when it does not follow so closely upon such an artistic success as his portrayal of the Cardinal undoubtedly was, his Shylock may be better enjoyed... To appear in the same evening as Shylock and as Petruchio, and to do so successfully is by no means an easy matter; but it may be claimed for Mr Dewhurst that what he undertook he thoroughly carried out.'

The *Age* commented that:

'…we may say in the words of a great critic, regarding Mr Dewhurst's Shylock

   "This is the Jew
   That Shakespeare drew."

The character was well made up and cunningly played, Mr Dewhurst's impersonation being quite on a par with any ever given on former occasions in Melbourne.'

However the *Weekly Times* took a different view:

'It appears to us that an intelligent and educated actor like Mr Dewhurst, with good natural qualifications, could give a clearer and more impressive reading of Shylock were he not so determined to be singular and original, even as he could a less boisterous and farcical Petruchio, were he so minded.'

His Hamlet was so well-received by the public that it was continued for two nights longer than intended. the *Age* said:

'His Hamlet is far superior to anything which Mr Dewhurst has hitherto attempted and compared with his previous Shakespearean performances, stands out prominently. The audience was entirely with him and applauded frequently and heartily, as well as insisting upon a recall after each act.'

The *Weekly Times*:

'His rendering of this part, notwithstanding its great difficulties, was far more successful than any of his previous efforts in classic drama upon this stage. His delivery was at times marred by inequalities of force, and he had in many instances adopted undesirable alterations in the text; but a very creditable moderation marked his performance from beginning to end, some of the scenes in the early part of the play being particularly impressive. In place of the boisterous declamation which so nearly approaches the melodramatic in the efforts of many actors, Mr Dewhurst interpreted the part of Hamlet with a quiet intensity which evinced a highly intellectual appreciation of the spirit in which the character is conceived.'

The *Daily Telegraph* considered his Hamlet 'superior to any representation we have had since the days of Montgomery and Kean'. Claudius was played by Charles Holloway, younger brother of W.J. Holloway, the founder of the theatrical Holloways in Australia. Later in his tour Dewhurst would join the Holloways at Ballarat, where they ran the local theatre.

It is evident from the press reviews that, although there had been some adverse criticism, it was far outweighed by the praise that Dewhurst received from the press. He had drawn large and responsive audiences and at the end of the four-week season the presentation he received was an indication of his popularity with his fellow artists. The *Age* recorded that:

> 'Mr Dewhurst received a benefit at the Theatre Royal last evening. He again played Richelieu and met with a very hearty reception, being honoured with several recalls. During the evening Mr Dewhurst was presented by Mr B.N. Jones, stage manager, with a handsome silver trophy subscribed for by members of the company and of the profession. Mr Dewhurst acknowledged the compliment, and in the course of his address referred to the press criticisms of his performance, which he said were such as other men might have succumbed under, and hardly a sufficient reward for the trouble he had taken to present his pieces in a worthy manner.'

His response to the presentation betrays the hurt caused by the criticism, and also perhaps a feeling that giving 100 per cent was sufficient justification for expecting favourable criticism on every occasion. Hurt pride probably explains his feelings, rather than a fear that the public might note the adverse comment and stay away – which happily for him they never did. Dewhurst may have felt ill-used by the Melbourne critics, but that was before he had sampled the work of the drama critic of the *Sydney Bulletin*. The newspaper pages we have been able to examine detail the reviews in which we are specifically interested, but also include other notes and critical comments by the drama critic of this newspaper. He displays clear likes and dislikes, a somewhat satirical, not to say dyspeptic view of things and a very entertaining turn of phrase. We have included below a few unrelated gems merely to give a little added flavour and a little posthumous exposure to this gentleman's literary efforts. Dewhurst's Sydney season lasted until late September and contained his usual repertoire. He opened at the Queen's Theatre with *Hamlet*. The *Bulletin* enjoyed itself, if not the performance, and despite the length of the reviews they represent such good value that we feel quite justified in reproducing a selection of them in their entirety:

'The piece Mr Dewhurst chose in which to make his debut in Sydney, was a tragedy in five acts, called *Hamlet*, and popularly supposed to have been written by one William Shakespeare, an author of some repute in his time, but whose reputation has been, in our era, eclipsed by the splendid genius of that Owl bard who penned their inaugural address. With regard to the play itself, we think we may fairly risk the assertion that it is a creditable production. We admit that in some parts it lacks the sparkle of Scott and the polish of Hopkins, and also that it has the disadvantage of not having been adapted from the French – still as a specimen of the work of a young man who lived in an age before Lewis was known, or Darrell dreamed of, it can fairly lay claim to a modicum of merit. Perhaps if Mr Shakespeare were living we would give him a little more kudos, but there is so little "hanging to" praising a man when he's dead, that we really can't afford him any more space this issue.

'So far as the play was concerned, then, Mr Dewhurst hadn't much to grumble at. Let us now glance at the cast. The backbone, of course, consists of Hamlet, the King, the Ghost, Ophelia and the Queen. With these characters left out, we consider that the tragedy would lose a good deal of its interest: but doubtless this is only a matter of opinion. Mr Dewhurst of course took the title role, and as this is called in the programme his "Grand Creation", and as the piece was written in the year of grace, 1580, we were rather surprised to find Mr Dewhurst looking so young. The King was entrusted to the "celebrated English character actor", Mr Newton Griffiths. Mr J.B. Steele played the Phantom, Miss Melville the Queen, and Miss Marian Willis Ophelia. This is the strongest combination that has shown at the Queen's since Mr Keogh's lesseeship, and, to judge from the crowded attendance, the performance excited considerable interest in the minds of the public. We ourselves, plead guilty to having, on Friday, passed a sleepless night.

'Mr Dewhurst is a tragedian of very fine presence indeed; being, in fact, anatomically sublime. He has, also, a fine resonant voice, and his "get up" exhibits great taste and discrimination. His reading of the part, however, is quite antagonistic to the conception we have formed of it. Of course Mr Dewhurst may be right and we wrong; but if we are wrong, why we have the satisfaction of knowing that we err in very good company. To us the performance became, after a time, wearisome in the extreme. Mr Dewhurst displayed so fine (and indeed such little) action that his role resembled – more than anything else – a long sermon. We have an objection to acting of the "robustious" school, but certainly the coldness of Mr Dewhurst is, to our mind, quite as grave an error even as ranting. His madness was of the mildest character, and in the closet scene he upbraided the Queen for her conduct in marrying his uncle very much in the same manner that a father would chide his eldest girl for lingering too long with her "chap" on the family doorstep. He made nothing of the "O what a rogue and peasant slave am I" speech, the lecture to the players was delivered – like a lecture; and the reception by the audience of his "To be, or not to be," sililoquy [sic], was as quiet as the manner of Mr Dewhurst itself.

'In his reading we could detect nothing that was original, but there was in it much that was crude and unscholarly. For instance, when Rosencrantz says, on his exclaiming he "lacks advancement", "How can that be, when you have the voice of The King himself for your succession in Denmark?" instead of giving the answer as punctuated by the author – "Ay, sir, but while the grass grows, – the proverb is something musty", he delivered the reply in one breath, thus: "While the grass grows the proverb is something musty." Such carelessness (for it can be nothing else) is inexcusable, and by passing it over the critic would be as lacking in his duty as a writer as Mr Dewhurst was in his emphasis as an actor. Finally, we must confess – and we are sorry to have to do so – that Mr Dewhurst's *Hamlet* was a great disappointment to us. Not only did it never rise above bare mediocrity, but it was very often below it. We are, of course, just as sorry to say this as Mr Dewhurst will be to read it. Doubtless, however, the "taffy" he will receive from some of our contemporaries will console him. We hope so.

'Mr Newton Griffiths's King was an astounding performance. His costume beggars description, and he went about with the largest fire insurance plate upon his kingly breast that was ever seen off a five-storey building. His voice was so deep that it seemed to come out of his boots, while his face was so ferociously made up that murder gleamed in his optics, and burglary was branded on his brow. You could see the moment he came on that he would stick at nothing, and we fully expected to see him bore a hole through Hamlet before the piece was half over. In the middle of Hamlet's speech about the "witching hour of night", this ferocious monarch caused some confusion by "coming on" at the wrong time, but Polonius who (being fond of the drama) was yet lingering near the players platform, proved equal to the occasion, by taking his majesty by the shoulder and butting him back into the wing. Mr Newton Griffiths may be (and possibly is – for he

76

ought to know) a "celebrated English character actor", but, if so, the King in *Hamlet* doesn't suit him. Perhaps, though, that is because it isn't an English character, but a Danish one.

'Mr George Melville made a good Polonius, but his costume was too suggestive of the Cock-lane Ghost to be pleasant. His cloak (and what a lot of it there seemed!) was of some white material, and his doublet and trunks being slashed with the same fabric, he looked like a chessboard in front, and like a ghost behind. And two ghosts in one *Hamlet* is rather rough on a law-abiding public.'

Richelieu fared somewhat better at the hands of the *Bulletin*, but not to any extent that would have pleased Dewhurst:

'... We have already delicately hinted that Mr Dewhurst's conception of *Hamlet* would not have been likely to revive Shakespeare had that extinct person ever been treated to a view of the performance while suffering from low spirits. And, when the eminent tragedian remarked, in the character of the moody Dane, that "By Heaven, I'll make a ghost of him that lets me," we felt sorry for Mr Steele, who had let Mr Dewhurst make a Ghost of him.

'Perhaps it's easier to interpret Lytton than Shakespeare. Possibly a man may glow through the romantic historical melodrama with intelligence, yet fall short of elucidating the subtle philosophies of "Hamlet". Anyhow, Mr Dewhurst makes a much more satisfactory Cardinal than he does a Prince of Denmark, and if we continue to have any influence with Pope Leo he shall ere long – but, no matter. We have been told that when Mr Dewhurst read our opinion of his Hamlet he became purple. Having seen him in his Cardinal's robes, we now understand that that was only returning compliment, as there can be no doubt that purple becomes Mr Dewhurst. That eminent tragedian is perhaps too robust to make his presentment of the Cardinal entirely satisfactory. The hollow eyes are belied by the very substantial frame and well-nourished cheek. The hectic cough business doesn't fit in well, and Mr Dewhurst would be wise to tone his pulmonary demonstrations down. Hawking at intervals, and then looking to see what he hadn't brought up on his handkerchief may suggest a decline, but on the whole the effect might be produced by more agreeable means.

'The play opens, as everyone knows, very quietly. Richelieu, on his first appearance, is *chez lui*, and tells his people lies about his feats at the siege of Rochelle, and brags about the plays he has written. The first hit of the performance was made when His Eminence called for his falchion, and brought Defries immediately into the minds of the audience. When François (Miss Marion Medway) hauled forward the weapon, with an elaborate demonstration of having as much as she – we mean he – could manage, even the family weapon of the Defrieses was surpassed. Richelieu's little vanities were seen through at once. The weapon was so obviously and transparently constructed for pantomimic purposes, and the probable equipment of giant Fee-Fo-Fum, that a unanimous wink went round the house; and it was decided that Richelieu, as a statesman, reminded one very much of Parkes, and that Joseph, for his agreeable complaisance, deserved to be made a C.M.G.–

> *The sword, my lord, which at Rochelle*
> *You handled with such ease,*
> *Reminds us of that other sell –*
> *The sabre of Defries.*
>
> *The falchion of Defries, my lord,*
> *Was steel, and bright and strong;*
> *Your weapon's wood, and, on my word,*
> *As broad as it is long.*
>
> *Oh, put away your trusty blade,*
> *And never mind its faults –*
> *Brag of the thousands you have 'slayed'*
> *When taking Rochelle-salts.*

'Mr Dewhurst, when disassociated from this preposterous sword and during the intervals between his coughs, presented a very satisfactory impersonation of the Cardinal. He did not "tear the passion in tatters" – in fact, had he ripped it a trifle more than he did, his piece might have gone none the worse.'

Our selection from the *Sydney Bulletin* concludes with *Othello*:

'At the Queen's Theatre, Shakesperian drama has been presented during the week. We are great admirers of Shakespeare's plays ourselves, and so – haven't been much at the Queen's. We looked in, however, on Friday, to see *Othello*, with Mr Steele in the title role, and Mr Dewhurst as honest, honest, Iago. Mr Steele defers to modern prejudice against

Mr. H.W. Chapman gave, on Wednesday week, a Shakespearean, dramatic and humorous recital at the Protestant Hall, of 21 pieces, all of them more or less hackneyed. Admission was by invitation and, therefore, we suppose we have no right to be critical. For Mr. Chapman we can say this much and we say it with pleasure, that he is very persevering. When he gives a recital to which a charge (however trifling) is made for admission we will say a good deal more. In the meantime we would delicately hint to Mr. H.W.C. that it is just possible to have too much of even a good thing. Twenty-one pieces – Eureka!

We are pleased to be able to record one success for this young gentleman and shall be more pleased still when we can conscientiously record another.

Miss Clara Hamilton, a Scottish lady, gave on Monday night a concert at the Protestant Hall which entertainment with considerable originality, she entitled 'Twa 'oors at Home'. We don't quite know what this means just now, but will try and construe it before we are called up to do the trump and angel business in a brighter sphere.

Miss Clara is a lady who possesses a very large amount of confidence, but not a very large voice. Of what she has, however, she makes the best possible use, and her dialect ballads appeared to find immense favour with the audience. They found immense favour with us, too, and we should have been quite more than excessively enchanted had we been able to gather even a glimmering of what they were about. But for all the meaning we could make out of the ballads of Miss Clara, she might have been singing translations of the inscriptions from off the Chinese tea-chests, or warbling free renderings of 119th dissertation by Confucius on abstract theology.

There are amateurs and amateurs. There are the curled darlings of fortune, whose performances, always 'under distinguished patronage', draw crowds of other curled darlings to witness them; and there are the clerks and warehousemen whose entertainments attract other clerks and warehousemen to attend them. Well, during the past week we have attended – and are consequently in an exceedingly feeble condition – performances given by both these types of amateur societies. And, at the risk of forfeiting forever the favour of the horny-handed, we must confess to preferring the patchouli and rose-leaf contingent. Our reasons for this are manifold. In the first place the Government House people can talk English; in the second they look pretty, and in the third they (the audience is included in this reason) smell nicer.

22   Snippets from the *Sydney Bulletin's* drama critic.

gentlemen of colour, and carries the whim, common of late years to many distinguished tragedians, of representing the Moor as only lightly touched by the sun, to so great a degree as to induce in the minds of observers as strong suspicions of the honour of Othello's mother as the unhappy husband of Desdemona nourished respecting the honour of his wife. Mr Dewhurst's pourtrayal [sic] of honest Iago is a respectable one. He, also, adopts the modern conception and discards the diabolical for the insinuating ideal. His Iago is a bland and dexterous individual, as, beyond doubt, he should be represented to preserve the unities of the drama, and to relieve Othello from the imputation of being a fool altogether.

'To carry out this conception demands, however, infinitely more of art than to growl and scowl through the part in the fashion of former days. The by-play, and, above all, the subtlety of facial expression, required to convey to an audience a sense of Iago's duplicity, while yet preserving his fair outer seeming, are very exacting, and demand peculiar qualifications alike of mobility of feature and inner inspiration. We venture to suggest that in these essentials Mr Dewhurst is some-what deficient. His Iago is too stolid. His face is devoid of expressive-ness. Only the eyebrows had motion, and not the most gifted actor could convey a thousand contending passions with voice and eyebrows alone. Mr Dewhurst suffered from a severe cold, which affected his voice even in speaking. We never yet heard a tragedian of eminence who could sing any better than an opera-bouffe comedian at the Royal. The more eminent the actor, as a rule, the worse he sang. In this respect, Mr Dewhurst – thanks in some degree to his cold – towered to an unrivalled eminence. Iago's chants about letting the canakin clink, and concerning King Stephen's breeches, were nearly as blood-curdling as ever Mr Harwood's chansonnettes [sic] in *Olivette*. Poor G.V. Brooke himself never croaked more horribly.'

Dewhurst, who alternated Iago with Othello, would have turned purple at such criticism, certainly by far the worst we have found and probably the worst that he received during his career. Even allowing for the fact that his performances could not have been expected to please everyone (except the audiences), the impression can perhaps fairly be gained that the drama critic of the *Bulletin* was at least as interested in demonstrating his own literary intellect – and ability to entertain – as anything else. His views were not shared by others, the *Tasmanian Mail* commenting on Dewhurst's Othello that:

'In Sydney Mr Dewhurst's success continues at the Queen's Theatre: *Richelieu*, after a good run, has given place to *Othello*. Concerning his performance of the valiant Moor a local paper said his portraiture was in keeping with his conception of the outer man. He represented the early scenes with grace and dignity, delivering the famous speeches with a quiet power, which as the poison was gradually instilled by the demon Iago, became a fury; he gave the reins to his passion unchecked. And the strain which affected his voice during the later scenes seemed the natural result of such a stormy outburst. The impression was so realistic at times one could scarcely avoid a fear that his grip on Iago would become a fight indeed, and that the fragile Desdemona would be actually strangled by her incensed lord.'

The *Sydney Morning Herald* said of Dewhurst's Richelieu that 'his assumption of the name-part in Bulwer-Lytton's famous play is one of unusual power. He seems to have studied the character of the great minister... with sagacity and ardour, and the result is that he is able to paint in living colours a stage picture of one of the most remarkable figures of the Age in which he lived'.

Brisbane's Theatre Royal was the next port of call. Dewhurst's season was for three weeks, although he was engaged for a further two weeks before the theatre closed for alterations. He recalled later that his visit clashed with the first appearance in Australia of Wilson's Great World Circus, the 'Greatest Show that has ever visited Australia'. The circus was booked for only one week, but was so popular that it stayed for three. Unfortunately the rival attraction of the circus was too much for the Brisbane public, which attended the theatre in enthusiastic but small numbers. Dewhurst and others suffered a substantial loss. At the theatre he was supported by the resident company and other specially engaged artists, including Miss Maud Brandon, a 'charming young English actress recently arrived in Australia'.

From the press reports it seems that the support he received was, on the whole, of an indifferent standard and that Miss Brandon in the leading female roles took some time to get over her initial nervousness. In *Richelieu* the *Brisbane Courier* reported that 'Miss Featherstone, as François, forgot her lines and spoiled the effect of what would otherwise have been one of Mr Dewhurst's most effective scenes'. The *Brisbane Courier*, reporting on *Richelieu* and *Hamlet*, raises an interesting point and one which we should like to consider in some detail. When we first started researching Jonathan Dewhurst it was apparent that he was a man of impressive physique and commanding presence with equally imposing vocal equipment. In our uninformed imagination, and bearing in mind the theatrical fashions of the day, we could picture him centre stage adopting an exaggerated dramatic pose and declaiming loudly to the audience, regardless of the requirements of the role he was assuming. That he was not like this became clear quite quickly, but the more we have delved the more we have discovered that he was an actor who thought deeply about the characters he portrayed and who sought to show his interpretation of the inner man however radical this might appear to the critics. The review of *Hamlet* by the *Brisbane Courier* illustrates this aspect and perhaps suggests that in some ways Dewhurst's interpretations might have been ahead of their time:

'There was a rather better house at the theatre last night to witness *Hamlet*. In noticing this performance it is necessary to preface our remarks by saying that Mr Dewhurst's conception of the character is evidently quite different from that ordinarily presented. It is usual to represent the Prince of Denmark as a young man full of noble impulses, anxious to do right, but of weak mental fibre, so that throughout the play the dread task imposed upon him weighs down his soul, and if it does not actually madden him, at least tortures his whole being. The wildness of his outbreaks are indications of the mental storm raging within. This is the usual conception, but Mr Dewhurst's Hamlet is a man of quite a different stamp. Strong in mind, as in body, his purpose grows upon him, and his vagaries are deliberate – the part which he has coolly determined to play, and is playing. To such a man the breach with Ophelia is not heart-rending, and Laertes was quite right in his warning to his sister, for with Mr Dewhurst's Hamlet love would be more of a diversion than the governing motive of life. Whether this conception is the right one or not we are not now concerned to inquire, but it must be acknowledged that Mr Dewhurst carries it out. Such a man would scorn the dotard Polonius, and allow no qualifying touch of pity for Ophelia's father to lessen the sentiment. Accordingly Mr Dewhurst is uniformly bitter in his jibes to the old man, and the look of concentrated contempt with which he rebukes Polonius when he interrupts the player with his comments is – from this point of view – very fine. Even when he draws the curtain to look upon the old man's body there is nothing but coldness in the tone with which he pronounces the line – "Thus bad begins, and worse remains behind".

'Still keeping up the same conception, he is rough and almost brutal in the scene with Ophelia. There is passion rather than love in the embrace he gives her, not the clinging tenderness of the Hamlet we have been accustomed to see. When by a natural gesture he allows the audience to see that he has discovered the watch set upon him, there is very real bitterness in the wild words with which he continues the interview. He lashes Ophelia with his sarcasm, taking a savage delight in thus chastising what he supposes to be her deliberate treachery. But an inconsistency follows. When he re-enters the room to give his instructions to the players he picks up the casket Ophelia has returned to him, which is lying on the floor, and kisses it. Mr Dewhurst's Hamlet would not have done this.

'The advice to the player is exceedingly well given, and indeed – assuming Mr Dewhurst's conception of the character to be a correct one, so also are most of the soliloquies. The interview with Guildenstern and Rosencrantz is very natural. This Hamlet has no difficulty in playing a part, and he affects the friendly tone with complete success. The idea of ending the second act seated at the table and beginning to write the lines intended to be spoken by the players, makes the action suit the words – "The play's the thing Wherein I'll catch the conscience of the king".

'Another innovation introduced by Mr Dewhurst is in the commencement of the well-known "To be or not to be". He enters musingly, idly fingering his dagger, and pointing it almost unconsciously at his breast, thus giving the key-note to the idea of suicide which is running through his brain.'

Of his Richelieu:

'Mr Dewhurst opened last night to a fair audience in *Richelieu*. His enunciation of the splendid language put into the mouth of the great cardinal was clear and distinct, but he maintained at first a high declamatory level which became rather monotonous at times, and his conception of the character differs widely from that usually formed. Richelieu is generally played as a very feeble old man, whose invincible mind triumphs over physical infirmity when a crisis demands the full exercise of his powers. Mr Dewhurst has evidently formed a different idea of the part. The cardinal, as he presented him in the earlier acts, was an old man certainly, who had lost some of the lusty vigour of youth – who could not raise the great two-handed sword he wielded at Rochelle – but who was still hale and strong, with a body quite able to carry out the designs formed by his imperious mind. The extreme tottering feebleness he displayed in the last two acts was, according to

Mr Dewhurst's interpretation, merely the ruse of the wily politician at bay, and summoning all his craft to outwit his foes. The sudden outburst of vigour in the closing scene, when the king committed his whole power into his hands, became, therefore, not the conquest of the strong mind over the feeble body, but the triumphant flinging aside of a disguise which had served its turn, and was no longer needed. This interpretation of the character of course deprived Mr Dewhurst of many "points" which other actors are in the habit of making by contrasting feebleness of body with strength of will, but it enables him to give intensity to other passages. Towards the close of the play he carried the sympathies of the audience with him very heartily.

'*Richelieu* is a play which always draws, and it is probable that it will run successfully for the nights for which it has been announced. And Mr Dewhurst, whatever opinion may be formed of his conception of the principal character, plays with power, and, as an artist, is far above the average standard to which we have been accustomed.'

On the penultimate night of the run Dewhurst appeared in *Still Waters Run Deep*, receiving his complimentary benefit, and after the performance a presentation was made to him by 'Members of the Company and a few Friends'. Following the end of his short season, he was re-engaged by the theatre for two weeks of comedy and burlesque, supported by the resident company. He managed to avoid the burlesque and appeared in plays such as *Don Caesar de Bazan*, *Faint Heart Never Won Fair Lady* and *Katherine and Petruchio*, but had the satisfaction of ending the two weeks with *Louis XI*. With the departure of the circus, the audiences had returned and financial losses were reduced. *Louis XI* played 'to the largest audience ever assembled in the theatre' and 'Mr Dewhurst, as the crafty old tyrant, appeared to better advantage than in almost any character he has assumed. He was better supported also than usual, the crowded house spurring the company to unusual exertions'. And while Jonathan Dewhurst was appearing in Brisbane, what was happening to Henry Irving? The *Tasmanian Mail* reported that 'Mr Henry Irving has been decorated by the Grand Duke of Saxe-Meiningen with the Knight Cross of the Ducal Saxe-Ernestine House in recognition of his great services to the dramatic art'.

After the theatre closed Dewhurst played a week at the Ipswich (Brisbane) School of Arts and the account of the first night in the *Queensland Times* illustrates only too well the perils of touring in those days:

'Mr John Dewhurst, supported by the Brisbane Theatre Royal

Company, appeared in the School of Arts last evening, Shakespeare's tragedy of *Hamlet* being the play selected for the occasion. A little delay was experienced and at some minutes after eight o'clock Mr Marsh came before the curtain and craved the indulgence of the audience for a short time; he explained that Mr Dewhurst's wardrobe, though sent to the Brisbane station in time for the morning train, had not come to hand, and he would have to appear before them at a disadvantage, and in the best make-up procurable. Before the last act, Mr Dewhurst himself came forward, and apologised for the defects of the evening, which, he assured the audience, was not the company's fault. He would not feel a bit like Hamlet that evening, and he hoped they would excuse him, and not take the night's performance as a specimen of their acting. Tomorrow, they would have all requisites, and be able to appear before them to better advantage in *Richard III*. In the face of this, it would be out of place to attempt to criticise the performance. The company certainly are deserving of credit for appearing at all under such untoward circumstances. Due allowance, however, was made by the audience, and a very good hearing was accorded the performers. Most of the members of the company are well-known to Ipswich playgoers as careful and improving actors. Mr Dewhurst, himself, was frequently applauded during the evening, and his acting, though not up to his own standard, was not by any means without merit.'

Following the week at Ipswich, Dewhurst records that:

'I then went up the country with a small company and played Shakesperian and other pieces in schools, barns, or other buildings that we could get hold of. We had only sheets for scenery but our productions were very acceptable to the squatters, who, of course rarely had an opportunity of witnessing anything of the kind.'

On his return to Brisbane there occurred something unusual for which we have been unable to find a full explanation. Advertisements appeared in the press stating that the town hall had been hired for a short season of plays featuring Mr Dewhurst and all available theatrical talent. No details were given of the management or sponsors, but the first play to be presented was 'Pettitt's new and sensational National Drama *British Born*, or *Honour to Old England's Flag*'. On the first night the town hall was well filled but the performance was preceded by a speech 'from Mr Marsh, in which he explained why Mr Dewhurst had ceased to have any connection with the company

85

and stated their intention of paying their debts!' The *Brisbane Courier* reported that the play was 'excellent of its kind … a drama of the wildly sensational order turned into unintentional burlesque'. Although the company kept the audience in a state of 'high good humour', the second night was poorly attended, after which nothing more seems to have been heard of the company. Whether it was the play, or whether Dewhurst's fee was not forthcoming, we shall never know, but although he could be generous to a fault, he was not the kind of man to allow anyone to take advantage of him. So at the end of the year Dewhurst left Brisbane and, as far as we know, did not return.

10

Australia – 1882

Dewhurst records that at the turn of the year he called again at Sydney and Melbourne. We have traced no performances there for this period and possibly he intended to convey that he 'called' there – neither more nor less. What is interesting is that at this time the American actress Louise Pomeroy was appearing in Sydney, who, with her company, received very favourable reviews at the Theatre Royal. Our interest in showing a connection between Dewhurst and Pomeroy – or at least that they met – will become clearer a little later in the story. We next find Dewhurst appearing at the Royal Princess's Theatre in Bendigo, a town some 80 miles north of Melbourne. The *Bendigo Advertiser* complimented the lessees of the theatre for their enterprise in presenting to the theatre-going public of Sandhurst (the old name for Bendigo) a short season of tragedy, featuring the 'eminent tragedian Mr Dewhurst'. The season opened with *Richelieu*, and while the *Advertiser* felt that in one sense something better known might have been offered, nevertheless this was counterbalanced by the opportunity of seeing Dewhurst in 'what he must regard as his principal character and one which he has studied to perfection'. Here was not to be found the bile of Sydney: the press and the Bendigo public welcomed Dewhurst with open arms and much appreciation. Of his Richelieu, the *Advertiser* said:

'Indeed witnessing his performance recalls the days of that prince of tragedians G.V. Brooke and it is not saying too much in his favour that not since that time has Sandhurst seen so grand and powerful a delineator of the character of France's "all powerful Minister" as Mr Dewhurst. Mr Dewhurst has a commanding presence and a clear penetrating voice. His mimicry of age was excellent and in the latter scenes especially his infirmity was life-like. His changes of disposition, his hatred and contempt for Baradas, the indomitable will and power of

87

resources were qualities in the character of Richelieu which were prominent points in the performance. All the more powerful situations were brought out with a completeness which made the audience enthusiastic and made them recognise in Mr Dewhurst an actor of the first school and no ordinary merit. Mr Dewhurst was grandly powerful and thrilled the audience to an unusual pitch of excitement. Mr Dewhurst was recalled at the end of each act.'

Mr J.F. Cathcart, who had been specially engaged to support Dewhurst for the week, gave an 'excellent representation' of Baradas, Miss Kate Douglas as Julie, G.R. Ireland as De Mauprat and all the cast 'played very well'.

Dewhurst almost always received public acclaim from enthusiastic audiences. He had generally been accustomed to more appreciative criticism from the press than that which he had received from the Sydney Bulletin, but this was now behind him and Bendigo was an unqualified success. As Othello, his conception of the character 'is without doubt a very fine one' and the *Advertiser* referred to his 'dramatic power and energy'. As Shylock, 'each shade of passion was carefully preserved' in a character which was quite different from the others he had represented. The *Advertiser*'s critic, however, was not entirely happy:

'We have again to notice the faultiness of the scenic effects. The play last evening was decidedly marred by the want of knowledge of the stage manager, and a large portion of the action of the play was made to take place in the same scene, a liberty which is not sanctioned by any of the works we know of and which certainly spoiled many of the incidents. The audience do not go to the theatre to witness scene flats run out and drawn in again for no evident cause and the actors also would do well to be at their posts ready to enter upon the call-boy's announcement instead of letting the audience wait their arrival in suspense. We would not direct so much attention to this, but that last evening seemed to be an aggravation of the evening before.'

Dewhurst took his benefit on the penultimate night when *Hamlet* was presented. His interpretation, which earlier critics had questioned, brought forth comment, but the *Advertiser* was clear that it accorded closely with the words of Polonius:

'Though this be madness, yet there's method in it.'

The assumption, by many elements of the press, that the only possible interpretation of the role was that Hamlet was cracking up under the emotional pressure, may seem somewhat naive to us today, but in Australia in 1881 and 1882 there were critics who could accept an alternative reading, and in Bendigo as in Brisbane his performance in the terms in which he read the character was amply praised:

'Mr Dewhurst's rendition of the character of Hamlet must be regarded as a very fine one and the acting throughout was intensely powerful. The scene with his father's shade was full of dramatic power, and the intensity of feeling was shown in the oath of vengeance. The scene wherein he commences to reveal the secrets of his companions and then suddenly turns off to another thought was excellent. The scene with Ophelia was also very fine – the quick transition from trustfulness and love to doubt and disgust – being very clearly portrayed. The play scene was also another fine piece of acting, the climax being worked with an effect which thrilled the audience to a pitch of almost uncontrollable excitement. The lines before the interview with Ophelia, "To be or not to be", were rendered with a fund of thoughtfulness, showing how the mind dwells upon the question at issue. The scene with his mother was another most powerful piece of acting, the lines especially, 'Look here upon this picture, and on this', being given with fond remembrance and anon with startling vehemence, which chimed well with the situation and relations of Hamlet towards his mother, and was perhaps as powerful a piece of acting as any throughout the play.

'In the grave scene we saw sorrow once more overcast the brow and unutterable grief possess him upon the death of Ophelia. The last scene was also given with force and his death a very artistic closing to an unusually effective performance. There may be doubts as to the view which Mr Dewhurst takes of the character of Hamlet, but there cannot be any two opinions of the magnificent representation of the part at his hands. It ranks with his performance of Richelieu and we hardly know to which to award the palm for grandeur of perception and execution. Mr Dewhurst has been seen under circumstances which have not been altogether favourable to him. To do justice to his performances he should have support which is probably only obtainable in larger cities. The rendering is scholarly and his merit would appear brighter when surrounded by thorough exponents of Shakespearean characters. We say this much not out of any feeling that the company was incapable but that the circumstances and surroundings under which the parts were taken were really hardly favourable to a complete representation of Shakespeare's pieces. Mr Dewhurst is a great artist and we can congratulate ourselves that he has done us the honour of visiting us.'

At the conclusion of the engagement he was presented by the patrons of the theatre with 'a very handsome watch-guard made of pure Sandhurst gold' and the *Advertiser* greeted his departure with the words:

'Mr Dewhurst takes his departure, we understand, for Ballarat and we are certain that his splendid acting and talent as an exponent of Shakespearean character will meet with that recognition which is his due. The favour in which he has been held here by admirers of Shakespeare has been demonstrated very clearly by the demonstration of the same faces at the theatre night after night during his stay, perhaps the best tribute of praise that could be offered to an actor.'

In the mining town of Ballarat, Dewhurst was supported by the Holloway Theatre Company in a two-week season. The company was run by W.J. Holloway, its inspiration and leading man. Holloway was born in England in 1843 and his early life was spent in Seven Dials, London. In his book *Playing the Empire*, David Holloway, W.J.'s grandson, records that W.J. left school at the age of nine and was largely self-taught. He read avidly and was fascinated by the sound of words. W.J.'s son John (W.E. Holloway) later said of him:

'He was one of the most completely cultured men that I have ever known. His knowledge of the English classics was encyclopaedic and his understanding of history deep and accurate. He would answer my incessant questions on any imaginable topic clearly and fully, and rarely in the light of my later reading have I found him wrong. It is still more remarkable that he spoke beautiful English. There was never a trace of a false vowel sound, despite his boyhood in Clerkenwell and youth in the workshops of Sydney.'

Like so many actors, W.J. had been inspired by a visit to the theatre. In his case it was when he saw G.V. Brooke in *Othello* at the Olympic in London. Eventually W.J.'s parents emigrated to Australia, taking him and his three brothers with them. When Dewhurst visited Ballarat, W.J. had been running his company for less than two years. It was very much a family company – W.J. was the leading man, his brother Charles the heavy man, Essie Jenyns (his step-daughter) played juvenile roles and his three young children, Dora, Julie and John occasionally took suitable parts. W.J.'s wife Kate was the business manager. David Holloway's book indicates that the Holloway company had opened in Ballarat in the spring of 1880 at the Theatre Royal, but it seems that this could not have been so. *Lucky City: the first generation at Ballarat 1851–1901* (Weston Bate, [Melbourne University Press 1978] p.231) records:

'The great days of the theatre were the 1850s. Only the Theatre Royal was open in the sixties. Later it was converted into shops having been pushed out of business by the Academy which Sir W.J. Clarke built and then let in Lydiard Street, opposite Craig's Hotel. A company including many of Ballarat's best known citizens leased it for a time – until they found their "improving" ideas unprofitable. Why Clarke built it is a nice question. The Theatre Royal is said never to have paid.' (Defunct Trading Companies Files, no. 332, PRO, Star 1 Feb 1870, p.2, 8 June 1875, pp.2–3.)

The Academy referred to was the Academy of Music, the only theatre in the town in 1882. Advertisements in the *Ballarat Courier* show the lessees of the theatre to be George and Charles Holloway, two of W.J.'s brothers, and the Holloway Theatre Company as the resident company. The Academy was later renamed Her Majesty's Theatre and is still in existence today.

Dewhurst opened, with the Holloway company in support, in his favourite role of Richelieu. W.J., as was normal practice, stepped down from the lead role and gave an admirable performance as De Mauprat. W.J.'s leading lady, Annie Mayor, played Julie with 'her usual grace and display of discernment', Charles Holloway was Baradas and the young Essie Jenyns (soon to become one of Australia's leading actresses) played François. The *Ballarat Courier* went to some lengths to preface its review of the play with a lengthy critique of Jonathan Dewhurst the actor:

'Last night a new theatrical star was introduced to Ballarat in Mr J. Dewhurst, who won his way in the metropolis into the favour of most critical audiences, and who has played with marked success throughout the colonies; his last season, that at Sandhurst, being a series of triumphs for him.

'Mr Dewhurst's presence is certainly very good. He is over six feet in height and well – not massively – proportioned. His features are fairly mobile and expressive and his voice, though not one of unusual power or flexibility, has rather a pleasant intonation, and the quality of resonance. His enunciation is clear and distinct and his delivery easy and natural. Judging by first appearances – which are not always the most reliable data however – we should say that as an artist he appeals more to the intellect than the passions. Well versed in his profession – long practised, and with an evident appreciation of the higher influences of the stage – his playing commands general approbation, and he meets criticism by the consistency of his acting and the undoubtedly intelligent reading he gives of the author he undertakes to interpret.

'The intellectual force of Cardinal Richelieu's character makes its representation a display of intellectual activity rather than of stormy passion; of the courage of knowledge rather than physical power. The mind that moulds the destiny of others should be of irresistible force; and in the indomitable will of the aged Cardinal this necessary characteristic of power over others is graphically shown. This main feature of the Cardinal's sway marks the whole of the portion of his life represented in the drama, and it is upon this distinctive element that Mr Dewhurst casts his delineation. As a result, his representation of the character from first to last is profoundly interesting, and while it attracts it entertains and excites one's admiration. Never overstrained or stilted, his speech was always effective, and his gesticulation, even in the "very torrent, tempest, and (as we may say) whirlwind" of his passion, begat a temperance that gave it smoothness. If anything he was rather less energetic than unnecessarily vigorous; but whatever might be the opinion on that one point, it is certain that while he was before the audience his quiet but ardent emphasis of gesture and speech focused the interested attention of all upon his doings and sayings. On making his appearance as Richelieu Mr Dewhurst was very cordially received, and as he played with wonderful naturalness through the first act, that somewhat uneventful prologue to a stirring drama, the impression gained upon observers that the reputation he has won in the part was "not got without deserving". When the act closed he was loudly recalled and applauded.

'Through the second act the feeling of admiration for his talented acting deepened, and the politic old statesman was personated to the life. The performer had lost his identity in the character he had engaged to portray; and as the curtain fell at the close of the act increased applause told of the advance he had made upon the approbation of the audience. But in the third act he rose beyond the quieter successes of the previous ones. The varying emotions produced by Julie's tale of agony were admirably portrayed, and alternately the churchman, soldier and crafty statesman were displayed with emphatic individuality and independent vitality. His scornful address to the impetuous De Mauprat was superbly acted, and marked by cultured elocution. The verve and grace of the performer were so telling that the house fairly rose to the player and a burst of most hearty applause expressed its gratification and checked for a moment the action of the piece.

'The last two acts saw the impersonation of Richelieu carried out in the same effective and telling manner, repeated interruptions of applause and recalls at the close of the acts marking the delight of the audience. The new tragedian has commenced most auspiciously, his acting last night gained him numerous admirers, and he bids fair to obtain greater popularity than has been the lot of any tragedian here since the days of G.V. Brooke. It must not be forgotten that Mr Dewhurst dresses magnificently, omitting no detail of attire which would tend to the perfect representation of the character. He was most capitally supported last night and the production of the drama, taken as a whole, was of the most finished kind and worthy of the highest praise.'

Richelieu was repeated and then, interestingly, two performances of *Othello* with Dewhurst and W.J. alternating the roles of Othello and Iago. Dewhurst's interpretation of the title role was widely different from others Ballarat had witnessed, showing not so much 'the passion of a rough soldier perplexed in the extreme, so much as of a man of strong impulses hurried into actions he would rather evade, but being in them, accepting them and their consequences rather philosophically'. The force of his acting pleased the audience and he had many recalls, as did W.J., whose Iago was 'admirable in every respect'. The reviewer had some slight reservations about Dewhurst's Othello, but not on the following evening of his Iago:

'Of Mr Dewhurst's Iago it is impossible to speak in other than terms of the highest praise. Scholarly and skilful, and free from the least trace of over-doing, from first to last the delineation of the character commanded the admiration of all who could appreciate the character drawn by the master dramatist of the subtle Iago. Mr Dewhurst's Iago is not a heavy villain with melodramatic gait and speech but a keen reader of men resolved upon a villainous purpose, and determined to obtain his object in such a manner as shall be effective and yet not expose him as the author of the villainy. He played with such force and grace that the audience did not ever seem to tire of applauding him, but recalled him repeatedly to further applaud him.'

Dewhurst later recalled that Ballarat had perhaps been his greatest success in Australia, and from the reviews it is easy to see why. After his Hamlet, the *Courier* reported that 'his popularity increases' and that his acting in the role was 'magnificent, undoubtedly the finest that has ever been seen in the Academy of Music'. The season continued to increasing acclaim, with the whole company earning the most complimentary reviews. At the end of the first week Dewhurst placed a notice in the *Courier* thanking the public of Ballarat and vicinity for their kind and generous patronage and announcing his benefit in *The Lady of Lyons*. The review of *Macbeth* rather underlined Dewhurst's analytical and thoughtful approach to the roles he played and perhaps gave an indication of the different styles adopted by Dewhurst and WJ:

'Mr Dewhurst's performance showed the scholar and appreciative student of the master he essayed to interpret. He played carefully, and from the view he took of the character, most consistently. It is a characteristic of Mr Dewhurst's impersonations that they attract and interest by the culture, skill, and histrionic ability their portrayal causes him to display. There is an evenness of colouring noticeable through his every delineation, and the artist, never straining one feature of a character into the principal groundwork of his impersonation, makes every mode, show and speech work together towards the presenting to observers of a harmonious whole. No reaching after undue effect in one or other particular piece of business in a play is ever noticeable in his impersonations, but having conceived what he believes to be the whole character of the prototype he affects, he plays with the most comprehensive representation of that conception in view. In this almost indifference to applause he is somewhat singular, and the liberal plaudits he receives nightly must be considered by him as much endorsings of his opinions as tributes to his effectual way of expressing them.

'We do not like Mr Dewhurst's *Macbeth* so well as some others of the characters he has appeared in, for it was somewhat wanting in robustness, yet it could not fail to excite admiration, so consistently and artistically was his conception of the character carried out. As ever, Mr Dewhurst worked up the interest in his performance as the argument of the drama proceeded. His Macbeth in the first act did not bear in his features or voice a prophecy of what would happen to Duncan. He played Macbeth as Lady Macbeth described him, "full of the milk of human kindness", until crime and its sequent crime made of him a butchering tyrant, dead to all remorse. The audience grew more and more interested in the performance, each successive recall being heartier than its predecessor. The contest with Macduff and the death of Macbeth were so finely represented that the audience applauded vehemently and would like to have seen it over again.

'Mr W.J. Holloway made a soldierly Thane of Fife, and looked the character to the life. In contradistinction to Macbeth his Macduff was rather a vociferous one.'

One might be forgiven for thinking that things could not improve, but Dewhurst's performance in *Louis XI* was 'by far the best of the season. Throughout the drama to its close he played superbly and the scene which closed the piece was one of the most realistic that has been seen on the stage of the Academy'. *The Lady of Lyons* enjoyed more success and the season ended with *Richard III*. Ballarat was sorry to see him leave, and although the press suggested the possibility that he might return, this did not in the event happen.

Having left Ballarat, Dewhurst set sail from Melbourne for Tasmania for a two-week season at the Hobart Theatre Royal. Jonathan Dewhurst's agent in Australia was James Kitts, 'well and favourably known', as the *Mercury* observed, 'in connection with the Lyster Opera Company (who) has arrived in Hobart to make arrangements for the appearance at the Theatre Royal of Mr Dewhurst, the tragedian'. James Kitts was a businessman who had drawn forth some earlier light-hearted comment from the *Sydney Bulletin*, but also seems to have been a singer, having taken the part of the Second Singing Witch in *Macbeth*! The resident company at the Royal, which was to provide the support, was Walter Reynolds's Dramatic Company, with Walter Reynolds the lessee and leading man and Miss Carry George the leading lady. Newton Griffiths, the English actor who had been at the Queen's Theatre, Sydney in support of Dewhurst, was also in the company.

Dewhurst opened with his strongest suit – *Richelieu* – and the *Mercury* found his performance in 'this complex character ... unequal ... weak in some parts, strong in others'. He was compared unfavourably with William Creswick, and the *Mercury* saw him as an actor who was 'good in declamatory parts, but one who fails to catch the niceties of his art' – rather the opposite view to that expressed by most of the critics in Australia. The reviewer did urge the Hobart public to visit the theatre to see Mr Dewhurst's performance, which had many points to commend it. *Othello* however was another matter. His performance, restrained or powerful as required by the role, pleased the audience and the *Mercury*, which compared him very favourably with the German actor Daniel Bandmann, who 'ranted and roared about the stage'. The reviews during the two weeks became increasingly enthusiastic and there were many appreciative references to his physique and dress – both referring to the care he took and to the appropriateness and quality of his costumes. His Shylock was played with 'power and intensity', his Don Caesar with 'excellent dash and vigour', his Romeo displayed 'a manly beauty in regard to whom the enthusiasm of the fair Capulet seems in no degree out of place'. Macbeth was 'faultless; seldom, if ever, have Hobart audiences witnessed such an excellent piece of acting'. His final performance was as Richard III. The *Mercury* referred to 'an impersonation of considerable ability' and bade farewell to him with the salutation that 'his efforts were enthusiastically applauded by the large audience that had assembled to witness this his final appearance; and a general regret is felt that the stay of this versatile and powerful tragedian could not have been prolonged'. Dewhurst did prolong his stay for a few days, but not at the Theatre Royal, which was taken over by the young English singer and actress Miss Carry Nelson for a season of burlesque. He hired the Town Hall for two nights and gave his solo recitals of poetry under the title *A Night With The Poets*.

The *Mercury*, which carried advertisements and reviews of Dewhurst's season, also contained a note of two other matters of some interest. On the occasion of Dewhurst's first professional appearance at the Prince's Theatre, Manchester, back in 1865, Frederick Maccabe was giving his farewell benefit performance at that theatre. Now in March 1882, while Dewhurst was at the Theatre Royal, the same Frederick Maccabe was appearing at the Town Hall in his 'Original Monologue Entertainment' entitled *Begone Dull Care* – a 'Vocal, Ventriloquial, Musical and Sartorial Melange'. The other rather more bizarre item appeared as news and read:

'THE ARMLESS LADY – The armless lady continues to give her clever performances in the exhibition tent erected off Elizabeth Street, opposite the Rock Hotel. Mrs Thomson, by means of her toes, not only writes freely, conducting her own business correspondence, but embroiders with, and does other fancy work very creditably; she can also use a knife and fork with ease and dexterity. Altogether it is a performance well worth seeing. In the same tent is shown the pig – Bismarck – who is ready and accurate at arithmetic, tells the time by any watch, and can "euchre" good players at their favourite game.'

Evidently entertainment in those days was as varied as it is today.

Before leaving Tasmania, Dewhurst spent a few days in Launceston, where he presented two performances of *A Night With The Poets* at the Mechanics' Institute, both well-received by the press and by full houses. Elizabeth had not accompanied Jonathan to Tasmania, nor on most of his other trips — not for lack of interest, but for the very good reason that she was expecting their third child. Having lost her previous two children in infancy she was taking no chances. The baby was due towards the end of April and Jonathan had time to fulfil just one more engagement before he would have to give greater priority to his domestic life. His return to the Royal Princess's Theatre at Bendigo was a triumphant affair, both the press and the public welcoming him back in the roles he had presented only three months earlier, with the addition of *Louis XI* and *Richard III*. The pleasurable anticipation felt locally was well-expressed by the *Bendigo Advertiser* and if it reflects a response which Shakespeare might not have intended, then no one was the worse for that. The world of Bendigo in 1882 was rather different from the world of today in many ways:

'The opening of the dramatic season with *Richard III* seemed quite in accord with the fitness of things. Seeing that old English fairs have become so popular then why not encourage the taste for acquiring a deeper knowledge of England as it was in the days when the Houses of York and Lancaster, the Buckinghams, the Glosters, the Dudleys, and all the host of notable nobles held high revel in the Courts of Britain, and if so no historical lesson can be more pleasingly learned than by the medium of the stage, with cultivated and capable men and women to impersonate the various characters, robed after the fashion of the times, and provided with well-set pithy sentences to deliver with due emphasis and suitable action. This idea may have struck the management of the Princess's when engaging their present company to appear at this time, and so far a signal success has attended Messrs Dodge and McMahon's selections, notwithstanding the great difficulty experienced in getting together a company to support Mr Dewhurst. Talent to fill the minor characters of Shakespeare's plays respectably is not at all times available, hence much of the charm is dissipated and the legitimate has to give way for much that is not intellectual and so the stage halts its mission. The present dramatic season should receive substantial support if for no other reason than to show appreciation of something above sawdust and spangles.'

Despite the apparent difficulties of finding good supporting actors, this was clearly achieved: the whole cast was applauded throughout the week and superlatives were heaped upon Dewhurst for every role. The *Advertiser* commented, 'The more frequently Mr Dewhurst is seen, the more he is liked and the more his talents are recognised'.

The short season ended on 15 April and one week later Henry Melbourne Dewhurst was born. It is quite understandable that Jonathan would wish to spend some time with his wife and son, but, apart from one performance in Bendigo, we cannot place Dewhurst on any stage for a period of ten weeks, which for him was most unusual. The performance we have traced is of *A Night With The Poets*, which he gave at the Masonic Hall, Bendigo, on 24 May in honour of the Queen's birthday. At the conclusion The National Anthem was heartily sung by the enthusiastic audience and three cheers were given for Her Majesty. In June, however, tragedy struck the Dewhursts again with the death of Henry. To lose three infants in the space of three years was not perhaps uncommon in those days, but that would not diminish the

23   Entrance to the Theatre Royal, Sydney, 1882. This unprepossessing entrance to the stalls was through the bars in King Street. The main entrance was round the corner through a hotel in Castlereagh Street. The bill board advertised George Rignold's *Lights O' London* in which Dewhurst played Seth Preene.

pain and suffering of the parents. Jonathan had the stage, but now Elizabeth had nothing. We can only surmise how she felt. Her children dead, living so far from home and her husband frequently away pursuing his career. Did she insist on returning to England? Did their relationship suffer? We know only that they sailed from Melbourne in October and that in May, before Henry's death, Dewhurst had expressed the intention of returning directly to England.

Although his experiences in Australia do not seem to bear it out, Dewhurst felt that 'Shakespeare was now at a premium' and he took up a 14-week engagement with George Rignold at the Theatre Royal, Sydney. Two plays were presented – *Youth* by Paul Merritt and Augustus Harris, followed by *The Lights O' London* by George Sims. *Youth* was a spectacular success and ran for nine weeks. George Rignold played the lead, Frank Darlington, and Dewhurst his father, the Rev Joseph Darlington, both receiving excellent notices. *The Lights O' London* followed, with Rignold as Harold Armytage and Dewhurst as Seth Preene, a ruffianly north country poacher, which, according to the *Morning Herald*, was 'one of the best things in the cast'. *The Lights O' London* continued in Sydney until 6 October and a week later the production transferred to Melbourne, but it is unlikely that Dewhurst stayed in the cast, as on 26 October he and Elizabeth sailed from Melbourne. However, despite his earlier intentions, he did not return to England.

11

India

On 26 October 1882, Jonathan and Elizabeth sailed from Melbourne on the P.& O. steamship *Verona*. The *Verona* was a smaller ship than the *Cotopaxi* on which the Dewhursts had sailed to Australia, but was some six years newer, being built in 1879, and had three decks to the *Cotopaxi*'s two. The passenger list shows that the ship was bound for London and that *all* the passengers had contracted to disembark at London. We have already mentioned the American actress Miss Louise Pomeroy, who had been touring Australia with her company, the 'Pomeroy Dramatic Combination'. Miss Pomeroy's aim was to tour the world, acting in all the principal cities, and it appears that she did not rely entirely on local stock companies to provide support. She took with her a core group of players, who were supplemented as necessary by actors from the resident companies of the theatres in which she performed. She had been very successful in Australia and now on 26 October 1882 she, her maid, and seven members of her company were also sailing on the *Verona*, bound (as the passenger list shows) for London.

As will be readily apparent to the reader, we are from time to time confronted metaphorically by a brick wall. We know the outcome, but the reasons and the surrounding circumstances remain a mystery. So it is with Jonathan Dewhurst's next move. He had indicated some months earlier that he intended to return to London and Elizabeth must have desperately wanted to go home. Could it really have been a coincidence that Louise Pomeroy and her company were also on the *Verona*? In talking later to the *Leigh Chronicle*, Dewhurst had said, 'I then had the offer of a very lucrative engagement by Miss Louise Pomeroy to accompany her to India to play leading Shakespearean parts'. It is not credible that Miss Pomeroy and Jonathan Dewhurst happened to be travelling on the same ship, struck up a conversation and then decided to tour India together. Plans must surely have been made before this. We have not been able to establish that the two met in Australia, but presumably this happened and Louise Pomeroy saw the attractions of having Dewhurst as her leading man, at least for a period.

We do not know how Elizabeth viewed this change in their plans – in fact we do not know whether she toured India with her husband or whether she returned home on the *Verona*. It is unfortunate that, although there are very full records in Australia of ships' arrivals and departures, with full passenger lists, there are few records in England for this period. There was no requirement here for passenger lists to be kept before 1890 and many of those that were held have since been destroyed. Dewhurst later recalled that he 'sailed for Calcutta, calling on the way at Madras'. This is not strictly correct: the *Verona* arrived in Colombo (Ceylon) on 14 November 1882 and sailed for London the next day. The Pomeroy company with Jonathan Dewhurst would have disembarked at Colombo and from there travelled to Madras, where they commenced their tour. Here they played for two nights only. Dewhurst recalls that in Madras 'some unscrupulous scoundrel took the liberty of relieving me of a beautiful diamond and topaz ring worth thirty guineas'. The port of Madras was not the prime target however – a lengthy season had been booked at the Corinthian Theatre, Calcutta, and that is where they opened in the second week of December that year.

Calcutta was the seat of government and it is worth considering briefly the position of the British in India at that time. After the British had defeated, and recovered from the effects of, the Indian Mutiny (1857–58), control of this part of the British Empire was transferred from the East India Company to the Crown. In 1877 Queen Victoria was declared Empress of India and the Governor-General became the Viceroy, the semi-royal representative of imperial authority. The British were determined that a disaster such as the Mutiny should not be repeated, and while the intended limits of British 'interference' were made clear to the Indian Maharajahs, care was taken to ensure that all positions of authority in the Indian Civil Service and the army were filled by the British.

They built new towns and suburbs for themselves across India, and as they moved inland, military stations were set up all over the subcontinent. Instead of building forts, however, they laid out separate, self-contained enclosures for their communities, with their own military and civilian accommodation, their own markets, hospitals, churches and jails. Everything was laid out in orderly lines, with rows of spacious bungalows along wide, tree-lined streets.

The spirit was that of a little British world quite separate from the rest of India. These feelings also led to the development of 'hill stations', small European towns high up in the cool atmosphere of the hills. The most famous was Simla, 7,000 feet up in the Himalayas. It was the summer capital of British India and during the hot months it was the headquarters of the Indian Government, which would be moved up from the steamy heat of the plains. Simla was more like a distant part of England than any other part of India. The 'club' was another institution which represented an island of Britishness in the midst of an Indian sea. The club was a focus for the whole European community and often occupied the most spacious and elegant buildings in town. In his book *A Traveller's History of India*, Sinharajah Tammita-Delgoda says:

'For all the pristine splendour of European Calcutta, outside its boundaries there lay a chaotic, stinking mass of slums, described by Kipling as that "smokey, magnificent, many-sided city of Dreadful Night".'

Theatrical entertainment was almost exclusively intended for, and patronised by, the British. Theatres existed and the more important ones had resident companies, but acting standards were not high and the arrival of leading professional actors was an occasion to savour. It all tended to add to the 'Britishness' of life and visiting performers were greeted with great hospitality. Although numerically the theatre-going public in Calcutta was limited, support for Louise Pomeroy's 14-week season was considerable, helped by a regular change of programme. It was evident, too, that the quality of the entertainment was rather greater than that to which they were normally accustomed. Press comment such as the following (in the *Indian Daily News*) appeared regularly:

'The theatre is crowded nightly – a fact unparalleled in the history of drama in India.'

Plays were presented for no more than two consecutive nights at a time and, in all, 24 plays were presented in the 14-week season. The programme consisted generally of Shakespeare supplemented by the popular dramas and melodramas of the day.

Louise Pomeroy was one of those actresses who saw herself as Hamlet and she took the title part when the play was presented. The *News* considered her 'very good' and that she would 'bear a favourable comparison with Irving'. Dewhurst's performance as Claudius (for the first time in his career) was 'the best thing he has yet done'. Miss May Hill, one of the 'locals', as Ophelia was 'good but not as good as expected'. In *Romeo and Juliet*, Louise Pomeroy was 'first-class' as Juliet, and Romeo was played by Arthur Elliot, one of her 'core' actors. Dewhurst, again breaking new ground for him, 'made a splendid Mercutio'. Dewhurst must have had some misgivings when *Macbeth* was presented in January 1883 – Wilson's Great World Circus was also performing in Calcutta! However, the attractions of spangles and sawdust did not keep the audiences away. The review referred to the play being 'put on the stage in a way superior to anything of the kind yet seen in Calcutta'. In commenting on Dewhurst's Macbeth the review continued:

> 'The moral vacillation as contrasted with the physical resolution was admirably depictured and he was plainly a man insensible to bodily fear yet superstitious to a degree... The result of this fine acting was to permit Miss Pomeroy to show a character in every way the complement of Macbeth.'

Herr Bandmann had also been touring India. The *News* preferred Dewhurst's Macbeth to Bandmann's, whose farewell performance as Richard III at the Opera House was heavily criticised. It was thought that the length of *Cymbeline* might have taxed the patience of the audience, but it was well-received. Dewhurst was on familiar ground as Richelieu and his 'representation surpassed anything he has yet done in Calcutta', but there were several plays that were new to him. In *Ingomar the Barbarian*, Dewhurst as Ingomar, 'showed himself to be the fine actor he is. Ingomar lost nothing in his hands but was finely, even grandly, acted. The performances of Dewhurst and Miss Pomeroy (as Parthenia) were given in a manner far and away beyond anything seen in Calcutta for years'. As the Irish Earl in *Lady Clancarty*, Dewhurst's brogue was thought to be weak, but he 'pleased more than he has done in any previous part and fully merited the repeated applause which his rendering of the warm-hearted, faithful Irishman called forth'. All plays and performances appear to have been appreciatively received by audiences and critics – except for one. The American play *Pique* by Augustin Daly, introduced by Louise Pomeroy, was evidently a favourite of hers, but the critics did not like it, principally because of the distasteful female character Mabel Renfrew. They praised Pomeroy's skill in playing the part, which they felt must have been very unpleasant for her.

One of the high spots of the season was the Vice-Regal Night on 10 January, when the Viceroy himself, the Marquis of Ripon, was present and the theatre was packed. The programme comprised W.S. Gilbert's *Pygmalion and Galatea* with excerpts from *The School for Scandal*. The *News* commented:

> 'The extract (*School for Scandal*) was carefully and satisfactorily gone through, Mr Dewhurst gaining especial applause... The evening's

103

performance was under the Viceroy's patronage and a party from Government House occupied the old royal box. The house was full to suffocation, no spare seats being anywhere obtainable and the audience was extremely enthusiastic.'

There was a further comment in the next day's edition, which throws some light on critical attitudes to W.S. Gilbert as a literary figure:

'*Pygmalion and Galatea* is the best known of the series of plays produced in rapid succession some ten or a dozen years ago which placed their author Mr W.S. Gilbert for a time in the very front rank of our then living dramatists. Few of the remainder of the series are now heard of: *The Palace of Truth*, the most interesting and dramatically perfect of them is rarely to be seen, while another *The Wicked World* is quite lost sight of, though it obtained a transient renown through the success of *The Happy Land*, a political burlesque parodied from it, in which the leading members of the last Liberal Ministry were held up to laughter. Of late years Mr Gilbert has abandoned this road to fame and betaken himself to a more lucrative one, producing in conjunction with Mr Sullivan, *Trial by Jury*, *Pinafore* and the operettas with which their names will ever be associated.'

On Monday, 12 March, Dewhurst took his benefit in *Still Waters Run Deep* and on the Friday Louise Pomeroy took hers in *Led Astray*. The report in the *News* was a generous appreciation of Miss Pomeroy and the whole company in what had been a most successful 14 weeks of drama. It also mentioned that now that the season had ended, Miss Pomeroy was 'going to the Theatre Royal'. This did not happen. Miss Pomeroy gave one further performance at the Corinthian on the Saturday night, presenting selections from several plays that had been given during the season. But Dewhurst did not take part – he had already left the company to arrange his own season at the Royal!

For his two-week season Dewhurst was supported by Lizzie Gordon and the Royal's resident players, the Gaiety Company. Lizzie Gordon's claim to fame seems to have been that she had played Desdemona to the Othellos of Barry Sullivan and Charles Dillon, and now she played this role opposite Jonathan Dewhurst. The short run received good reviews but relatively poor audiences, the reason being the 'season' – the start of the hot season when 'everyone left for the hills'. Before he too went, Dewhurst took the opportunity of giving a recital to a very aristocratic audience at the Dalhousie

Institute, to which he was introduced by Mr Dave-Carson, proprietor of the Corinthian Theatre. On his benefit night at the Corinthian, Mr Dave-Carson had presented him, in the name of the public and on behalf of the patrons of the theatre, with a very handsome diamond ring and, in the words of Dewhurst, 'remarked as he placed it on my finger that "It was a bright gem, but of the two the wearer was the brighter gem".' It is reported by an English actor who was in India at the time (see Chapter 18) that Dewhurst had been 'the honoured guest of the leading European residents, the officers of the different regiments stationed there, at whose mess he was always welcomed when opportunity afforded, and particularly so by the ex-King of Oude, whose paradisical residence it is impossible to describe, or to be appreciated by anyone unacquainted with Eastern splendour'. Dewhurst then visited several places 'up the country', one of which was probably the Gaiety Theatre at Simla, where Kipling subsequently performed as an amateur. The theatre still stands, but the stage is in need of repair and the green room houses a club for Indian Army officers. Dewhurst recalled later that he found the heat excessive and, 'seeing so many of my friends and acquaintances dying off one by one, I took fright and decided to return to dear old England'.

We have been unable to trace the ship on which he sailed, or the date of departure, and whether he returned alone. We know that he must have arrived in London in June or early July, as by the end of July he was touring the North of England once more with his own company. But before we leave the sea and those distant foreign parts – more distant than they seem today – let us hear a little of what it was like travelling by steamship in 1882 and 1883.

★　★　★

Phillips Brooks was an American bishop who enjoyed travel and was a committed letter writer. He wrote regularly and very descriptively to his relations while on his extensive travels and his letters were published in 1895 under the title *Letters of Travel*.

Venice, 26 November 1882

'I have just come here to get a few quiet days of Venice before the *Poonah* sails. She is here, lying in the harbor; and I have been on board and looked her over. She is a beautiful, great vessel, with a big, broad deck and a bright, pleasant cabin, looking as if she might be a capital home for three weeks...

'My state room is on deck, with air all round it, and I have it to myself, so I am counting very much upon my voyage... The officers of the ship say that at this season the thermometer does not go above seventy, even in the Red Sea, and there is never any chance of bad weather in December between Suez and Bombay. It seems to be the very perfection of ship life.'

Steamship *Poonah*, lying at Brindisi
Sunday, 3 December 1882

'...The *Poonah* is an old ship, rather noisy, not at all fast, and not very clean. But she is well arranged and in good weather must be very pleasant. The sail from Venice to Brindisi has been cold, rough and rainy. The Adriatic has behaved badly.'

Steamship *Poonah* in the Suez Canal
9 December 1882

'You do not know what a queer looking thing this big ditch is, with long stretches of sand reaching out on either side and the curious effects of light everywhere in the distance, and the superb blue sky, and our great steamer slowly plodding along at about six miles an hour towards the Red Sea. And inside the steamer it is just as queer, a host of wild-looking ruffians for sailors, and a lot of Englishmen. It is all very pleasant and foreign.'

On the *Poonah*, 15 December 1882

'All this week we have been running down the Red Sea. The weather has been sultry and oppressive; not particularly hot by the thermometer, but such weather as makes one want to get in a draft and do nothing. In the great cabin, the punkas are hung up, long cloth fans, which are fastened to a rod that runs along the ceiling over the dining-table; every meal time they are kept swinging by a long cord, which runs through the skylight, and is attached at the other end to a small Mohammedan on deck who pulls and pulls and pulls. We could hardly live without it. This morning we were passing Mocha, where the coffee comes from, and this afternoon we shall go through Bab-el-Mandel. When we are once out into the Indian Ocean, the special sultriness of the Red Sea will be over and we shall have a week of charming sailing.

'The ship is very comfortable, but she is old and slow. She is four days behind her time and we shall not be at Bombay before Saturday the 23rd, more than three weeks from the time we left Venice. But it has been very pleasant. There is a miscellaneous and interesting company on board. Here is the general who led the cavalry charge at Tel El Kebir, and is coming back from England after being decorated by the Queen. Here is Lord Charles Beresford, who ran his boat up under the guns at Alexandria at the time of the bombardment and did wonders of bravery. Here is a young Cambridge parson going out to a missionary brotherhood at Delhi. Here are merchants of Calcutta and Madras, whom one pumps continually for information about India – Englishmen, all of them.'

Madras, 18 February 1883

'We had a beautiful sail down from Calcutta. For four days the *Rohilla* slid along over the most beautiful glassy sea, the sky was lovely at sunrise and sunset, the nights were the most gorgeous moonlight, and the sun at noon was hotter than Sancho. There were a good many pleasant people on board, two bishops, an archdeacon, and the usual queer lot of sailors who run the steamships in these Eastern seas. We arrived at Madras very early on Friday morning and I have been charmed with the place ever since. It was glorious last night. I drove five miles into the country to dine at Mr Sewall's. He is the archaeological director of the district and knows all about the Vishnu temples and the Buddhist Topes, of which the whole region is full. The road ran through long avenues of banyan trees, which looked like ghosts with their long arms; little temples peeped through the trees and picturesque groups of people were flitting about on foot, or in queer bullock carts, and it was all as unlike the Milldam as possible. We had a charming dinner with people who knew all about India and drove home at eleven o'clock through the February summer night.

'On Wednesday morning the *Verona* sails from Colombo, and will carry me to Suez, and the Indian trip is over. It has been one unmixed pleasure from beginning to end.'

P.&O. Steamer *Verona*, 11 March 1883

'It seems so strange to be on the sea again and thinking about the Indian journey as a finished thing. The days from Venice to Bombay keep coming back, when I was full of wonder about it all. Now I know at least a great deal about what I shall always think one of the most delightful and interesting lands in all the world. In some respects, the last bit of it was almost the best. The tropics had seemed to elude us before. Many a time in India it seemed as if the landscape were almost what one might have seen at home, but the minute that we touched Ceylon everything was different. One cannot conceive of the gorgeousness of nature. Only the night before we left we drove a few miles along the seashore with such groves of enormous palms and cocoanuts on one side, and such color of sunset on the water on the other side, as no dream or picture ever began to suggest. And the whole four hours' ride from Colombo to Kandy is marvellous. The mountains are superb and in the valleys there are depths of jungle which show what the earth is at only eight degrees from the equator.

'We have been four days on the *Verona*. The people are pleasant, the Captain is cordial and agreeable, and the weather is cool, so the voyage is charming. The Archdeacon of Calcutta is on board, and preached this morning. He is a very jolly sort of person. I am to preach next Sunday. There are some private theatricals in prospect, so the future looks lively. Next Sunday you shall hear how the week has gone.'

Steamship *Verona*, Sunday, 18 March 1883 [to his niece]
'We have been sailing up the Red Sea and on Monday evening we shall once more be at Suez, and there I say goodbye to my companion who stops in Egypt and goes thence to Palestine, while I hurry on to Malta and Gibraltar in the same steamer. She is a nice little steamer with a whole lot of children on board, who fight all the while and cry the rest of the time. Every now and then one of them almost goes overboard, and then all the mothers set up a great howl, though I don't see why they should care so much about such children as these are. I should think it would be rather a relief to get rid of them.'

Steamship *Verona*, 25 March 1883
'Last Monday night we reached Suez and put about half our ship's company on shore to go to Alexandria, Brindisi and Venice. Since then we have been dragging along the Suez Canal. There were twenty-six steamships in single file; we were the eleventh. Every now and then, No.1 or No.6 would get aground; and then we all had to wait till it got loose, five or six hours as the case might be. Every night the whole twenty-six of us pulled up and tied fast to the bank and waited for morning. So we crept along till yesterday (Saturday, Easter even), when we reached Port Said, where we stayed four hours and then launched out into the broad Mediterranean. Now all is clear. The broad sea is rolling merrily around us and we have a lot of sail set, and are scudding on towards Malta.'

When we first read Phillips Brooks's account of his voyage on the *Verona* and specifically his reference (11 March 1883) to theatricals on board, we became quite excited. Could this have been Jonathan Dewhurst returning to London? Unfortunately there proved to be no grounds for this romantic notion, as we later found that Dewhurst was in Calcutta long after the *Verona* sailed from Colombo. In fact he did not return to England on the *Verona* – the dates for the movements of the ship make this impossible. Dewhurst's return journey is shrouded in some mystery. But we do know that he would have sailed via the Suez Canal, that his journey, only weeks later, would have been similar in many respects to that described by Phillips Brooks, and that by the end of July he had once more returned to the theatre in England.

12

Back in 'Good Old England'

It is unfortunate that we cannot pinpoint Jonathan Dewhurst's return to England, either the date or the ship on which he travelled, or whether he was accompanied or returned alone. On arrival, however, he immediately formed another company and toured the 'northern circuit', presenting Shakespeare and his other favourites *Richelieu, Louis XI* and *The School for Scandal*, which had provided him with much success in India. He opened at the Theatre Royal, Wigan, on 30 July 1883, so it is reasonable to assume that he returned in June, or at the very latest early July. Dewhurst's return to the English stage was greeted in the *Wigan Observer*'s advertisement with the words:

'First appearance in England after his highly successful Tour Round the World of Mr Jonathan Dewhurst
Who will appear in his Great Impersonation of Richelieu, pronounced by the entire Australian and Indian Press to be the Finest Representation of the character ever witnessed in the Eastern Empire'

Stretching a point perhaps, but to some effect – the house was well-filled in all parts on the opening night. The audience was vociferously appreciative, and the *Observer*, while giving Dewhurst due praise, spent the major part of its review discussing Mr W. Lees, a Wigan gentleman, who was making his debut on the stage. He received appropriate encouragement for his Louis XIII and a flattering reception from the audience. It is interesting to note that playing Marian de Lorne was Mrs Walter Hill – the same Mrs Hill who had been in the Holloway Company when Dewhurst visited Ballarat and in Louise Pomeroy's Company at the Corinthian Theatre, Calcutta. She did not travel to India on the *Verona* with Dewhurst and Louise Pomeroy and we can only assume that her appearance in these three places was a matter of coincidence.

Charles Calvert died in 1879, but his wife Adelaide continued in the theatre for many years, dying in 1921 at the age of 85. She had joined Dewhurst's company, playing selected roles and reciting dramatic verse as a supporting feature. On the opening night her recitation of 'The Life and Death of Mary, Queen of Scots, illustrated in six tableaux' brought down the house, indicating that it was a sensible move by Dewhurst to have the popular and honoured name of Calvert in the company and, at the same time perhaps, to repay a little more of the debt that, no doubt, he felt he owed Charles Calvert. From Wigan the company transferred to Oldham's Theatre Royal and ran the established repertoire including Mrs Calvert's dramatic offerings. The *Oldham Evening Chronicle* carried the news that 'at the conclusion of his 18 weeks' engagements in England [Dewhurst] purposes revisiting many of the places where he has gained additional fame in his profession'. The implication seems to have been that he intended going abroad again, but whatever thoughts gave rise to that possibility, it did not come about.

Dewhurst opened with *Richelieu*, the *Chronicle* commenting:

'The above distinguished and eminent actor is so widely known, and his name so highly respected in Oldham, that he needs but little or no introduction from us on the occasion of his first visit to the town after a brilliant and successful tour round the World. The programme put forward for a week is in itself a proof of the great range of Mr Dewhurst's histrionic abilities, and although it would be asserting too much to say that he will be as successful (from an artistic point of view) in every individual character as he was last (Monday) evening in that of Richelieu, it will be universally admitted that he has a strong claim to being classed as being one amongst the finest of the legitimate actors of his day.

'The character of Richelieu tests the ability and powers of any man who has aspirations to the professional vocation alluded to, and coupled with his undoubted position as an elocutionist, Mr Dewhurst's impersonation of the Lord Cardinal must be pronounced as a veritable triumph of histrionic art. And while saying this we are not forgetting the great men who have essayed the role, some of whom have long since gone over to the majority. Probably it would be an insult to Mr Dewhurst to compare him in this particular character with some of those illustrious names – Macready, Dillon and Calvert for example – but we have no doubt that when he arrives at still maturer years he must lose that little of the young man which now and then he cannot help but display in those passages which have taxed to the utmost even greater actors than he.

'In the third, fourth and closing act Mr Dewhurst has a large amount of scope for his histrionic powers, and that he made the best use of them will be saying too little: he simply held the audience in almost breathless admiration and achieved such a distinction in declamatory and elocutionary power that has not been witnessed inside the Theatre Royal for a long time.'

The comment about Dewhurst arriving 'at still maturer years' is interesting. At the time of this performance he was 46 years of age: Calvert (for example) was playing Richelieu in his late 30s. Perhaps Jonathan Dewhurst carried his years well! *Othello* followed and although the role was not considered to be 'amongst the best of his splendid histrionic efforts', nevertheless, 'his rendering was a magnificent one from an elocutionary point of view'. Miss Edmiston's Desdemona was 'fairly excellent' and as Emilia, Mrs Calvert's rendition was 'beyond reproach'. *Hamlet* followed and:

'Mr Dewhurst was honoured with a further increased attendance at the Theatre Royal. The multitude of his admirers were provided with a rich treat. *Hamlet* was presented in as complete a manner as it is possible for the capacity of the stage to allow. The rendering of this magnificent creation of the immortal bard's, as given by Mr Dewhurst, is amongst the most supreme of that gentleman's histrionic efforts, and the audience vociferously cheered him in front of the curtain at the close of each act. His admitted high elocutionary attainments are probably seen nearer to perfection in Hamlet than in any other character contained in his repertoire.'

Dewhurst's Louis XI was a 'splendid effort, undoubtedly a great performance and lacked nothing in artistic touches', although for the *Chronicle* it was perhaps too robust. The *Chronicle* carried an interesting comment on Dewhurst's presence at the theatre some 15 years earlier, when on the threshold of his career. It also supported his own comments about standards in the theatre, standards not only in acting, production and dress, but also in the quality of the plays presented to the public:

'Mr Dewhurst's connection with the drama in Oldham has extended over a considerable period. It is now upwards of 15 years since he was a "stock" man in the old Theatre, when *The Green Hills of the Far West*,

Jack Long of Texas, and the like were the principal attractions offered to the play-goer. But he once cut the line and that was on the occasion of being requested to play "Sweeney Todd". But, no; he had played in almost everything to oblige the management – first heavy lead, then juvenile – and he must cut the line somewhere, and cut it he did. Mr Dewhurst never assumed the role of the barber. The now eminent actor, likewise, has done in Oldham what no man either dared to do before, or has ever attempted since, viz., "run" Shakespeare's *Macbeth* for 18 nights, and draw crowded houses.'

The tour continued with much the same repertoire, but although the bookings were good and he received acclaim from critics and audiences, Dewhurst records that over the next year he came to accept that 'Shakespeare was now somewhat of a drug in the market'.

In April the following year – 1884 – Dewhurst was able once again to demonstrate his generosity in helping a friend in need. A testimonial fund had been initiated by Tom Nash, a young barrister, to assist the Lancashire dialect poet, Ben Brierley, to go to America 'with his pockets well lined'. Ben Brierley was born in 1825 in Failsworth, Lancashire. His parents were poor hand-loom weavers and, although he started school, his parents moved to Hollinwood when Ben was five – and that marked the end of his formal education! Although on leaving school he had worked for his father as a bobbin winder, Ben was, like his friend Jonathan Dewhurst, a self-improver and a believer in Samuel Smiles's gospel of self-help. He had been encouraged by an uncle to read the works of Shakespeare, Byron, Shelley and others, and it was evident that his future lay in a direction other than the factory or the hand-loom. With the aid of the Mechanics' Institute, evening and Sunday classes, and a good deal of determination, he went on to become one of the most popular and amusing provincial dialect writers of his time.

He helped to form a mutual improvement society, which later became the Failsworth Mechanics' Institute and it was here that some of his early plays were performed. He later became sub-editor of the *Oldham Times* and was a founder member of the Manchester Literary Club. Eventually he turned to writing full-time and in 1869 started his own magazine *Ben Brierley's Journal* which ran for 22 years.

The similarities in the backgrounds and careers of Brierley and Dewhurst are obvious and both had strong beliefs in standards and the importance of self-improvement. It was hardly surprising that they were friends. In 1875 Brierley's only child Annie had died and this affected him considerably. He became ill and in 1880 took a trip to America in an attempt to regain his health. It was four years later, after losing most of his savings when a building society collapsed, that, struggling financially and in poor health, he decided to visit America again. So it was that on 22 April an entertainment was given in aid of the Testimonial Fund at the Prince's Theatre, Manchester, with the following programme:

PRINCE'S THEATRE.
TUESDAY NEXT, APRIL 22
In aid of the
BEN BRIERLEY TESTIMONIAL FUND.
And last appearance of Mr Brierley prior to his leaving for America.
The performances will begin at 7.30 p.m. with
Sullivan's Operatic Burlesque,
COX AND BOX

———

SIGNOR SALVINI
will Recite Schiller's Poem 'THE GLOVE.'

———

THE COBBLER'S STRATAGEM.
(A Farce by Ben Brierley.)
Solomon Makapenny, a retired grocer . . . Mr Ben Brierley
Sam Sly, an amorous cobbler   . . . . Mr R. Dottie

Twelve Dramatic Tableaux, entitled
A GAME AT CARDS.
By Chevalier-Lafosse, Mr Warwick Brookes, and others
The Fourth Act of Bulwer Lytton's Play.
RICHELIEU.
Richelieu . . . . Mr J. Dewhurst
Suported by Messrs Charles Arnold, C.K.Shute, Louis Calvert,
and James Power; and Miss Maggie Hunt of the Claudian
Company, by kind permission of Wilson Barrett, Esq.
Boxes, £1.1s.and £2.2.; stalls, 6s.; circle 5s.; upper circle, 2s 6d.;
Pit, 2s.; gallery, 1s.

The success of the performance was assured. Tommaso Salvini was regarded by many as one of the leading tragedians of the day; as Richelieu, Dewhurst, a great local favourite, was a natural draw, and Ben Brierley appeared in his own farce. *Cox and Box*, which Arthur Sullivan had written some 17 years earlier in conjunction with F.C. Burnand, the editor of *Punch*, was an ideal way in which to get the evening off to a rousing start. It seems, however, that enthusiasm triumphed over organisation and in the event there was no time for *A Game at Cards*, leading to a somewhat huffy notice being placed in the *Manchester Guardian* four days later. Brierley stayed in America for almost three months, but unfortunately the money from the Testimonial Fund was not paid over to him until well after his return. In failing health he died in 1896 at the age of 71.

In 1884 it appears that Dewhurst was having doubts about the popularity of Shakespeare and this would not have pleased him. What happened next would have acted as a tonic and provided the change in direction which he evidently needed. In his words, 'As luck would have it, however, I received a telegram from Mr Wilson Barrett offering me an engagement to play the Holy Clement in *Claudian*.' Jonathan Dewhurst and Wilson Barrett became great friends and we have frequently wondered when and in what circumstances they first met. We have found nothing conclusive, but the above quotation gives a strong clue. Dewhurst usually referred to 'my friend Wilson Barrett' and the reference to a telegram from *Mr* Wilson Barrett indicates that this may have been the first occasion on which their paths crossed. They would have known of one another, of course, and Barrett now wanted Dewhurst to tour in his production of *Claudian*.

Wilson Barrett was a fascinating and talented man of the theatre and it is a matter of some amazement to us that no biography of him appears to exist. Born into a farming family in 1846, Wilson Barrett soon realised that his future lay in the theatre. His handsome features were set in the classic mould and with a resonant voice and a manly and graceful bearing he 'lacked only height to make him a fine figure of a man'. His looks fitted him for melodrama, particularly that with classical pretensions, and at this he excelled. It was thought by some critics that he wasted his looks and talents on inferior material, but he did not receive much critical acclaim for his Shakespearian roles and it is reasonable to assume that Barrett knew better than his critics the directions in which his talent should be used. In much the same way Arthur Sullivan was criticised for using his musical talents in partnership with William Gilbert, rather than pursuing a career in 'serious' music, but there can be no doubt that he achieved greater success, gave greater pleasure to more people, and contributed more to the musical and theatrical life of the nation through the Savoy operas than would otherwise have been possible.

Wilson Barrett was noted for his roles in such popular melodramas as G.R. Sims's *Lights O' London* and the H.A. Jones/Henry Herman collaboration *The Silver King*. But he was also a prolific writer, creating many melodramas in which he also acted, and adapting novels such as *Quo Vadis* for the stage, while his collaboration with the novelist Hall Caine led to successful productions of *The Manxman* and *The Bondman*. His greatest success, however, was with his own *The Sign of the Cross* – a strong melodrama with religious overtones – which suited the mood of Victorian England and appealed to the church as much as the theatre. The play revived his financial fortunes, which were in decline at the time, and was an enormous success with audiences for years to come. It was filmed with equal success in 1932 starring Charles Laughton and Claudette Colbert.

Barrett was a versatile optimist who threw himself with enthusiasm into everything he did. He made money, lost it and made it again; he toured America six times and Australia twice; he managed theatres in Leeds, Hull and five in London – the Court, the Princess's, the Globe, the Olympic and the Lyceum – following Irving at the last named without the success achieved by that gentleman. In 1866 he married Caroline Heath, actress and reader to the Queen. Caroline was eleven years older than Barrett and well-established in the theatre. For several years he supported his wife's leading roles and her reputation overshadowed his. Caroline died in 1887 and Wilson Barrett in 1904, only a few weeks after visiting Liverpool to produce his last play *Lucky Durham*, and make his final stage appearance as Wilfred Denver in *The Silver King*.

Wilson Barrett's production of the poetic drama *Claudian* was first staged at the Princess's Theatre in 1883 with Barrett in the title role. As ever with

24   Leonard Boyne played the leading role in the tour of *Claudian*, in which
Dewhurst played The Holy Clement.

his productions, stage spectacle was of great importance and *Claudian* contained a sensational earthquake scene. In May 1884 he decided to change the programme: at the Princess's he would take the title role of the boy-poet in Jones and Herman's new drama *Chatterley*, while *Claudian* would go on provincial tour with an appropriately changed cast. Leonard Boyne took over the title role and Dewhurst joined the cast as the Holy Clement. The play was as successful in the provinces at it had been in London and, with various cast changes, it ran well into 1885. In October 1886 Barrett took it to New York, following a successful opening there with a profitable six-months' tour of America. Dewhurst however did not join the tour.

In October 1884, when Jonathan Dewhurst had been touring with the *Claudian* company for almost five months, Wilson Barrett asked him to leave *Claudian* and join his new production of *Hamlet* at the Princess's. Dewhurst was presented with a very handsome Army and Navy album, containing photographs of each member of the *Claudian* company. The inscription on a shield in the front was 'Mr Jonathan Dewhurst, from the members of the Claudian Company, Nottingham, October 3 1884'. Dewhurst was ecstatic – a return to Shakespeare, a first-rate company and London! The cast was a strong one: Wilson Barrett would play Hamlet to Miss Mary Eastlake's Ophelia. Edward Smith Willard (Barrett's highly regarded heavy man) was Claudius and Polonius was played by the experienced Clifford Cooper who, back in 1867, had engaged Dewhurst for the Victoria Theatre at Oxford. Barrett's brother George was First Gravedigger and Jonathan Dewhurst was to play the Ghost. The *Stage* printed an interesting comment about the cast:

'It is a fact worthy of notice that the company engaged by Mr Wilson Barrett for the production of *Hamlet* at the Princess's Theatre includes no less than four leading actors who have identified themselves with the Prince of Denmark. Mr Barrett, it is well known, has before now acted Hamlet in the provinces; Mr John Dewhurst has made the part a favourite in his repertory both in the country and the English colonies; Mr Walter Speakman has also delighted large audiences in the character, and Mr Frank Cooper has impersonated the Prince with remarkable intelligence and success. Two other members of Mr Barrett's company – Mr E. Bulwer, one of his stage managers, and Mr Belton – have also appeared in the role. It is also interesting to note that Mr Clifford Cooper, the Polonius of the forthcoming revival, has played every part in the tragedy excepting that of Hamlet.

'By the way, there is no truth in the report that the Ghost, as represented by Mr Dewhurst at the Princess's, is to be invisible.'

117

ROYAL

PRINCESS'S THEATRE.

LESSEE AND MANAGER - MR. WILSON BARRETT.

EVERY EVENING, AT 7.45,

SHAKESPEARE'S TRAGEDY OF

HAMLET

The Archæology of the Play by E. W. GODWIN, F.S.A.

Scenery by Messrs. W. R. BEVERLEY, W. L. TELBIN, STAFFORD HALL and WALTER HANN.

New Music by Mr. EDWARD JONES.

PRODUCED UNDER THE SOLE DIRECTION OF

MR. WILSON BARRETT.

BUSINESS MANAGER - Mr J. H. COBBE.

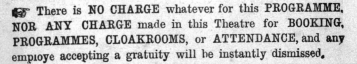

☞ There is NO CHARGE whatever for this PROGRAMME, NOR ANY CHARGE made in this Theatre for BOOKING, PROGRAMMES, CLOAKROOMS, or ATTENDANCE, and any employe accepting a gratuity will be instantly dismissed.

25   Wilson Barrett's *Hamlet* at the Princess's Theatre, London, ran for 116 performances.

"HAMLET" AT THE PRINCESS'S.

THE OPH'A.

FIVE-AND-TWENTY years ago a small boy clad in the corduroys and comforter of the period stood upon the flags of Oxford-street outside the Princess's Theatre. He had parted with his last sixpence to witness the performance of *Hamlet* by Mr. Charles Kean, and had been so improved thereby that he sworn—happily to himself—that he would some day or other be the manager of the Princess's, and play *Hamlet* there. This "poor friendless lad," who, according to his own statement—or at any rate the published reports thereof—had, in 1859, sat in a gallery and then built was no other than Mr. Wilson Barrett. The conjoint outcome of his oath and of the prominence in the dramatic world achieved by him, thanks in many respects to works produced by the pens of Messrs. G. R. Sims, H. A. Jones, and H. Herman, stands revealed in the production last week of Shakespeare's tragic masterpiece.

Every earnest reader of Shakespeare—and who does not pretend to be an earnest reader of Shakespeare nowadays?—is supposed to carry his own ideal Hamlet in his mind's eye like an undeveloped photographic negative; but for him ever to expect to find this ideal fully realised on the stage is out of the question. Still, there are Hamlets that will please him more than others. I do not claim to be an earnest reader of Shakespeare but Mr. Barrett's Hamlet pleases me less than others. He has framed for himself a consistent conception of the character, and of this he gives a careful, earnest, and thoughtful reading, marked by sundry variations from the ordinary text, that have been so thoroughly commented on from all points that it will say nothing critical about them. His "Is it very cold?", his short-vowelled "kind," and his "siege" of troubles, are mere details. On his own stage, too, he has a right to make himself up as he pleases, and who shall gainsay him when he ducks some ten years from Hamlet's age? But I do not like his conception, and I have a strong antipathy to his delivery. His conception rather suggests the schoolmaster than the scholar. He lectures on Yorick's skull like a professor of anatomy, and in his lighter passages is a perkily pedagoguish punster. "Oh! for an hour of Dundee," exclaimed the Highlander at Sheriffmuir when his leaders refused to order the charge that would have turned a drawn battle into a decisive victory. Oh! for one burst of genuine impulsive enthusiasm, such as will thrill an entire audience. Mr. Barrett delivers the text of Hamlet trippingly from the tongue like macadam swiftly dribbling over the tailboard of a cart to a hard road. Chop, chop, chop, the words drop from his lips like so many pebbles. Now and again the tail-board is shifted, and the result is that a cacophonous clatter of polysyllables streams out with a rush. This is especially noticeable in some of his soliloquies, wherein he rattles along with a roar and a rush like that of an express train going through a tunnel. Continually recurrent contortions almost suggest the application of a galvanic battery to his facial muscles, and as

did not give her a little longer neck, are does not step in to keep her from raising her shoulders from time to time to the level of her ears. But her shortcomings were nobly atoned for in the mad scenes, played with a tender, winning pathos hard to be excelled. Madness is not a pleasant thing in real life, and can be made a very repulsive one on the stage, but she manages to simulate dementia thoroughly and with dramatic force, and yet to excite throughout a sense of tender pity rather than disgust. Being a leading lady, Miss Eastlake is allowed those changes of costume, a luxury not even enjoyed by the feminine majesty of Denmark, who has to be content with a couple. Ophelia is lectured by Laertes in blue, rated by Hamlet in pink, and goes mad in the orthodox white satin. But with all the flourish about archæological accuracy, these high-heeled satin shoes are surely out of place.

Mr. E. S. Willard represents Claudius King of Denmark as a red-headed gentleman of audacious disposition and usurious propensities. There is no mincing matters with him; he is a man of action, prompt and decisive, though the action is to some extent hampered by the circumstance that as king he is compelled to wear more clothes at a time than anyone else in the piece. In certain junctures he must find the regal petticoats awkward. Nothing could be better than his acting in the opening scenes, and in his interview with Laertes in the fourth act, but he is somewhat overweighted in the long soliloquy in the oratory. Miss Margaret

fails to make anything out of his scene with the King. Horatio is presented by Mr. J. R. Crauford after the manner of a tame cat—a very tame cat indeed; a young gentleman of the mild admiring school, whose "Where, my lord?" in answer to Hamlet's remark that he thinks he sees his father, is delivered in the mean tone as though Denmark's buried majesty were not defunct at all, and had just been caught a glimpse of by his son through the window. So his "Heaven secure him," when he and Marcellus come in quest of the missing Prince after his interview with the Ghost, is uttered with a placid indifference as to whether such a result may or may not be arrived at that is really amusing.

Mr. John Dewhurst is an affliction rather than an afflicted Ghost. No wonder he is let out at intervals, for they could not endure him for four-and-twenty hours consecutively even in Purgatory. Fasting in fire, too, evidently fails in his case to do anything towards bringing down a serious redundancy of "flesh, too solid flesh." Surely he might be shod with felt by the management, so that his approach might not recall by its thunder that of the bare-backed steed in the drama of *Mazeppa*. After his ponderous tread, his majestic buried business, in conjunction with his disappearance, becomes a mockery, though in the days of realism he might be provided with a rock-tomb to vanish to. His partly presence is, however, belied by a meek, feeble, and altogether unimpressive delivery of the lines allotted to him. The Rosencrantz of Mr. G. R. Foss and the Guildenstern of Mr. C. Fulton are of respectable mediocrity, and Mr. H. Evans is a satisfactory Marcellus. Why, by the way, does Hamlet swear him and Horatio on the cross-hilt of his sword? The oath was always taken as it still is in Spain on the blade. The most conspicuous thing about the Osric of Mr. Neville Doone is the wonderful pair of boots wherewith he has been endowed by the costumier. Mr. Walter Speakman, as the First Actor, gives a fair elocutionary display, rather academical than moving, and Miss Mary Dickens admirably realises Shakespeare's conception of the Player Queen—as expressed in Gertrude's pungent criticism. That argumentative old deliver, the First Gravedigger, is played by Mr. George Barrett. Personally, I entertain a high respect for this character. The First Gravedigger is the only man in the play who will not stand being preached at by Hamlet. The Prince manages to preach at everybody else, from the Ghost downwards—or upwards. Hence it was a delicate attention on Mr. Wilson Barrett's part to allot the character to his brother.

The mounting of the piece shows that Mr. Barrett was in all things impressed by Mr. Charles Kean, and is bent on carrying out that tradition inaugurated at the Princess's by the man who was one of the first to realise that upholstery might be made a substitute for acting. Well, the days are gone by when a great actor could go down to Drury Lane with the accessories for Shylock tied up in a pocket-handkerchief, and Shakespeare would stand but a poor chance without scenic and sartorial embellishment. So the manager has called to his aid Mr. E. W. Godwin, F.S.A., and has given up a pseudo-representation

THE GRAVEDIGGER.

OPHELIA.

affected tapping of the head might imply hollowness equally well as the loss of memory it is supposed to denote. Personally Mr. Barrett's Hamlet is of the curled and oiled Assyrian bull order, bearing the marks of the hairdressers' tongs on his sable locks and rather recalling the conventional representation of an Italian artist of the seventeenth century than that of a Danish prince of the days of the Vikings.

Miss Eastlake is the fair, the almost flaxen, Ophelia. In the opening scenes she does not show to very great advantage, and her trick of simultaneously rounding her eyes and mouth is rather painfully apparent. It is a pity, too, that, since Nature

ALAS, POOR GHOST!

Leighton enjoys the inestimable privilege of being allowed to make up younger as Gertrude Queen of Denmark than any prior performer of the part. She also has the regal prerogative of going to bed by the light of red lamps, which lend to the royal chamber something of the aspect of a railway terminus in miniature. Red is the royal colour of Denmark, so I suppose this is correct. She plays the rejuvenated part very well, but I wish she did not sob quite so harshly when Hamlet reproves her. It must be uncomfortable for her to evolve those spasmodic gusts.

Polonius is very respectably presented by Mr. Clifford Cooper. Not too much of the comedy that used to be aimed at the gallery, but just enough to serve as a foil to the more serious characters with whom the venerable word-spinner is brought into contact. But how about that brocade robe? I have not the history of the silk trade at my fingers' ends, but I question whether such stuff would have been found in Scandinavia in Hamlet's day, as dated by the other costumes worn. The Norse Vikings would have to have sailed pretty far afield to glean such spoils, and while they were about it might just as well have brought back Claudius's black boy, and have given him that part in the piece for which rumour says his soul is sickening. Mr. Frank Cooper is a Laertes most terribly didactic in his advice to Ophelia. Perhaps this is a delicate touch on the part of the performer intended to indicate that had not this young man's career been untimely cut short by the poisoned rapier, he would have grown into just such an old proser as his sire Polonius. He

of Danish Court life of the tenth or eleventh century that is not always in keeping even with the scenic architecture shown on the stage, and that, in my opinion, only serves to heighten the anachronisms with which the piece as a whole bristles. It would be traversing an oft-worn track to point out the countless instances in which the language, manners, and customs are those of Shakespeare's own day. Why, then, this straining after archæological accuracy that can never be wholly realised? Why not boldly mount Shakespeare's plays as if the scene were laid in the Kingdom of Reconciled Impossibilities. The rebel jar would be less felt by the student, and the mounting could be all the more gorgeous.

THE KING!

26   The 'Captious Critic' took a somewhat jaundiced view of *Hamlet*.

27   Wilson Barrett as Hamlet.

In general, Wilson Barrett's *Hamlet* does not appear to have gained the approval and commendation of the critics. The 'Captious Critic' of the *Illustrated Sporting and Dramatic News* found little to praise in either the production or the acting, but was evidently writing to amuse and entertain his readers, as the following snippets illustrate:

Of Hamlet –   'Mr Barrett delivers the text of Hamlet trippingly from the tongue like macadam swiftly dribbling over the tailboard of a cart onto a hard road. Chop, chop, chop, the words drop from his lips like so many pebbles. Now and again the tailboard is shifted and the result is that a cacophonous clatter of polysyllables streams out with a rush. This is especially noticeable in some of his soliloquies, wherein he rattles along with a roar and a rush like that of an express train going through a tunnel.'

Of Ophelia –   'Being a leading lady, Miss Eastlake is allowed three changes of costume, a luxury not even enjoyed by the feminine majesty of Denmark, who has to be content with a couple. Ophelia is lectured by Laertes in blue, rated by Hamlet in pink, and goes mad in the orthodox white satin. But with all the flourish about archaeological accuracy those high-heeled satin shoes are surely out of place.'

Of Gertrude – 'Miss Margaret Leighton enjoys the inestimable privilege of being allowed to make up younger as Gertrude, Queen of Denmark, than any prior performer of the part. She also has the regal prerogative of going to bed by the light of red lamps, which lend to the royal chamber something of the aspect of a railway terminus in miniature.'

Of the Ghost – 'Mr John Dewhurst is an afflictive rather than an afflicting Ghost. No wonder he is let out at intervals, for they could not endure him for four-and-twenty hours consecutively even in Purgatory. Fasting in fire too evidently fails in his case to do anything towards bringing down a serious redundancy of "too, too solid flesh".'

Rosencrantz and Guildenstern were of 'respectable mediocrity'. On a more serious level, the critic J.R. Towse said of Barrett's performance:

'A more utterly prosaic, laborious and trivial interpretation of the character was never seen. The lack of comprehension displayed in it was almost shocking. The reflective, melancholy "sweet prince" posed, gesticulated and ranted like the hero of a modern melodrama, whose one anxiety was to keep himself in the middle of the limelight.'

Clement Scott, in his book *Some Notable Hamlets*, felt that Barrett's presentation of an unconventional Hamlet was surprising, almost audacious and the determination to eschew theatrical tradition in favour of a 'contribution to the school of natural acting' ultimately 'exhausted the actor and fatigued the audience as well'.

Fatigued they may have been, but it did not deter them from returning time and again to the Princess's. The production ran to full houses for 116 consecutive performances, giving us a fair idea of public appreciation of the attraction of the production and of the actors' performances. A different opinion was expressed by the *Illustrated London News* (25 October 1884). This account deals fully with Barrett's view of the play itself and with his performance as Hamlet and we make no apology for quoting from it at some length:

'The immediate and unqualified success achieved by the production by Mr Wilson Barrett at the Princess's on Thursday October 16 of

Shakespeare's tragedy of *Hamlet*, with the actor-manager himself as the still inscrutable Prince of Denmark, may be considered as due to two leading causes. In the first place Mr Wilson Barrett has with equally happy skill and audacity largely altered the ordinary acting version, not with the intent of further curtailing, mutilating and "Bowdlerising" the poet's text, but of giving back to Shakespeare that which is Shakespeare's own, and of which, so far as the modern stage is concerned, he has been deprived by the stupidity of dramatic hacks, or by the egregious vanity of actors who, paraphrasing in their minds the notable saying about Eclipse, the racehorse, resolved that in the case of the performance of Shakespeare's masterpiece, that it should be "Hamlet first and the rest nowhere".'

'Mr Austin Brereton, in his just published and very valuable monograph, "Some Famous Hamlets from Burbage to Fechter", has told us of the fantastic alterations which Garrick in his old age made in the grandest of English tragedies. He thought the first act too long and divided it into two. He entirely changed the scenes in which the King and Laertes conspired to kill Hamlet, so as to make Laertes's character more estimable. He left the audience in ignorance of Ophelia's fate; and the Queen, instead of being poisoned on the stage, was led from her throne and was "said to have become insane from a sense of her guilt". When Hamlet attacked the King in the last scene, the latter drew his sword, defended himself and was killed in the encounter. Finally, the Gravediggers were wholly expunged from the play; Osric was as ruthlessly excised and Laertes was provided with a "high falutin" dying speech. Garrick's "revised version" soon fell into oblivion; but since his time there have been many pedantic or simply idiotic versions of *Hamlet* played and printed, full of incongruities, suppressions and obscurities.

'Mr Wilson Barrett has, so far as ever he could, given us not the pedant's or the Prompter's or the conceited actor's acting version, but Shakespeare's; and the strange but pleasing result has been that a tragedy, which on the stage may to many seem stilted, artificial and cloudy, becomes a most picturesque and animated melodramatic play, quite coherent and sequential and full of the liveliest human interest. The episode of the murder of Polonius and its consequences in the sedition led by Laertes is by the restoration of long-omitted scenes clearly and fully set forth; more scope and verge are given to the characters of the King and Queen and more light (complete illumination is impossible) is thrown on the relations of Hamlet and Ophelia than has been ven-

122

tured upon for many a long year; and the final catastrophe is naturally and not violently suggested. To very many of the spectators – merely play-goers and not Shakespearean scholars – who have crowded the Princess's since Thursday, the Sixteenth inst., *Hamlet*, owing to the sensible and generous restorations effected by Mr Wilson Barrett, may have seemed, comparatively speaking, a new play. And it is certain that they liked the new play immensely, although all that seemed new was Shakespeare's glorious and immortal own.

'The second reason for the unmingled success of the tragedy lies in the singularly novel, intelligent and original presentation of the character of the Prince of Denmark. I have seen many Hamlets, and have a distinct remembrance of them all. Macready, magnificent in elocution, but uneasily and sometimes grotesquely melodramatic (as in the pocket-handkerchief fluttering passage); Charles Kean, exceptionally graceful and romantic in early youth, harsh and cynical in age; Phelps, Edwin Booth, Lawrence Barrett, Creswick, Barry Sullivan, Fechter and Henry Irving – the last two supremely princely, tender and emotional. And I have heard Charles Young and Charles Kemble read Hamlet.

'I do not intend to compare Mr Wilson Barrett's Hamlet with that of any previous impersonator of the part. A few living play-goers may remember Edmund Kean in the character. The elder Booth, George Frederick Cooke, Macklin, Garrick, John Kemble belong in their Hamlets as hopelessly to ancient history as do Burbage, Taylor and Betterton. But I can frankly say of Mr Wilson Barrett's rendering of the part that I never before saw anything like it. He has at least created a Hamlet of his own; and the performance seems to me in the highest degree natural, intelligent and artistic. He has, it is true, left the spiritual side of the part pretty much where he found it. The psychological character of the Royal Dane is, and must continue to be, an insoluble mystery.

'Mr John Cordy Jeaffreson has found out nearly all that is discoverable, perhaps, about "the Real Lord Byron"; but the secret of the "Real Lord Hamlet" is locked up with the dust and ashes in that grave at Stratford-on-Avon. Succeeding generations of tragedians have laboured to conceal their inability to fathom the mystery of Hamlet's being by giving him now a classical and didactic, now a dreamy and romantic, individuality. Now he has stalked and solemnised, towering in sable plumes, majestic and austere, with the Danish Order of the Elephant round his neck, as he does in Sir Thomas Lawrence's picture of John Kemble. Now he has ranted and roared, mouthed and sputtered, thrown himself into antic attitudes, or burst into fits of hysterical weeping. All this has been mainly dust thrown in the public eyes. The actor seems to be continually saying, "I must not, for occult reasons, tell you precisely what manner of man Hamlet, Prince of Denmark, really was; but you must gather it from my tricks and my manners". There is neither manner nor trick about Mr Wilson Barrett's Hamlet. The poses of Claudian, the studied mournfulness of the Silver King have disappeared. Mr Barrett's Hamlet is altogether natural and unaffected. We see a very young man – eager, restless, impulsive, impetuous, full of loving and lovable qualities, prompt to forget and to forgive, implacable and ruthless only towards the murderer of his father, the obligation to revenge whose death has been laid upon him by supernatural command.

'The magnificent speeches assigned to him he delivers easily, gracefully and with perfect elocution, but wholly unconventionally and, as it were, incidentally. There is, in fine, throughout this noble performance distinct and pervading evidence that the actor is thinking much less of Wilson Barrett, tragedian, than of William Shakespeare, Poet of all Time; and that he is working heart and soul to place before us "The Tragical Historie of Hamlette" as Shakespeare meant it to be played, and not merely in a manner most conducive to the principal character having the stage to himself during the major part of the evening.

'Devotees of the classical school of declamation may object that Mr Wilson Barrett's delivery of the "To Be or Not to Be" soliloquy was slightly undignified. So it was from the strictly classical point of view. It would scarcely have pleased the excellent Hannah More, who remarked of Garrick's Hamlet that, "Whether in the simulation of madness, in the sinkings of despair, in the familiarity of friendship or in the meltings of tenderness, he never once forgot he was a Prince; and in every variety of situation and transition of feelings, you discovered the highest polish of good breeding and courtly manners". Whether it was consonant with the highest polish of good breeding and good manners among the Princes of Hannah More's time to indulge, as Hamlet does, in the grossest *double entendres* in the presence of ladies; to describe with loathsome particularity the decomposition of a murdered corpse; and to allude to the ghost of his father as "True-penny" in "the cellarage", must be left to students of the Georgian Era. Mr Wilson Barrett was certainly not conventionally princely; but there may have been Princes quite as outspoken and as animated as he is at many mediaeval courts besides that of Elsinore.'

124

Were the critics swayed by the departure from what had become tradition, finding the interpretation difficult to accept even though the text may have 'given Hamlet back to Shakespeare'? And was Wilson Barrett's performance another example of an actor being ahead of his time? Of the other performances the *Illustrated London News* said:

'Mr Wilson Barrett was supported with tolerable efficiency. Miss Eastlake as Ophelia revealed in the mad scene a gleam of true dramatic genius. Otherwise she was vaporous and nebulous – very graceful and floating in mien, but mainly unsubstantial. Miss Margaret Leighton – whose comely port and visage might excite the enthusiastic admiration of M. Max O'Rell – was not half matronly enough. Mr E.S. Willard, as the King – usually a ponderous and morose villain – acted as an alert and vivacious man of the world, with a propensity to commit capital offences. Mr John Dewhurst was respectable as the Ghost and Mr Clifford Cooper was most painstaking and discriminating as Polonius.'

For some time Elizabeth Dewhurst had been ill. We have been unable to show whether she returned to England on the *Verona* without her husband, or whether she stayed in India with him. The deaths of all her infant children and the possible disaffection with her life as the wife of a busy actor must have weighed heavily on her. On the 3 February 1885 she died, the cause of death being cirrhosis of the liver. This – and the death certificate – leave us with more unanswered questions. Was Elizabeth so unhappy that she had taken to drink and become an alcoholic? What latterly was her relationship with her husband? Did he spare any time during *Hamlet* to look after his wife and, if not, was this because he needed to maintain their income while caring for her in his 'spare time'? Or was it that their relationship had deteriorated to the point that he no longer cared or was even living with her? Certainly he did not register her death. That was done by Wm. Plumer, present at the death, who lived at 98 Prince of Wales Road, Pancras. What was the connection with Wm. Plumer – and perhaps, more to the point, what was the connection with 98 Prince of Wales Road? Elizabeth Dewhurst died at 29 Malden Crescent and this house was just round the corner from Prince of Wales Road. In the following year when Jonathan remarried, 98 Prince of Wales Road was given as his address. One can postulate various scenarios to explain what facts there are, but unfortunately we have no definitive explanation of what exactly happened in the Dewhurst household in February 1885. All we know is that Elizabeth died and Jonathan continued to play the Ghost in *Hamlet*.

On the completion of the run of *Hamlet*, Dewhurst resumed his role of the Holy Clement in *Claudian*, touring the provinces until May. His involvement with Wilson Barrett had cemented their friendship which lasted for the rest of their lives, but at the end of the *Claudian* run he decided on another change of course. While involving himself in a short reciting tour, he made plans for his next 'powerful legitimate company' – and further plans in other directions which would change the pattern of his life significantly.

13

Fanny Rivers

Despite his pleasure at being involved with Wilson Barrett in the long runs of *Hamlet* and *Claudian*, Jonathan Dewhurst's domestic life in London had been troubled, to say the least, possibly with growing difficulties in his marriage and ultimately the death of Elizabeth in what could not have been happy circumstances. We do not know precisely when Jonathan became acquainted with the actress Fanny Rivers and her family, or the circum-

28   Fanny Rivers, who became Dewhurst's third wife.

stances under which they met. The Dewhursts and the Rivers were at the time resident and involved with the theatre in London, so it would have been quite understandable that their paths should cross.

Frances Clara (Fanny) Rivers was 26 years old and an established actress with a long tradition of the stage in her family. Her parents, Henry Rivers and Fanny Morelli were actors, as were her three brothers Charles, Robert and Alfred. Henry Joseph Rivers was born in 1819 and had been in the theatre all his life. He had been associated with the principal London and provincial theatres from the age of 19, but never rose to take the leading roles. He was a wholly reliable, experienced and professional supporting actor, always in work and from 1860 based almost exclusively at the leading London theatres: for many years with Alfred Wigan at the Olympic and with J.B. Buckstone at the Theatre Royal, Haymarket. For Buckstone he also acted as stage manager and in those days the stage manager virtually ran the production. J.R. Towse comments that:

'The stage managers of those days, if not themselves expert actors, were, at least, experts in the whole art of acting and of stage production, knew how things ought to be done, and could and did show the actual players how to do them. They licked tyros into shape and converted wooden supernumeraries into living human beings. They had the faculty of blending discordant details into one harmonious whole.'

Henry toured with the Vezin-Chippendale Comedy Company in 1875, appearing in *The School for Scandal* (as Rowley), *She Stoops to Conquer* (Stingo), *London Assurance* (Martin) and *The Rivals* (Coachman). In 1878, when Adelaide Neilson was appearing at the Haymarket, he was in the supporting cast throughout her season. In *Romeo and Juliet*, with H.B. Conway as Romeo and Adelaide Neilson as Juliet, Henry played Friar John, his wife Fanny Morelli was Lady Capulet and daughter Fanny was Page to Paris. *H.M.S. Pinafore* by Gilbert and Sullivan was so popular at the time, that in December 1879 a *Pinafore* company was formed entirely of children. Not only did they perform in London but also toured the provinces. Alfred and one of his brothers were in the company and it seems that, at least for part of the tour, Henry and daughter Fanny travelled with the company, providing the occasional supporting feature and no doubt keeping an eye on the two boys. In May 1881 we find the Children's *Pinafore* appearing at the Theatre Royal, Bradford, supported for the week by the 'Farcical Absurdity', *An Awkward Adventure*. No author is named on the poster and, hoping it might be a two-hander suitable for us to revive, we have made every effort

R owley

29　Henry Rivers, the father of Jonathan's wife Fanny, as Rowley in *The School for Scandal*
– detail from programme, 1875.

to trace the play. All to no avail! There is no mention of the play in the Lord
Chancellor's records, nor in Allardyce Nicoll's list of plays of the nineteenth
century. The Lord Chancellor's records list two similar titles, *An Awkward
Mistake*, which is dated later than the performance of *Adventure* and *An
Awkward Affair*, which has entirely different characters. Henry ended his 60
years in the theatre with Wilson Barrett at the Lyceum. His final perfor-
mance was as Gaffer Pottle in *The Silver King*, the leads being taken by
Barrett and Maud Jeffries – and the stage manager was Henry's son Alfred.
But that was in 1899, some 14 years later than the point reached in our
narrative.

Frances Rose (Fanny) Morelli, whom Henry married in 1858, was the
daughter of the noted actor and clown Charles Francis Morelli, who, as a
boy, had acted with the celebrated Joe Grimaldi. There is some suggestion
that Fanny was the step-daughter of Charles Morelli – she is so described in
his will – but on her marriage certificate he is given as her father. As she is
the only one of his many children to follow in the theatrical tradition a
blood relationship may seem more likely. Her obituary tells us that she had

129

started her career at an early age with Samuel Phelps at Sadler's Wells, and played such parts as Albert in *William Tell* and Prince Arthur in *King John*. When she outgrew boys' roles she joined James Rodgers in the Worcester circuit as singing chambermaid. She had an excellent singing voice and, having a good musical education, could undertake the most difficult music. She stayed with James Rodgers for many seasons, following which she worked in Liverpool and then London when the Strand Theatre opened under the name of Punch's Playhouse. She subsequently played many stock engagements at the principal provincial theatres before she and Henry joined J.B. Buckstone at the Haymarket.

Dewhurst, we believe, must have met the Rivers family when in London with Wilson Barrett. But following Elizabeth's death he appeared to leave all his London connections behind and throw himself once more into touring the North of England with his own 'powerful legitimate company'. His leading lady was Rose Murray ('the favourite Liverpool actress') and the repertoire consisted once more of the well-tried Shakespearian tragedies and popular historical plays. One of his first engagements took him back to Leigh, his old home town. On his last appearance there the theatre had been the old Assembly Rooms (or the 'Sems' as they were known locally), but in 1884 a new theatre, the Theatre Royal, had been built. After its first season the theatre was closed for almost three months while improvements and renovations were effected, and in August 1885 it was ready to re-open. Jonathan Dewhurst and his company were specially engaged for a week to celebrate the grand re-opening. The programme for the week consisted of *Hamlet*, *Richelieu*, *The Lady of Lyons*, *Louis XI*, *Othello* and *Macbeth*, and was heartily welcomed by the *Leigh Chronicle*, which took the opportunity of explaining to its readers, in its review of *Hamlet*, why the play appealed to all types of audience:

'Mr Jonathan Dewhurst, as we have just stated, opened the Theatre on Monday evening when the famous tragedian received a very hearty reception, after an absence of nearly five years. Mr Dewhurst's critics say that he shines best in Shakespeare's play of *Othello*, but whether this be so or not, his personation of Hamlet on Monday evening, before a large and fashionable audience, far exceeded anything we have yet seen from him, for he has indeed placed on the records of the stage a thoroughly acceptable reading of Shakespeare's work. In the whole range of human compositions, there is probably no example which for poetic beauty, wit, philosophy and dramatic force, can compare with the moving story of "Hamlet, Prince of Denmark", as told by

130

Shakespeare. It is popular with all classes alike. Those to whom its wit and wisdom are as dumb show revel in the sensations which succeed each other in such unexpected profusion. The illiterate feel amply compensated for the loss of the verbal points by the ghost and the unstinted sword practice; the habitues of the pit are thrilled by the real or simulated ravings of the Royal Dane, and the elite of the house is swayed into abnormal excitement by the craft of the actor.

'This to some extent was the case on Monday night, but the crowded "house" was eager and attentive, bending forward in perfect stillness to catch the accents of the performers and, when the occasion came, as it very often did, for a demonstration of hands and feet, the unanimity and heartiness were irresistibly impressive and significant. The appearance of Mr Dewhurst in the second scene was the signal for an outburst of loud applause, which was some time before it subsided. Then the audience were given a rich and intellectual treat such as they never had before in their own town. The applause was loud and prolonged, but perhaps the finest piece of praise that could be bestowed was that of a man in the back pit, who exclaimed "Good lad!" with the utmost heartiness when Mr Dewhurst finished his lines. At the close of the play Mr Dewhurst appeared in front of the curtain, when he was received with rapturous applause. He thanked them for the reception given to him, and expressed the pleasure it gave him to meet them in such a handsome theatre. It was a pretty building and should prove a means of education in Leigh if the management brought high intellectual entertainments. (Applause). It was a credit to the town and should prove as great an instructor as the church. (Applause).'

Quite what happened next is not clear, but only three months later, when the Dewhurst company appeared again at the Theatre Royal, Fanny Rivers was with them. Dewhurst's leading lady was Kate Varley, who took all the leading female roles except for that in the supporting comedy *Faint Heart Never Won Fair Lady* on the Friday night, when Fanny Rivers took the lead opposite Jonathan Dewhurst. It is interesting to note that for the previous week the theatre had engaged Mr F.A. Scudamore and his Powerful Company – the same F.A. Scudamore who had been in the Dewhurst company five years earlier. There was a complete change of programme from that of the previous visit and the local press found much to praise in all the performances, particularly in that of Dewhurst's Shylock. It was unfortunate that the week at Leigh coincided with the approach of the general election, which was generating considerable excitement and resulted in the recovery

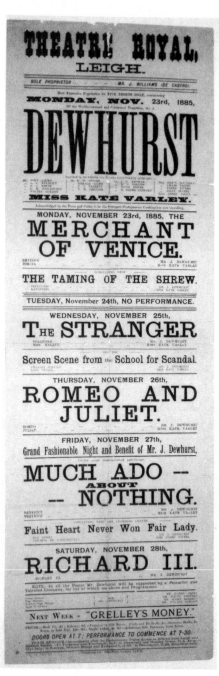

30   This poster of 1885 shows a typical week for a touring rep company.

of power in February 1886 by Gladstone's Liberals from the somewhat short-lived administration of the Conservatives, who, led by Lord Salisbury, had been in power only since June.

Jonathan Dewhurst was 22 years older than Fanny Rivers, but that did not present a problem. They were attracted to each other and shared the major influence in their lives – the theatre. Whereas Margaret Mary and Elizabeth may have been described as actresses, Fanny *was* an actress: she came from a theatrical background and the theatre was in her blood. She well-understood the pressures exerted by life in the theatre and the concerns which could be engendered by what was frequently a precarious way of making a living. She and Jonathan shared all this – it was the only life they knew – the only life they wanted. And, touring with Jonathan's company, they could be together all the time in a way which had been impossible before. Touring continued throughout the North of England until 16 August 1886 when they married.

Marriage was probably their intention in any event, but now it was the only action possible for them when Fanny found that she was pregnant. They were married at the Pancras Register Office, their witnesses being Fanny's parents, Henry and Fanny Rivers. The marriage certificate shows the address for both of them as 98, Prince of Wales Road – the address given by Wm. Plumer who was present at the death of Elizabeth. Was this the home of Henry and Fanny Rivers – and if so what was their connection with Wm.Plumer – or was it a boarding house? We have failed to find answers to these questions. Henry Rivers is, naturally, described as an actor on the marriage certificate, while John Dewhurst, Jonathan's father, now deceased, is described as a Gentleman. The change in their domestic circumstances marked the end, at least for the time being, of Jonathan's touring company and a break in Fanny's acting career. They remained in London and Jonathan was invited to join Mrs Conover's production of *Macbeth* at the Olympic Theatre.

Mrs Anna Conover, a young American actress, had been running the Olympic for almost three years but, despite her every effort, success had eluded her. The critics were unimpressed and, in the views of some observers, were cruel and destructively critical in their comments. Her lease of the theatre would expire with the final performance of *Macbeth*, which she then planned to take on tour. The play opened with J.H. Barnes in the title role opposite Mrs Conover's Lady Macbeth, with Dewhurst as Banquo. The *Stage* commented:

'If energy, courage and a lavish expenditure of time and money go for anything in these days the production by Mrs Conover of *Macbeth* at the

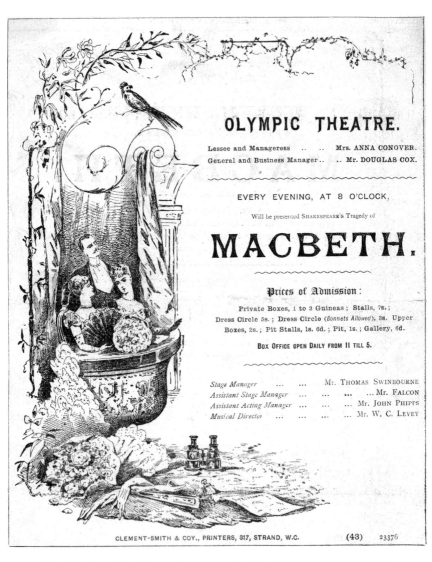

OLYMPIC THEATRE.

Lessee and Manageress   ..   ..   Mrs. ANNA CONOVER.
General and Business Manager..   .. Mr. DOUGLAS COX.

EVERY EVENING, AT 8 O'CLOCK,

Will be presented SHAKESPEARE'S Tragedy of

MACBETH.

Prices of Admission:

Private Boxes, 1 to 3 Guineas; Stalls, 7s.;
Dress Circle 5s.; Dress Circle (*Bonnets Allowed*), 3s. Upper
Boxes, 2s.; Pit Stalls, 1s. 6d.; Pit, 1s.; Gallery, 6d.

Box Office open Daily from 11 till 5.

Stage Manager   ...   ...   Mr. THOMAS SWINBOURNE
Assistant Stage Manager   ...   .Mr. FALCON
Assistant Acting Manager ...   . Mr. JOHN PHIPPS
Musical Director   ...   . Mr. W. C. LEVEY

CLEMENT-SMITH & COY., PRINTERS, 317, STRAND, W.C.   (43)   23376

31   Dewhurst joined Anna Conover to play Macbeth to her Lady Macbeth
at London's Olympic Theatre in September 1886.

134

Olympic Theatre should meet with a warm welcome. No pains appear to have been spared in the effort to make the revival worthy of the subject. If the good intentions of those interested in the venture had been carried out all would be well, for it is evident that no labour has been lost in the process of preparing the play for the stage. But it unfortunately so happens that what has been attempted is a little beyond the reach of those making the attempt. The poetry, the weird significance, the sublimity and the tragedy are wanting. The production only succeeds in modernising, and, consequently, in lowering the Shakespearean work. Its general tone is essentially colloquial and reminiscent of the second-class drama of today. For a lady of Mrs Conover's limited experience to attempt to act a part which taxed the powers of Sarah Siddons at the same moment that her playing of it had brought her fame, and in which Sara Bernhardt has failed, was, indeed, a bold, hazardous venture.

'Mrs Conover is seen at her best in the sleep-walking scene, where she is calm and impressive enough to thrill her audience. Mr Barnes is a bluff, burly Macbeth; he speaks his lines broadly and with good effect, but he does not try to reach the subtle under-side of the character. Mr Beveridge, unfortunately, is the most modernised Macduff imaginable. Mr Palmer as the King and Mr Dewhurst as Banquo are not strikingly well-suited.'

Dewhurst played Banquo for two weeks and then, when J.H. Barnes left the cast, he assumed the role of Macbeth. The *Stage* saw this as an improvement:

'Mr Barnes having been compelled to fulfil his American engagement, the title role is assumed by Mr J. Dewhurst in a manner that accentuates his reputation as an actor of ripened and varied experience. His reading is a robust one and, as was to be expected, smacks of the "old school" of Shakespearean acting. It is full of animation, and marked throughout by a thorough insight into the character. The Dagger Scene is particularly well-rendered, the doubt of the reality of his vision, his persuasion that it is no optical delusion, and his disappointment on finding that it is only the phantasy of an o'erwrought brain are well-conceived and executed; and there is poignant regret in his utterance "I could not say Amen" to the half-muttered prayers of the murdered king's grooms. The depiction of horror at the apparition of Banquo's ghost was masterly, if over elaborate in execution, and the recurring qualms of conscience as the king has to steep his soul deeper in murder and ill-doing are never lost sight of in the portrayal. Mr Dewhurst's whole performance was warmly applauded and he was called at the end of each act. A further change was the substitution of Sir Randal Roberts for Mr Dewhurst as Banquo and, without wishing to say anything unkind of one who evidently tries his utmost, audiences are certainly losers by the alteration.'

At the end of the month the lease expired, *Macbeth* closed and did not go on tour. Mrs Conover stayed at the Olympic, accepting an offer from the new lessee to appear in several productions.

While Dewhurst had been involved with *Macbeth*, Augustus Harris, the manager of Drury Lane, had produced there a new and sporting drama, *A Run of Luck*, which was an immediate success, and customers unable to obtain tickets were turned away every night. The play ran at the theatre until the end of October and then went on provincial tour with an almost entirely new cast. The cast was large and the production opulent. The *Stage* wondered 'how the scenery, the horses and the hounds, let alone the company are to be carried from town to town so as to keep the receipts on the right side is a mystery that only a manager like Harris can solve'. Dewhurst was engaged to play the bluff Squire Selby, a part which suited him admirably and in this role was required to ride a horse on stage. The *Leigh Observer* reported that on one occasion, when he and the horse rode off the stage, 'his hack shied at the limelight. The girths of the saddle being loose, the squire had a veritable cropper. Mr Dewhurst being a man of substance fell rather heavily, but fortunately was not much hurt'.

It seems likely that during this period Jonathan and Fanny were staying with Henry and Fanny Rivers. On 15 March 1887 Fanny gave birth to their first child, a son whom they christened Harold Brotherton. We have been intrigued by the choice of the name 'Brotherton'. We have found no family connection and only two references that may possibly be relevant. There is a village in Yorkshire of that name, but there seems no reason why this location should be honoured by having their first child named after it. The second possibility is perhaps more likely. Edward Brotherton was a wealthy Manchester cotton merchant, an author of pamphlets on spiritualism and a Swedenborgian. He was also devoted to the cause of popular education and did much to further it in Manchester. Is it possible that in his youth Jonathan had benefited from Brotherton's efforts and was now showing his gratitude? This is quite possible, but there are two other considerations. Jonathan's sister Rebecca, who married Joseph Taylor, gave the second Christian name 'Brotherton' to one of her daughters and, secondly, there was a younger actor (of Harold Dewhurst's generation) H. Brotherton Rivers, of whom we have found no connection either with 'our' Rivers family or 'with the Dewhursts. The reason for the selection of the name may well remain a mystery.

Jonathan and Fanny returned to the north after the birth of their son, taking a house in Manchester. Work involved both of them; in the recital tour of *A Night With The Poets* Jonathan was assisted by Miss Fanny Rivers (Mrs J. Dewhurst). They both appeared at the Theatre Royal, Manchester, in *The Duke's Motto*, the romantic play from the French by John Brougham and then, on 19 December that year, an event was arranged that gave Jonathan Dewhurst – and no doubt his wife – enormous pleasure. The Prince's Theatre, Manchester, where he had started his theatrical career 22 years earlier, was the venue for a 'grand benefit performance' arranged for him by friends and admirers. The main offering was a performance of *Still Waters Run Deep* starring Jonathan and Fanny, for which Mrs Adelaide Calvert travelled expressly from London to take part. The play was followed by a 'miscellaneous entertainment and concert' given by local artistes. All involved gave their services and the theatre was placed at the disposal of the committee by the manager, Mr J.C. Smith, free of all cost. Dewhurst recorded that the event was given 'under the patronage of a whole host of theatrical, literary and artistic friends, including Messrs J.L. Toole, Wilson Barrett, Barry Sullivan and many more'.

Taking part in the pantomime at the Manchester Theatre Royal at this time were members of the De Castro circus family, who performed under the name of 'The Wonderful Craggs'. The De Castros also owned the Theatre Royal in Leigh, where Jonathan and Fanny had recently performed *A Night With The Poets*. At his benefit performance Jonathan Dewhurst was introduced to Mr John Williams De Castro, the proprietor of the Leigh Theatre, and the possibility of his taking over the theatre as lessee and manager was raised. This certainly gave the Dewhursts something to think about. On the one hand it could spell the effective end of travelling the country with his own company, or of being in a position to respond to lucrative and attractive offers, such as Wilson Barrett's *Hamlet*. It would also mean that his future success would depend on the tastes and support of the Leigh public. On the other hand Dewhurst recognised that his career was in the 'mature' stage and that theatre management would not only offer a stable income, but would also enable him to present whatever entertainment he felt appropriate, while still having the occasional opportunity to appear with Fanny before the public. In addition to this Fanny was now expecting their second child, underlining the growing family responsibilities with which he was faced. A firm home base, even if the job was the management of one of the lesser

32   The programme cover for Mrs Saker's farewell benefit when she left the
Royal Alexandra Theatre, Liverpool, in 1888.

provincial theatres, did have significant attractions. Earlier in his career he
would not have considered the offer for a moment, but now it was different; now the prospect of being the successful and respected businessman in
the town where he had grown up, with the support of 'his own' people, was
something he could not ignore.

He did not make up his mind at once. Did he consider that if management was the next logical step he should perhaps seek a more important
theatre? Or was he concerned that management at Leigh would effectively
settle his career for the rest of his working life? No doubt these thoughts and
many more went through his mind, which may explain why eight months
elapsed before he reached a decision. And then on 11 March 1888 their second son, William Henry Bostock, was born. Unusually for him, Dewhurst
was not very active in the theatre at this time, apart from an engagement for
Mrs Saker at the Alexandra Theatre, Liverpool. His thoughts were on his
family and the opportunity at Leigh. And in August 1888 he made up his
mind and accepted the offer.

14

Leigh Theatre Royal and the Way Up

Jonathan Dewhurst's attitude and aims regarding the running of the Theatre Royal in Leigh were entirely consistent with the views he had formed throughout his life about drama, the theatre and public entertainment generally. They were summed up by him in his words to the *Leigh Chronicle* on 3 August 1888:

'My one desire will be to see things well done – I shall carefully exclude everything of a degrading character. The object of the drama and the stage is not to pander to the low and vulgar, but to elevate and refine. That being so it will be my endeavour always to provide for my Leigh patrons such productions as will combine instruction with amusement; and having done my part, I can only trust that the public of Leigh will willingly accord me that amount of support which they may consider my humble efforts deserve.'

His objectives could not have been stated more clearly and for the next 18 years he did all in his power to carry them out. In his favour was his reputation and popularity as a son of Leigh, who had achieved considerable success, one who had reached the heights of his chosen profession, and one who had always been welcomed most enthusiastically on his regular visits to play in the theatre. But it would take more than this to persuade the Leigh public to fill the 1,800-seat Theatre Royal on a regular basis.

The late Dr John Lunn recorded that a Leigh Theatre existed in 1778, attached to the Golden Lion Inn in Windymill Lane. The Golden Lion was situated on what is now the corner of Albion Street and Bradshawgate. Up to 1863, the only other place available for theatrical entertainment was the old Town Hall Assembly Rooms in King Street and these continued to be used even after the establishment of a regular theatre in the town. The first

33 The Theatre Royal, Leigh, opened in 1884 and closed, as a theatre, in 1954.

purpose-built theatre (if so it can be called) was the large wooden building erected in 1863 by a Mr Wardhaugh, to which we referred in Chapter 2, and this continued for some years on the site where the 'Imperial Theatre and Constitutional Assembly Rooms' subsequently stood, referred to variously as 'the Theatre', 'the Assembly Rooms' and 'the Sems'. It was here in the Assembly Rooms that Dewhurst had performed on his earlier visits to Leigh. In 1884 the Theatre Royal was built in Lord Street by the De Castro family and opened under the title of De Castro's Theatre of Varieties, providing entertainment along music-hall lines. However, as mentioned in the previous chapter, the new season in 1885 opened with Jonathan Dewhurst's company presenting legitimate drama and this indicated a change of emphasis, which culminated in Dewhurst taking up the position of lessee and manager in the summer of 1888.

Dewhurst recalled that, as soon as it became known that he was to manage the theatre, he was 'flooded with letters and telegrams of congratulation from friends, acquaintances and brother artistes, wishing me every success'. One such was a letter from his old friend, the poet Ben Brierley, addressed to the Editor of the *Leigh Chronicle*:

140

34 The Theatre Royal, Leigh, detail.

'"JONTY" DEWHURST

To the Editor of the Chronicle

Sir, – I have been told that Mr Jonathan Dewhurst, better known as "Jonty", has become lessee of the Leigh Theatre. "Jonty" is an old friend of mine and a conscientious and a painstaking actor. If he is not a Kean or a Kemble, he has attained a standard in his profession higher than most actors of the present day. I saw his "Shylock" a few evenings ago and I consider it far above the "Shylocks" we are accustomed to see, and betrays a dramatic intelligence we rarely meet with. He is worthy of all the assistance he can obtain. – I am yours etc.,

> BEN BRIERLEY
> The Poplars,
> Harpurhey,
> Manchester, Aug. 3, 1888.'

The *Chronicle* reported that before he opened, Dewhurst gave the theatre a thorough overhauling

'cleaning, beautifying, redecorating and the whole of the scenery renewed. The services of Mr Robert Rivers [presumably Jonathan's brother-in-law] have been secured as resident scenic artist and stage manager, and this is a guarantee that every piece and every production will not only be carefully mounted, but upon a scale of magnificence which has never before been attempted in the town. Mr Dewhurst is sparing neither pains nor expense to make the Theatre Royal a credit to the town, and we are confident that lovers of the drama will gladly accord that patronage which he deserves, and his success will be assured.'

The re-opening was reported in the *Stage*:

'After being closed for over a couple of months this theatre was re-opened on Monday, when a vast number of the drama-loving public attended to welcome the new manager Mr J. Dewhurst. During the recess this capitally constructed opera house has been splendidly decorated, a new act-drop has been painted by Mr R. Harrison, and special scenery has been procured so that altogether the building presents as taut and neat an appearance as any provincial theatre in the country. The opening, which was under the patronage of the local gentry, was signalised by the presentation of *The Lucky Star*, by Miss Emma Rainbow's Co., in which the principal artists are well-supported throughout by capital all-round performers, the interest in the piece, never at any period of the performance, lagging. The scenery and incidents are really admirable.'

It is not clear who in the end painted the scenery, but as the later report credits Mr Harrison we must assume that Robert Rivers was unable to carry out the work. The fare presented by Dewhurst in the new season was a mix of drama, melodrama, a week of opera by Arthur Rousbey's English Opera Company and, in December, prior to the pantomime *Robinson Crusoe*, he and Fanny appeared in a week of legitimate drama. The week of the Dewhursts' performances was an unqualified success, with full houses every night. Such a reception must have confirmed to Jonathan Dewhurst and all concerned that industrial Lancashire could respond to Shakespeare without reservation. Four months in management had robbed Dewhurst of none of his old power. The *Leigh Chronicle* greeted his return to the stage rapturously:

'An illustrious Shakespearean actor has said that whenever he takes part in Shakespeare's plays he always finds something new in them – some new and precious jewel that he has not previously discovered –

142

some additional flight of the imagination that confers greater lustre on Shakespeare's immortal name. The same may be said of Mr Dewhurst. Whenever he assumes one of his old characters, all his old fire seems to burst forth anew and the scenes of his success seem to pass before him as the ghosts of Banquo's descendants. Again he is at the other end of the world, thrilling an audience of enlightened Australians with his splendid elocution; once more he is bowing in response to the deafening cheers that greet some exceptional triumph. Again he is achieving still greater success, and he sees his star rising in the heavens, and attaining a higher altitude than before. The waves of time roll on in their ceaseless course and he once more confronts an audience of fellow townsmen.'

His Macbeth displayed 'all that robustness and energy for which he has ever been remarkable' and all aspects of his performance were 'admirable specimens of the excellence to which Mr Dewhurst has brought his interpretation of Shakespeare'. *Macbeth*, *Hamlet* and *Richard III* were performed and there was one non-Shakespeare play, Kotzebue's *The Stranger*. In this play, Dewhurst in the title role:

'Proved that he possesses not only the instincts of a great tragedian, but can on occasion become exceedingly tender and touching. The last act where, after frequent mental conflicts between duty and love, he becomes finally reconciled, is pathetic to the last degree and, in this part, both Mr and Mrs Dewhurst touch the audience to the heart. Mrs Dewhurst appeared for the first time as Mrs Haller, the unfaithful wife, and secured a brilliant success. Her nature is one that causes her to shrink from the display of power, vigour, sarcasm and declamation which are essential to a tragic actress, but she is admirably gifted for a role like the one she assumed on Tuesday evening, where she can display her womanly tact and pathos and arouse the sympathy of everybody by depicting beauty in distress. The quiet, rich, musical tones in which she spoke quite charmed the audience whilst her passionate appeals to her husband (both real and pretended) cannot be characterised as less than a signal triumph. The gentle, though inexpressibly touching manner in which she recalled the happy days of her early womanhood was peculiarly striking by its deep pathos, and the shriek of joy at beholding her children restored to her must have moved a heart of stone. The final scene was in all respects an unqualified success and fully deserved the hearty cheers of the appreciative audience.'

143

Dewhurst took his benefit with *The Merchant of Venice*, performed before the elite of the district. There was an added bonus: the very popular Craggs, who were appearing in Liverpool, rushed to Leigh to pay Dewhurst the compliment of giving an exhibition of their skills in support of the main production. *The Leigh Chronicle* reported:

'The vast attendance spoke much of the popularity of Mr and Mrs Dewhurst and the Cragg family. The latter had, at great inconvenience, come over to Leigh for the purpose of giving an additional lustre to the evening's proceedings, and had to be back in Liverpool about nine o' clock, in order to perform there. Their display on Friday evening even excelled that of the previous week, their feats arousing unbounded enthusiasm. They were recalled again and again, and repeatedly greeted with storms of applause.

'After their departure the curtain rose on Shakespeare's great drama *The Merchant of Venice*. Great pains had been taken to make the play a thorough success and the costumes were on a gorgeous scale. Mr Dewhurst, of course, appeared in his old character of Shylock the Jew and his display was fine to the last degree. His "get-up" was admirable. His long, venerable beard, white with the hoar frost of age, his Jewish gown, with a red cross on the left shoulder, his grey hair and his skull cap, caused him to assume such an ancient appearance that even his most intimate friends would not have known him had not his well-known voice and gesture betrayed his identity. On Friday night he merged his own individuality into that of Shylock and appeared to all intents and purposes as a Venetian Jew of the fourteenth century.'

There then followed a lengthy panegyric on Dewhurst's portrayal of Shylock, ending with the words:

'It was a rare treat to see Mr Dewhurst's final display. In an agony of rage and despair he makes a strange noise like the hiss of a snake, dashes his knife on the ground with the fury of a fiend and toddles off the stage, babbling like an old man in his second youth and shedding bitter tears.'

Fanny Dewhurst as Portia:

'...was as queenly, lovable, mild, and charming as ever. Her acting,

though falling short of that intensity of feeling necessary in a tragedi-
enne was rendered pleasing by the delightful manner in which she
acquitted herself in the love passages. In this part she was seen at her
best, and her smiling, cheerful, pleasant face made her the beau–ideal
of a lovable woman.'

In his book *A History of Leigh*, John Lunn refers to Dewhurst's incident
with the knife in somewhat greater detail:

'It was during a performance of *The Merchant of Venice* on 7 December
1888 that Dewhurst, playing Shylock, worked himself up to such a
pitch of frenzy, that he threw the knife against the stage, where it
glanced off and wounded a spectator sitting in the pit.'

By the end of the year the Dewhursts had successfully established themselves at the Theatre Royal and their first season had been a success. They
had moved to 12, Wilkinson Street, a terrace house close to the centre of
Leigh, and within easy walking distance of the theatre in Lord Street. Their

35   12, Wilkinson Street, the Dewhursts' first home in Leigh.

near neighbours included two schoolmasters, a solicitor, a journalist, a retired grocer and a retired blacksmith. At No. 26 were the Hiltons, to whom in 1900 was born a son, James, who in later life would achieve fame as the author of *Lost Horizon* and *Goodbye Mr Chips*. Wilkinson Street was a very respectable address and the census return of 1891 shows that the Dewhursts had a domestic servant, a Miss Jessie O'Neil. Perhaps for the first time Jonathan and Fanny could feel settled in their domestic and professional lives.

Jonathan had one eye on his position in the Leigh establishment and in 1889 joined the Leigh Literary Society, remaining a member for the next 17 years. The Society met on a weekly basis for six months of the year and featured speakers on a wide range of subjects, as well as the occasional musical and dramatic entertainment. Jonathan Dewhurst was a regular contributor, presenting *A Night With The Poets* and, later, recitals of selections from Shakespeare and even recitals from memory of complete Shakespeare plays – *Hamlet*, *Macbeth* and *Othello*. In November 1889 Fanny presented Jonathan with their third child, another son, Percy Jonathan. Fanny's brother Alfred, who in September 1889 was in Liverpool with the Wilson Barrett company, took the opportunity to visit his sister. His diary records that he:

'Went for a long country walk with my brother-in-law in the morning and a long talk in the afternoon with my sister who I found very well considering her worries with three babies which are fine little fellows, all boys. Went for a walk in the town with sister and her husband in the evening. This is a very dull town and the people hang about the streets in crowds not knowing what to do.'

The Theatre Royal continued to present a weekly change of programme throughout the year, the accent being on melodrama, with old favourites such as *The Silver King* and *The Sign of the Cross* making regular appearances. Then in June 1890 Dewhurst was invited to join H.C. Arnold's company to play Seth Preene in *The Lights O' London*, which Arnold was taking on tour to the northern theatres. There can be little doubt that he welcomed the chance of performing once again and he stayed with the tour for ten weeks, leaving Fanny to look after the children and his business manager, James Smith, to run the theatre.

In October Dewhurst took what can only be considered an enormous gamble. He decided to get together a company to present *King Lear* in Leigh for six consecutive nights. Nothing like that had been attempted there before, nor, as far as we know, ever since. Amazingly the gamble paid off and the Leigh public filled the theatre. Dewhurst played Lear for the first time in his career and Fanny played Goneril. The *Chronicle* reported that the production was a great success and that, unlike some visiting companies, all the characters were strongly played. Dewhurst had offered local employers block bookings at reduced rates for their employees and many of them responded positively.

In January 1891 Dewhurst offered something not seen in the town before – a melodrama entitled *The Streets of Leigh*, described in the publicity as 'The Great Drama, adapted and localised from Boucicault's *Poor of New York*'. It was 'produced under the personal supervision of Mr Dewhurst' and had new local scenery depicting:

'– The Market Place, Leigh (By Moonlight)
– Exterior of the Theatre Royal, Leigh
– The Great Fire Scene, in which Captain Crompton and the
  Leigh Fire Brigade will appear Each Evening'

The *Chronicle* reported that:

'Friday evening has been very generously set apart by Mr Dewhurst for the benefit of the genial and capable acting manager Mr J.R. Smith, and as Mr Smith is well-known and highly respected and does his duty in a conscientious manner there should be a "bumping" house. Special attractions will also be provided.'

James Smith was Dewhurst's nephew, the son of his sister Lucy and her husband Richard Smith. As reported in the newspaper he had a high reputation in the town and remained with the Leigh theatre for many years. The Dewhursts were happy to be established in the Leigh theatre and in particular in a settled family life and, on 13 March 1891, their fourth child, Daisy Adelaide, was born. Jonathan, however, missed the active stage work that had occupied the major part of his working life, and he and Fanny took the opportunity whenever possible to appear on the stage at Leigh. The comment was made on more than one occasion by the local newspapers that it was a pity that this did not happen more often.

On 24 May 1891 William, Percy and Daisy were all baptised and the register records the parents as Jonathan and Frances Clara Dewhurst. Nothing unusual, until we come to 'father's occupation'. Dewhurst, surrounded by success and aware of his position in the community, as usual gave

147

his occupation as 'Tragedian'. Presumably the clerk mis-heard, or did not understand, and it is certain that Dewhurst did not see the entry – for all three children their father's occupation is given as 'Comedian'!

A year after *The Lights O' London* tour, Dewhurst received an offer from Wilson Barrett to tour with him, acting as his understudy for the leading roles and taking specific supporting roles as well. Rehearsals took place in July 1891, and the tour opened at the Plymouth Theatre Royal on 20 July that year. The tour was genuinely national, visiting major provincial theatres such as Leeds, Birmingham, Liverpool and Hull – and the Grand at Islington – as well as lesser theatres which included Ramsgate, Hanley and Blackburn. Three, four or even five plays were performed each week from a programme which included *Othello, Hamlet, Claudian, The Acrobat, The Lights O' London* and *The Silver King*. The tour was an enormous success, critically and financially, selling out wherever it played and (according to the *Stage*) breaking all records. Wilson Barrett received lavish praise from the *Stage* and the provincial press – a clear indication of his popularity throughout the country. The tour also introduced Maud Jeffries as Barrett's new leading lady – a successful association which was to continue for many years. Dewhurst also had earned excellent reviews, but after five months he decided to leave the tour and, at the end of November, he returned home. This was not with the intention of resting, as the following week he and Fanny appeared at the Royal Court in Wigan presenting *Richelieu, Louis XI* and *The Lady of Lyons*. Wilson Barrett was sorry to see him go and sent the following message:

'December 3, 1891. Dear Dewhurst, – I can quite understand that your presence is good for business for the good of your theatre, but I feel a little jealous that Leigh takes you from your place in my company. I miss you very much, and Leigh's gain is my loss. Sincerely I wish you every success, my dear Dewhurst. You deserve to prosper. Believe me, yours always, WILSON BARRETT.'

From the moment he took over the theatre, Jonathan Dewhurst had been concerned to treat his staff well and with every consideration. He gave an annual dinner for them to which were also invited local dignitaries and the report of the dinner provided on 31 December 1891 gives not only a fair account of the proceedings, but also the feelings regarding Dewhurst's progress with the theatre in Leigh. It is interesting to note that Mrs Dewhurst was not present, but no doubt she was fully occupied with the children:

Theatrical Dinner at Leigh

★   ★   ★   ★   ★

'On Thursday evening Mr Dewhurst, the lessee and manager of the Leigh Theatre Royal, invited the employees at the Leigh Theatre and a few friends to a dinner which took place at the Crown Hotel, Leigh. Mr W. Prescott catered in his usual excellent style. About twenty persons were present, including Messrs J. Dewhurst, O.P. Lancashire, J.P., W. Tunnicliffe, J.P., Smith Lancashire, T. Youd, J.R. Smith (business manager of the theatre) and Horace Allen, the clever actor.

'The usual loyal and patriotic toasts having been duly honoured, Mr O.P. Lancashire proposed the health of Mr Dewhurst and in doing so spoke highly of the efforts Mr Dewhurst had made to improve the dramatic taste in this district.

'Mr Dewhurst, in reply, alluded to Mr Lancashire as one of the dearest friends of the theatre and hoped he would continue to be so. He (the speaker) always tried to be a straight fellow, and to do that which was right and just. He thought they would all acknowledge that so far as the theatre was concerned they knew they had had a very uphill fight, but they had fought it and he thought they were bringing the theatre into the haven of success. (Hear, hear.) There was no question as to the theatre being a noble and good institution, both from an educational and an entertaining point of view and he wanted to make it more so in the future. He had secured some very good bookings and he thought that in spite of the opposition – some of it honest and some of it unworthy opposition – they would still manage to steer the ship to success. He wished to see the Theatre Royal much bigger and the town much better from a dramatic point of view, and when that was the case they might depend upon it that they would all be better citizens and better men and women. A well-conducted theatre meant a good community, as it required a good community to make a successful theatre.

'This was followed by numerous speeches and toasts and "a convivial evening was spent". It was evident from several of the speeches that the Dewhursts had experienced some difficulty at first, Mr W. Tunnicliffe commenting that "...though the Leigh people were a little prejudiced when Mr Dewhurst came, that prejudice had now been overcome and the people of Leigh had come to appreciate him. They admired him and he (Mr Dewhurst) was now getting his reward".'

149

MR. J. DEWHURST.

MRS. DEWHURST.

The great event in the Leigh theatrical season—the appearance of Mr. and Mrs. J. Dewhurst—took place at the Leigh Theatre Royal on Tuesday evening, which had been set apart for the benefit of Mrs. Dewhurst. The piece selected for production was Shakespere's "Merchant of Venice," and when Mrs. Dewhurst appeared as Portia in the second scene of act one, she was very cordially received by a large and highly appreciative audience, but when in the next scene, Mr. Dewhurst came on as Shylock, the exacting Jew, his popularity was evinced by the hearty and continued applause which greeted him. The story of Antonio borrowing 3,000 ducats from Shylock for the purpose of assisting his friend Bassanio to win the fair Portia and the bond which was entered into with regard to the pound of flesh, is well known. Mr. and Mrs. Dewhurst were supported by Mr. J. F. Preston and his company who have been appearing at Leigh during the past fortnight; and considering the short time the artistes have had to rehearse their parts, the play was very successfully rendered and without any hitch of any kind being noticeable. With reference to the acting, the accomplishments of Mr. and Mrs. Dewhurst are widely known. Mr. Dewhurst's pourtrayal of Shylock was given with a force and completeness which could scarcely be excelled. Bassanio had a very efficient exponent in Mr. Rutland, whilst Mr. Preston's rendition of Gratiano strengthened the high opinion already entertained of his powers.

Mr. Fitzsimmons, a popular Manchester amateur and pupil of Mr. Dewhurst, made a very successful *debut* on the real stage, and he filled the rôle of Antonio very creditably. Mr. G. De Lara as Launcelot, and Miss Georgie Walton as Nerissa, were also very good. We must also give a word of praise to Mrs. Dewhurst for her splendid wardrobe. At the conclusion of the piece, Mr. and Mrs. Dewhurst were called before the curtain and vociferously cheered. Mrs. Dewhurst was presented with a beautiful bouquet.—Mr. Dewhurst said he thanked them most sincerely for their presence that evening for the benefit of his dear wife; he was more proud of their presence than if it were for himself. He was very glad they had received the play so well, and that they were pleased with it. It was very pleasing to him to see so many present, especially in the front portion of the theatre; it certainly showed that since they came to Leigh they had done some good in trying to raise the standard of the drama produced. When he got the theatre altered he should try and do better than in the past. He would rather make £5 out of something that was good than £150 out of anything that was bad. He hoped they would also remember that on Friday evening it was his benefit. The performance was brought to a close with the farce, "Raising the Wind," in which Mr. J. F. Preston as "Jeremy Didler," created much amusement. To-night (Friday), Mr. Dewhurst will perform the title rôle in "Othello, the Moor of Venice."

36   Mr & Mrs Dewhurst, as seen by a local newspaper in 1893.

Several of those present were members of the Marquis of Lorne Lodge and in May Jonathan Dewhurst joined the lodge, of which he subsequently became Junior Warden and Secretary.

In April 1893 J.F. Preston's company played at the theatre for two weeks, during which they supported Jonathan and Fanny for special performances of *The Merchant of Venice* and *Othello*. The *Leigh Journal* referred to the appearance on stage of the Dewhursts as 'the great event in the Leigh theatrical season'. Several additional rows of stalls were provided for both performances and the theatre was packed. The *Chronicle* reported on *The Merchant of Venice*, which was given for Mrs Dewhurst's benefit:

'Three rows of additional stalls had to be provided for the convenience of Mr Dewhurst's patrons, and the manner in which both Mr and Mrs Dewhurst were received testified to their popularity. Mr Dewhurst's fame rests on a solid basis, his reputation as a Shakespearean actor having been acknowledged in various parts of the world. He gave a most graphic and picturesque rendering of the part of Shylock. Especially was he seen to advantage in the court scene, where the eagerness with which he pressed forward his deep-laid scheme for revenge prepared the audience for the great contrast presented between the man Shylock, as the grasping moneylender conscious of success and the whining, broken-hearted wretch that he became when he saw all his schemes shattered by the eloquence of a second Daniel. At this point Mr Dewhurst fairly thrilled the audience by his dramatic intensity and the curtain fell down upon a wonderfully realistic scene. Mrs Dewhurst is always extremely fascinating whenever she appears on the stage, and if there is a character in her repertoire which suits her immensely it is that of Portia. No wonder that Bassanio falls madly in love with her. Her fine stage presence, her rich musical voice and the delightfully charming little touches she gives to her renderings of the character all combine to awaken enthusiasm.

'At the close Mr Dewhurst was greeted with tremendous cheering on appearing before the curtain. He thanked them most sincerely for their presence there, and he was very glad they had received the play so well. He hoped they had pleased them all. In their little way they had put the play on quite as well as in many more pretentious theatres. He was not well-supported when first he had come, but the attendance had since greatly improved and when he had got the place altered they would have a very nice theatre. They could believe him when he said that he would rather make £5 out of something good than £150 out of something bad.'

In the following week:

'Friday night was fixed for Mr Dewhurst's benefit and the theatre was filled with a large and appreciative audience. A further enlargement of the stalls had to be made to accommodate the large number of local gentry who had arranged to come and see the popular and respected Leigh actor-manager. The play chosen was Shakespeare's *Othello*, a piece which admirably suits Mr Dewhurst. Physically a better Othello could not be desired: his huge, massive shoulders and ponderous chest making him look every inch a warrior. But it is not to his physical advantages so much as to his mental acumen that Mr Dewhurst owes his success in this part. From the moment he first appears on the stage it is evident that he has realised to the full the idea that Shakespeare wished to convey by Othello. It is that of a man strong, not only in his body, but possessed of strong over-mastering passions – passions which can be made capable of doing a tremendous amount of good when used rightly or, when perverted, of doing a great deal of harm. The strong man wrestling with his passions and with the insidious poison that Iago craftily instils into his ears presents a fine characteristic study and the audience decidedly appreciated those subtle touches which give such a finish to Mr Dewhurst's acting. The applause that greeted his efforts fully testified to the appreciation in which he is held.

'Mrs Dewhurst was a decidedly fascinating Desdemona, and her melodious voice rippled pleasantly in some of her most striking scenes. She was evidently quite at home in the part and she fully maintained her reputation.'

Jonathan and Fanny continued to maintain their acting connection with the theatre, appearing in *Much Ado About Nothing* and *Hamlet*. It is interesting to note that in the former, one of the supporting actors playing the part of 'a boy' was 'H. Brotherton', Jonathan's eldest child, Harold, who a week earlier had celebrated his seventh birthday.

The variety of visiting companies and productions continued, with average attendances running at 75 per cent throughout the year. In September 1894, Wilson Barrett came to the theatre with his company to present *The Acrobat*, adapted by Barrett from the French. The company included Austin Melford, one of Wilson Barrett's leading players, and his assistant stage-manager was Alfred Rivers, Fanny's younger brother. Dewhurst, of course, knew most of the visiting actors personally, and from time to time the companies he booked were led by actors who had been in his own companies in the past. Miss Ellen Cranston (who had toured with him in 1880) was one such and another was F.A. Scudamore, who not only toured with his own company, but by 1895 was also the author of several successful melodramas.

In the same year, looking to make a contribution to the life of Leigh other than through the theatre, and also perhaps to establish himself more fully in the civic life of the town, Jonathan Dewhurst put his name forward as one of the Conservative candidates for the St Paul's Ward in the Leigh Urban District Council elections. Three candidates were elected, one Labour, one Liberal and one Conservative: Jonathan was one of the four who were unsuccessful, polling only 80 from a total of 1,493 votes. There were many local people who regarded him highly and who felt that the St Paul's electorate had made the wrong decision. In typical fashion he put this reverse and his disappointment behind him – but he made no further attempt to enter local government.

Jonathan Dewhurst's 59th birthday was marked by a presentation to him by some of his friends at the Courts Hotel, Leigh. Mr George Shaw, the wealthy brewer of Pennington Hall, presented him with a solid silver bowl, saying that 'Mr Dewhurst's friends wished to show the appreciation and esteem in which he was held by them'. Dewhurst, taken by surprise, expressed his gratitude for the kind remembrance of his birthday and said that 'those whom he would leave behind him to look upon that bowl would say, as he did, that he had some good and true friends in Leigh'.

1894 ended with the annual dinner that Dewhurst always provided for staff and employees of the Theatre Royal and was held at the Saddle Hotel. The *Chronicle* reported:

'Mr Chadwick proposed the "health of their host, Mr Dewhurst". In doing so he said he was sorry that he could not congratulate Mr Dewhurst on being returned for the first District Council of Leigh. If the electors of St Paul's Ward had returned Mr Dewhurst they would have done themselves a great honour. He was a native of the town and was an honour to his profession, and Leigh was noted for possessing a son who was in the front rank of the theatrical profession. (Loud cheers). In responding, Mr Dewhurst said he had done his utmost for the good of the town. At first when he took the theatre it was a question of whether the good ship would sink or swim, but now he thought it was on its way to success. With regard to local affairs, if he had been returned he would have done what he could for the good of the town without regard to creed or politics, but as it was he would have more time to devote to the theatre and make it a still greater success in the future. During the evening, songs, recitations and instrumental solos were given and the party broke up after toasting the hostess and singing the National Anthem.'

The following was the

MENU

Soup
Hare-Soup

———

Joints
Roast Ribs Beef
Boiled Turkey and Oyster Sauce
Roast Goose and Apple Sauce
Roast Chicken and Bread Sauce
Ox Tongue

———

Sweet
Plum Pudding and Mince Pies
Jellies and Cream

———

Celery
Dessert

The 1896 season began in August with Morris Bandmann's company in *Trilby* and each performance was preceded 'by an exhibition of the *Cinématographe*, a most wonderful optical entertainment; the views are changed each night'. In the last decade of the century '*cinématographe* entertainment' was starting to make its presence felt, and it was frequently used in theatres as a support feature to the main entertainment. Dewhurst was certainly up with the times. In December F.A. Scudamore's company visited Leigh and, taking advantage of the support offered by a capable company, Jonathan and Fanny were delighted to accept Scudamore's invitation to appear with them in *Richelieu*. The *Leigh Chronicle* reported that this was the play in which Dewhurst had 'in time past achieved some of his greatest triumphs'. Enormous trouble had been taken to stage the play in a manner worthy of the occasion and the result was a 'gratifying success'. The *Chronicle* went into raptures over Dewhurst's portrayal of Richelieu and found Fanny as sweet, winning and fascinating as ever in the part of Julie. Mr W.D. Clifford showed 'considerable dramatic skill' as Baradas, Mr Leighton Leigh 'made a dashing and impressive De Mauprat', and Mr F.A. Scudamore was a 'capital Joseph'. Apart from the pleasure it gave the Dewhursts to appear

in *Richelieu*, the evening was a considerable success attracting to the theatre
the largest house, financially speaking, that had ever 'assembled within its
walls'. After the performance the artistes and some friends of the Dewhursts
gathered in the smoke room for what must have been an emotional
occasion. The *Leigh Chronicle* reported it thus:

'Mr F.A. Scudamore addressed the assembly and said that the object of
that night's entertainment had been to pay a substantial compliment to
their mutual friend Mr Dewhurst (hear, hear) – a man who had made
a position as a distinguished actor in almost every English-speaking city
in the world. (Hear, hear). Mr Dewhurst was a man of a very domestic nature, and some few years ago he got weary of the life of a travelling actor and determined to retire from that life and make a permanent
home for his charming wife and his young family in Leigh. Leigh was
not the most beautiful spot on earth – (hear, hear) – but Mr Dewhurst
in the course of his travels had been a keen observer and student of
human nature, and wanted something more than beautiful scenery –
honest, true-hearted friends, and he had found them in Leigh. (Hear,
hear). He thought the magnificent house which had assembled there
that night to do him honour spoke volumes for him, and showed that
his sterling qualities had been thoroughly recognised and appreciated.
(Hear, hear). Several of Mr Dewhurst's personal friends, brother actors,
and brother managers, who regretted very much that they could not be
present there that night, had determined not to miss that opportunity
of doing honour to their old friend and comrade, Jonty Dewhurst, and
they had therefore deputed him (Mr Scudamore) to present to Mr
Dewhurst an illuminated address and a purse containing banknotes to
a substantial amount. (Applause). He had great pleasure in making that
presentation to Mr Dewhurst, and in asking him to accept that token
of esteem and regard, he hoped the recipient would have a long and
brilliant life, and be able for many years to ornament the profession
which he loved so much, and would have very many great compliments
paid to him before he took his final exit from the stage of life.
(Applause). Mr Scudamore read the address, which was as follows:
  "To Jonathan Dewhurst, Esq.,- We, the undersigned, beg leave to offer
our sincere and hearty congratulations on the occasion of your benefit.
  "We also take this opportunity of presenting you with the accompanying testimonial, subscribed for by a number of your brother actors,
friends and admirers, which we ask you to accept, not on account of
its intrinsic value, but as a slight token of our loving admiration and

esteem for you as a good fellow, a fine actor, and a genial manager, and in recognition of the earnest and valuable work you have done in cultivating a taste for the drama in Lancashire.

Mrs Bandmann Palmer,	Wilson Barrett,
F.A. Scudamore,	W.H. Hallatt,
T. Sergenson,	W.W. Kelly,
Lester Collingwood,	J.F. Elliston,
T. Morton Powell,	W. Morton.
Harding Thomas,	John H. Morton,
Sydney Vereker,	H. Burkinshaw,
James Carr.	

Theatre Royal, Leigh, 22nd December 1896".

'The address, which was in brilliantly illuminated colours relieved by a quartering of the arms of England, was the work of Messrs Elkington & Co., and was enclosed in a massive gilt frame.

'Mr J. Dewhurst, in response, said it was customary in every city and town in England, and in the County of Lancashire more particularly, for managers of theatres to take a benefit once a year, but he had not

37   Jonathan and Fanny Dewhurst – the successful businessman and his wife.

done so. He had hitherto used his name for the benefit of others, and if he had been put up for a benefit at that theatre it had been for others and not for himself. The last time he and his wife gave a benefit was for his friend Charles Melville, who had now joined the great majority. They (his wife and he) did not get a single penny of benefit out of it. One reason why he had not taken a benefit was that the Leigh folks were very peculiar. He himself was a native of Leigh, so he might perhaps be numbered in the same category. (Laughter). He remembered once putting up his name for a benefit, and someone remarked "What does he want a benefit for; is he hard up?" (Laughter). A benefit was a matter of showing appreciation of the good work of a man who had striven to do the best for the community in which he lived, and that night he had had the greatest compliment that had ever been paid to him in Leigh. (Hear, hear and applause). That benefit performance had been brought about by the instigation of his friend Mr Scudamore, who insisted that he (Mr Dewhurst) must have a benefit, and his company would play for him. His (the speaker's) reply was that they were queer folks in the district and he did not know how they would go on, but they had come out wonderfully and that night they had played to the biggest house that had ever been in Leigh during his nine years of management – (hear, hear and applause) – and moreover they had appreciated a poetic drama, which was not now the fashion. He was very proud that he had put up *Richelieu*. He thought that the people would not come, that he would have no pit, no gallery, but only a few friends in the circle, but they had never had such a crowd and such bookings since he had had the theatre, not even for his dear friend Mr Wilson Barrett, with whom he had served and acted for many, many years, off and on, nor even for Mr J.L. Toole, and the week before Christmas was not a very good time. He did not expect the response and the exhibition had been worthy of the occasion, he believed. The people in this district had done well and nobly, and he was very grateful indeed to them. Their thanks for that performance that evening were however due to Mr Scudamore, for he (Mr Dewhurst) once really made up his mind that he would never act in Leigh again, because he thought there was a lack of appreciation. That evening, however, had shown him clearly and distinctly that he had many friends outside his little circle who had some little love and admiration for him. He had done all he could for the welfare of the town, and hoped and believed he had never done a dishonourable or disgraceful action in Leigh. He had helped every charitable object, no matter whether it was football,

Catholic or Protestant, Liberal or Tory, if it was for a good cause. He could not afford to put his hand in his pocket and give them £10 out of his purse, but with the little ability with which God had endowed him, he had given his services willingly. He could not sufficiently thank Mr Scudamore for his kindness. They had been old friends for nearly thirty years and had a mutual admiration for each other, and Mr Scudamore admired him (Mr Dewhurst) as an actor perhaps more than he deserved. On behalf of his dear wife and himself he wished all present a Merry Christmas and a happy and prosperous New Year. (Applause).'

The review in the *Chronicle* of Jonathan Dewhurst's 10th Season at Leigh gives a fair idea of the variety of entertainment offered. There were 49 productions: 37 melodramas, 2 pantomimes, 2 comedies, 2 burlesques, 4 variety companies and 2 Shakespearian evenings, both of which featured the Dewhursts. In his paper on 'The Theatre in Leigh' (October 1973) Mr Stephen Hampson, commenting on changing tastes, said:

'Under Mr Williams (De Castro) and Mr Dewhurst, until the arrival of the Cinematograph (experimented with in the Theatre Royal in the 1890s), Leigh Theatre flourished on the merits of its stage performances. What I term as the Golden Years of Leigh Theatre can be dated between 1880 and 1914 approximately, and it was the Theatre Royal which served as the centre for professional public entertainment, until the appearance of the Hippodrome in 1908. Mr Dewhurst continued "legitimate" theatre through the 1880s and 90s according to the Leigh Journal with ... minimal burlesque and musical variety.'

On 16 September 1898 something occurred that gave Jonathan Dewhurst the greatest possible pleasure, something that he would not forget for the rest of his life. The week of Monday 12 September 1898 was booked for a presentation of *The Silver King* by G.M. Polini and Austin Melford's London Company. A high standard of production was eagerly anticipated, as the company had been rehearsed by Wilson Barrett, the original Wilfred Denver, the Silver King of the title, and the members of the company were very well-versed in their parts. The role of Wilfred Denver was taken by Claude King, but despite his, 'masterly delineation' he was not to play the part on the Friday night. The *Chronicle* reported:

'An evening of more than usual interest will occur at the Theatre Royal, Leigh, this (Friday) evening, when Mr Austin Melford, the well-

38 Austin Melford, who in 1898 with his London Company gave a special performance
of *The Silver King* in honour of Jonathan Dewhurst.

known London actor will journey here specially to appear, for this one
night only, in *The Silver King*. Lancashire audiences are well-acquainted
with this versatile actor who has been leading man to Mr Wilson
Barrett for a number of years, accompanying him through his English
and American tours and playing in his repertoire of pieces so well-
known to Lancashire play-goers. Mr Austin Melford comes as a compliment and a tribute of long-standing friendship to Mr Jonathan
Dewhurst. That his impersonation of the Silver King will be a great
treat there can be no doubt, in view that the London Press have pronounced him the best Silver King in this Country. Mr Dewhurst's
patrons would do well not to miss this occasion as they will not only
pay a compliment to Mr Melford, but a double and substantial one to
their worthy lessee.'

The following week the *Chronicle* added the following note:

'An artistic treat was provided for the patrons of the Theatre Royal,

THEATRE ROYAL LEIGH.

GRAND COMPLIMENTARY BENEFIT TO . . .

Mr and Mrs Dewhurst

TUESDAY DECEMBER 20th, 1898

The Curtain will Rise at 7-30 prompt on . . .

"THE STRANGER"

In 4 Acts
(By Augustus Von Kotzebue.)

The Stranger - Mr.	JONATHAN DEWHURST
Francis, his Servant	Mr Wellesley Draper
Baron Steinfort -	- Mr P. B. Sewers
Count Wintersen -	- Mr Ernest Jeffries
Solomon - -	- Mr T. Percival
Peter, his Son -	- Mr C. Cruikshanks
Tobias -	- Mr Maurice Ainsworth
Mrs Haller -	- Mrs DEWHURST
Countess Wintersen	Miss Jennie Thomas
Charlotte -	Miss Lilly Morgan
Savoyard -	Miss M. Lilly
Count Wintersen's Son	Master W. H. Dewhurst
The Stranger's Son	Master H. B. Dewhurst
Stranger's Daughter	Miss Daisy Dewhurst

RECITATION BY

Mr Leighton Leigh.

To be followed by Shakespeare's Comedy in 3 Acts, as adapted from the "Taming of the Shrew," by DAVID GARRICK,

"Katherine and Petruchio"

PETRUCHIO . .		Mr DEWHURST
Baptiste \ Gentlemen		Mr T. P. Percival
Hortensio / of Padua		Mr H. Nelson
Music Master .		Mr Maurice Ainsworth
Tailor .		Mr Ainsworth Cook
Biondello \ Servants of		Mr Wellesley Draper
Grumio / Baptiste		Mr C. Cruikshanks
Pedro . .		Mr Harry Morgan
Nathaniel . .		Mr Walter Edmond
KATHERINE, Daughter of Baptiste		Mrs DEWHURST
Bianca, her Sister, married to Hortensio		Miss Lanoma
Curtis, Housekeeper to Petruchio		Miss Sankey
Ladies, Gentlemen, Servants, &c., &c.		

In Consequence of the great demand for Reserved Seats, the Management has decided to place Numbered Chairs in the Entire Circle, for which Patrons desiring to be present on this occasion are advised to Book at once.

		PRIVATE BOXES.	
Seats Behind Dress Circle and Promenade, 1s. 6d.		Centre Boxes to hold 4 persons	12s. 0d.
Reserved Circle Chairs -	2s. 6d.	Top Boxes to hold 5 persons	12s. 6d.
Pit Stalls Reserved, -	2s. 6d.	Bottom Boxes to hold 4 persons	10s. 0d.
Pit - 1s.	Gallery - 6d.		

"CHRONICLE" OFFICE LEIGH.

39   The handbill for *The Stranger* in 1898 shows Jonathan and Fanny in the leading roles, and three of their children taking part.

Leigh on Friday when Mr Austin Melford appeared for that night only in his great impersonation of the Silver King, as a tribute of friendship to Mr J. Dewhurst. The following telegram was sent to Mr Dewhurst from the Grand Theatre, Leeds, and read from the stage by Mr Melford:

"I join in spirit with my old friends Polini and Melford in the tribute paid to you tonight, and wish I could annihilate space and appear in one act of the play as a small token of my regard for Jonathan Dewhurst, true artiste, good fellow and honest gentleman, – Yours always, Wilson Barrett, the other Silver King".'

Melford's reading from the stage must have been a very emotional moment for Jonathan Dewhurst and for all those present. The telegram from Wilson Barrett, which he framed, became one of his most prized possessions, and he regarded the words used by Barrett as the best compliment that he had ever been paid. His friendship with Wilson Barrett, he said, was one which could only be broken by death.

The following year, with the support of the visiting Giffard Company, *Richelieu* was presented for the first time for three years. Dewhurst played the Cardinal, showing that his old powers were unimpaired and, as Julie, Mrs Dewhurst was as charming as ever. 'It is to be regretted', said the *Chronicle*, 'that he does not appear more frequently before the Leigh public in some of his favourite roles'. One role in which Jonathan did appear was the name part in Kotzebue's *The Stranger*, put on at the theatre in December 1898. Fanny played Mrs Haller and it is of interest to note that Harold, William and Daisy all appeared in the production. Was there parental pressure or did the children volunteer? Certainly as the century drew to a close the Dewhurst family appeared prosperous, successful and united.

161

15

Leigh Theatre Royal – the Way Down

The turn of the century was reached, and popular taste indicated an increasing need for comedy, burlesque, musical comedy and variety, all of which would show some profit to provide for improvements to the theatre and help fill its 2,000-seat auditorium. Dewhurst by now must have realised that his aims of improving the minds and tastes of Leigh audiences were not to be fulfilled. In November 1900 Dewhurst gave his solo performance of *Othello* in Manchester and repeated it a week later for the Leigh Literary Society. We quote at length from the report in the *Chronicle*:

'In previous years Mr Dewhurst has earned the warm admiration of the members by his recitals of *Macbeth* and *Hamlet*, but as Shakespeare has it these paled their ineffectual fires before his *Othello*. A long experience of Mr Dewhurst's style has convinced the public that Othello is one of his best creations. Although Mr Dewhurst was without the adjuncts of scenery and the usual accessories of a stage he succeeded by one of the most extraordinary mental and physical feats ever achieved, to thoroughly rivet the attention of the audience. To stand before an audience for over two and a half hours and repeat with that elocutionary power which has made him his reputation, at the same time exhibiting all the varied emotions which move the characters he represents, is certainly a triumph of memory calculated to arouse the utmost admiration, apart from the consideration of the physical exertion entailed.

'Although Mr Dewhurst was suffering from a cold, which somewhat hampered him at the outset, he exhibited the distinct articulation, the correct pronunciation, the due regard for light and shade and the variations of tone demanded by the particular emotion expressed, that characterise the true dramatic artist. It was certainly a triumph for Mr

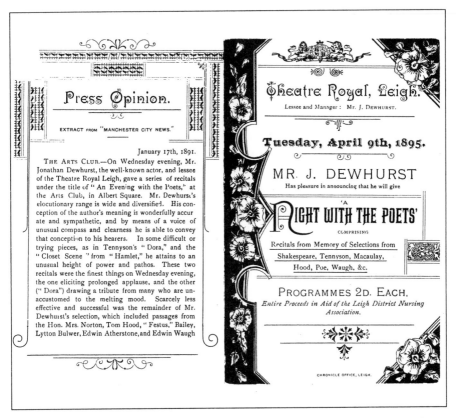

Theatre Royal, Leigh.

Lessee and Manager : Mr. J. DEWHURST.

Tuesday, April 9th, 1895.

MR. J. DEWHURST

Has pleasure in announcing that he will give

'A NIGHT WITH THE POETS'

COMPRISING

Recitals from Memory of Selections from Shakespeare, Tennyson, Macaulay, Hood, Poe, Waugh, &c.

PROGRAMMES 2D. EACH.

Entire Proceeds in Aid of the Leigh District Nursing Association.

CHRONICLE OFFICE, LEIGH.

40   *A Night With The Poets* of which the Leigh press said, 'In these recitations Mr Dewhurst stands unequalled and from beginning to end the audience is simply held spellbound'.

Dewhurst and the audience did not forget to show their appreciation. His versatility was remarkable. The hypocrisy and cunning of the ruthless Iago, the high-minded emotions that ennobled the soul of Othello, the rapid changes of feeling that came over Cassio in his scene of degradation and his subsequent remorse, the passions of the weak-minded and vacillating Roderigo, the radiant purity and love of Desdemona even when under the cloud of her husband's jealousy, and the steady unwavering loyalty of Emilia were all held up to the strong light of criticism and so spellbound were the audience held in the more dramatic and exciting scenes that literally one could have heard a pin drop.

'Mr Dewhurst played upon the feelings of the audience as upon the strings of a harp, striking hidden chords here and there and so fascinating his hearers as to cause them to see the scene he wished to depict as if it were real. There were many curious examples of this spell that held the audience. At those intense passages where, for example, Desdemona kneels at Othello's feet, or where she lies in bed at the last pathetic scene, many of the audience at the back of the hall could be seen half rising from their seats to get a better view of the supposed second occupant of the bare "stage". Several passages stood out as fine examples of elocutionary art that could with advantage be imitated. The veiled irony contained in the words of the hypocritical Iago, "Who steals my purse steals trash", was given with characteristic emphasis by Mr Dewhurst and as an example of declamatory force one needs only point to the great scene in the third act with Iago.

'That he is a past master in the art of depicting pathos was seen by his fine expression in the famous bedchamber scene. Indeed his representation in the whole of this scene – a scene which made greater demands upon him than any one previous – was marked by that high dramatic power and that ability to give voice to all the dramatic emotions that surge through the human soul which have made Mr Dewhurst what he is today. There is probably no man in this country who could do what he did on Monday evening – hold a large audience absolutely spellbound for over two and a half hours unaided and by the sheer force of his intellectual and dramatic genius. He stood alone on the bare stage, without scenery and without a prompter, yet not once from beginning to end did he falter at or miss a single word. It was a magnificent triumph of memory, of physical stamina and dramatic art. The whole performance was simply marvellous from every point of view.'

At the end of 1900 Leigh received a visit from two of Dewhurst's old friends – Edmund Tearle and his wife Kate Clinton with their 'powerful London company'. They provided fare of which Jonathan approved – *Hamlet* and *Macbeth*, with the historical romances *The Three Musketeers*, *Virginius* and *Ingomar the Barbarian*, but this was a lone voice crying in the Leigh wilderness. The following year Dewhurst decided to carry out extensive improvements to the theatre. The auditorium was enlarged, increasing seating capacity to 2,600, and the more expensive seats and boxes were made more comfortable and attractive. The stage was also considerably enlarged, so that it would be possible to stage any play. Altogether, 'a wonderful transformation' and to match it, the name of the theatre was changed to the 'New Theatre Royal and Opera House'. In June 1901 Jonathan and Fanny presented *The Merchant of Venice*, originally intended for one night only, but as the Tuesday night was completely sold out the play was presented again the following night to another full house. Dewhurst's portrayal of Shylock was again a notable success, as was his wife in the part of Portia. In a supporting role, their son, Harold, who was just 14, 'was a dashing Lorenzo'. On the Tuesday night Jonathan was presented with two large-sized photographs of himself in the characters of Othello and Macbeth, and Fanny received two beautiful bouquets with another on the Wednesday night. Shortly after *The Merchant of Venice*, Jonathan Dewhurst gave his last performance for some time – it was to oblige his old comrade, Osmond Tearle, who sent him an urgent wire asking him to come to the Comedy Theatre, Manchester, to play Richard III that same night. When he arrived he found that he was also to play Othello the following night! Tearle's health was failing and he died shortly thereafter.

In 1900 Fanny's mother died at the age of 75 and her father, Henry Rivers, then came to live with the Dewhursts. He survived only until the next year, dying in December 1901 at the age of 82, and was buried in Leigh Cemetery. Convinced that Jonathan and Fanny would have erected an appropriate headstone for this old and respected actor, we were amazed to

41   Osborne Terrace, Leigh, to which the Dewhursts moved in 1903.

165

find that none existed. We had the correct plot and grave numbers, but the grave itself was unmarked. How could this be? Henry's daughter and her husband, with whom he had been living, were local people of substance – so why? Unfortunately this, again, is one of those questions that will not yield an answer. The theatre in Leigh was now splendid indeed. Jonathan was also well-established in the town – he was on very friendly terms with all the leading local figures, he was a Freemason, a member of the Literary Society (the leading intellectual and cultural organisation in the town), and a member of the Arts Club, Manchester and the Conservative Club, Leigh. In 1903 the Dewhursts decided that a change of house would be appropriate and they moved from Wilkinson Street to the recently built Osborne Terrace (No.30 Railway Road). The move was one of only a few hundred yards, but Osborne Terrace offered a much larger and more imposing home.

The public requirement, however, was not for serious drama. Music-hall/variety was what appealed and sold seats. In 1904 the *Leigh Courier* commented, '...shortly we are promised a return to drama ... variety is good, but a complete change is sometimes better. Our regret is that the public of Leigh is content with Variety and Variety only'. The tide had certainly turned, as it had for much of the entertainment business. Dewhurst was now finding life in the theatre more difficult and it was starting to affect his health. The week commencing Monday, 16 April 1906 proved to be significant for the Dewhursts.

Mr Ian Maclaren's Shakesperian and Classical Repertoire Company was visiting the theatre and supported Jonathan and Fanny in a performance of *Othello*. By special request of the company they also appeared in *The Merchant of Venice* on the penultimate night of the week. Basil Dean, who joined the Maclaren company the following year, described Maclaren as 'a competent work-horse of an actor, devoid of subtlety, but with a good voice and a certain straightforward charm.' His 'buxom wife, even more simple-minded than her spouse, played all Shakespeare's heroines with buoyant inadequacy'. The significance of the Dewhursts' appearances with the company was that *Merchant* would be their final appearance in any play on the Leigh stage, and their final performance while still involved full-time in the acting profession. As a valediction to his 18 years at Leigh it is appropriate for us to quote in full the *Chronicle's* review of *Othello*:

'Lovers of Shakespearean plays, and those who take a pleasure in splendid acting, had a great treat on Wednesday evening when Mr and Mrs Dewhurst and the members of Ian Maclaren's Company gave *Othello*. The occasions on which one can see Mr Dewhurst are all too rare

166

nowadays, and it was not surprising to find the stalls crowded, and the other parts of the house well-filled. The part of Othello, the dusky Moor, has long been regarded as one of Mr Dewhurst's best, and no finer performance than that on Wednesday evening could be desired. It is questionable if he himself ever shone to greater advantage. Voice, gesture, the power of illustrating the various emotions of passion, jealousy and rage were all excellent, and it seemed as if Mr Dewhurst improves, like wine, with age. He brought all his ripened experience to bear in his performance and the result was a striking success.

'It would perhaps be difficult to find one so well-adapted by nature for the part of Othello, for Mr Dewhurst has a dominant personality and a fine physical presence, and his long acquaintance with the stage and with some of the finest tragedians that ever trod the boards, enables him to give due point to every incident in which he plays a part. One hardly knew which to admire most in his Wednesday night's performance, his tenderness for his wife at the outset, his gradual change in demeanour as Iago's poison circulates through his veins, his storms of passion alternating with doubts and misgivings, his icy calmness when at last he makes up his mind that his wife must die, his terrible remorse when he learns that he has murdered one of the purest of God's women, his terrible outburst of mingled rage and contempt when he confronts the villainous Iago, or his last dignified farewell to the world prior to stabbing himself to the heart.

'Mr Dewhurst has superb declamatory powers and these he exhibited to the fullest advantage. He dominated the stage throughout and towered above the others not only by his physical height but by his magnetic personality. He gripped the audience from the start and they did not fail to repeatedly testify their approval of his skill. It is a matter for regret that Mr Dewhurst does not emerge from his retirement oftener and give us more of his classic representations of Shakespearean characters.

'It is some years since a Leigh audience has had the pleasure of seeing Mrs Dewhurst on the stage, and it is with feelings of pleasurable anticipation that her reappearance in the character of Desdemona was awaited. It is almost needless to say that she fulfilled every expectation. To judge from her performance she might have been acting regularly for months past, for she resumed her accustomed manner with a facility and gracefulness that were much admired. She always shone in parts that required tenderness and femininity, rather than fierce outbursts of passion, and her voice has always been noted for its rich musical tones.

Hence she is eminently suited to play the part of Desdemona in which she has to exhibit the various gentle qualities and fascinations that endear a woman to a man; and notwithstanding her long absence from the stage she was as effective and as bewitching as ever, and formed an admirable foil to the stern, rugged grandeur of her husband's passionate emotions. In the bedchamber scene she was especially brilliant, and throughout the evening her voice rose and fell in gentle undulations, and her enunciation was as clear and distinct as ever, the various notes rippling forth with a cadence as pleasant as a moorland stream. It was indeed an exquisite performance and Mrs Dewhurst evidently retains all her old powers unimpaired.'

Ian Maclaren's company was strong indeed, many of the members of which had previously been connected with Frank Benson. In the Leigh production Iago was played by the young Ben Iden Payne, who would later achieve considerable success as actor and producer, and his wife Mona Limerick took the part of Bianca. The following year both of them would join Miss Horniman's company. The even younger Frank Cellier, now at the start of his brilliant career, played Cassio.

We know that Dewhurst took the opportunity of performing his favourite roles with suitable visiting companies and it is interesting to have some insight into how this worked. Many years after the visit of the Maclaren company to Leigh, Ben Iden Payne referred to it in his book *A Life in a Wooden O: Memoirs of the Theatre*:

'Spectators at an efficient but mechanical performance of a great Shakespearean tragic role are unaware that their emotional response would be much deeper, almost different in kind, if they were watching an actor borne along on waves of natural instead of forced emotions. All really fine acting, though differing in externals according to the social manners of the age, must have been natural in essence. Once during my tour in the Ian Maclaren company I saw the most striking proof of this in my experience.

'Mr Maclaren rather grimly explained that in his prime Dewhurst had been a secondary star in the provinces. He had "traveled," we were told, a proof that he had once been of considerable prominence. (In the days when stock companies were universal, actors of sufficient importance traveled from town to town, joining companies for a few days and acting their favorite parts.) We were convinced that we should see one of the worst embodiments of what we regarded as the bad old school.

Othello was in our repertoire and the title role, the part in which Mr Dewhurst had elected to appear, would surely give him many opportunities for old-fashioned ranting.

'When we met Mr Dewhurst at the run-through on Friday morning he merely wished to be informed about his entrances and exits and to be instructed as to where he was to stand. He made only one request. He was heavy and gouty and he begged me, as Iago, to assist him to rise from his knees after the vow of vengeance in act III. He ran through the lines in a rapid mutter, giving no indication of how he would speak them at night, so we continued to look forward to the fun his performance would offer.

'We went to the theatre that night to laugh and – if I may generalize from my own reaction – we left feeling much more inclined to pray. From the quiet but firm authority of "Keep up your bright swords," at the beginning to the final speech, all the verse was spoken simply and naturally, under the guidance of sincere emotion. It is true that in the more distressful scenes he wept more than a modern actor would; I can still see the tears streaming down his wrinkled cheeks. But it would be a poor spirit who saw in this a cause for ridicule.'

But in less than a month Dewhurst shocked friends and patrons alike by announcing his retirement as manager of the theatre, and his intention of leaving Leigh as soon as he was able to make appropriate arrangements. Friends had already formed a committee to raise a testimonial benefit for him: the arrangements proceeded, but instead of a 'thank you' the benefit became a leaving gift. Again it was an emotional time. The local press reported it:

'On Monday, May 14th 1906 and on Tuesday, May 15th 1906 miscellaneous entertainments were given for the benefit of Mr Dewhurst. Towards the latter part of the evening, to the strains of "Auld Lang Syne", played by the theatre orchestra, Mr Dewhurst, the late lessee and manager of the theatre, came upon the stage to bid his last farewell to the Leigh public. He seemed to feel his position keenly and he spoke in a voice broken with emotion. He said:
"I shall not interrupt the entertainment for more than a couple of minutes. I want to thank you for your presence here tonight. I should, of course, have liked after 18 years of hard service to have had a better send off. You can understand that, can't you? Tonight is the last time you will ever see me upon this stage. I want, first of all, to thank the

ladies and gentlemen who have so kindly given me their services tonight in entertaining you. I want to thank Mr Robert Youngson for a great deal of hard work in getting up this entertainment; and last, though not least, I want to thank my successor in the management of this theatre, Mr Rousbey, for placing the theatre at our disposal. (Applause) I want to thank you, ladies and gentlemen, again and again for your presence here tonight, and for the support that I have had during my long piece at this theatre. I thank you very much. So far as I am concerned the play is over and the curtain falls tonight. I cannot help feeling the severance after so many years, but I hope I shall be kindly remembered by some of you. I shall have many kind remembrances of Leigh and of my friends in Leigh; and I shall have the remembrance of much trial, hard work and suffering in trying to do all I could. I wish you all from the bottom of my heart all the good that can be done and I say to you, farewell". (Applause) The band at the close of the speech played "Auld Lang Syne".'

The presentation to Jonathan and Fanny was also reported:

'On Saturday evening at the Rope and Anchor Hotel, Leigh, a party of Mr Dewhurst's friends assembled to bid him farewell and to present him with a purse of gold containing £50. Mr J. Pygott presided and said they were met there for a very pleasurable though painful duty, for they were going to part with Mr Dewhurst. They as a testimonial committee had done their best for him. At the time that the testimonial was started it was for the benefit of Mr Dewhurst and they did not think they were going to lose him from the town. They knew that things had not been so well with him for months and they thought they might possibly alleviate his present necessities. Now all that they could hope for from what they gave him that night was that it might help him along a bit until he was able to work again and do something for his wife and family. They were all very sorry to lose him for he had always been very genial and willing to do anything for anybody. He had assisted every charitable object in the town without asking for fee or favour, and they could not do less than ask him to accept from them that night for Mrs Dewhurst that subscription book and a purse containing £50. (Applause)

'Mr Dewhurst, in reply, said he could not thank them as much as he felt, and unfortunately it was generally the case that those who were in the habit of expressing the thoughts and feelings of other men could not so well express their own. He was deeply grateful to them all for their kindness in assisting him in the hour of need. That present would at any rate give him the opportunity of going away and recruiting his health and help him to prepare to start the battle of life afresh. It was rather the wrong end of life to begin, but with God's help he thought he could make a home for him and his once more. (Hear, hear) He thanked them from the bottom of his heart. Again and again he thanked them most sincerely. He could not say any more and if he did he could not express half he felt.'

So after 18 years his managerial career ended. There was sadness that this should be so, and sadness for Jonathan Dewhurst that the tastes of the theatre-going public had changed, and not in his view for the better. When he and Fanny performed at Leigh they filled the house, but their personal popularity could not fill it with other worthy dramatic offerings. Dewhurst must have felt that the world had moved on and he did not wish to run to catch up with it. It was a different world and one that was not for him. So he went.

I recall visiting the Leigh Theatre Royal on several occasions in the early 1940s. The outside was unprepossessing, but the inside, though a little threadbare and faded, was the typical Victorian theatre so lovingly created by Dewhurst at the turn of the century. What I saw then was variety, and on one occasion I assisted a conjuror on the stage. Later, in 1954, its life as a theatre ended and the interior was gutted and re-formed to create a modern dance hall. It has since done duty as a bingo hall and is now Rueben's Nite Spot. In May 1954 the theatre had been empty for three months and the local press speculated on the possible fate of the building. The report commented on the involvement of Jonathan Dewhurst:

'Another lessee who could claim about 20 years service was the late Mr Jonty Dewhurst, whose efforts to raise the tone of drama in Leigh were so much appreciated that he was presented with a full-size oil painting of himself by his admirers – a picture which still hangs in the circle bar – one of the many reminders of bygone days. Mr Dewhurst was himself a Shakespearean actor of repute being the male lead in the Wilson Barrett Company, and it was he who persuaded Sir Henry Irving to come to Leigh.'

This paragraph immediately excited our interest. What had happened to the full-size portrait? We have written to museums, galleries, theatrical collections, libraries, but no one knows the fate of the picture. Could it have been thrown into a skip when the theatre was cleared? Surely not, but on the other hand such vandalism is not unknown today. We live in the hope that one day we may trace it. The reference to a visit to the theatre by Sir Henry Irving also intrigued us, as we have traced no report or mention of it.

But to continue with our story: Dewhurst had been 'down' before, but had always risen to meet new challenges. Now, though, with family responsibilities and indifferent health – what would he do?

16

His Last Bow

Jonathan Dewhurst made two decisions. The immediate one was to take himself to Blackpool for a few weeks to recuperate and to consider the future. The second decision, made shortly thereafter, was to leave the theatre permanently and, at the age of 69, to take up a new career. He considered his personal attributes: he liked being with people, being centre stage, conversing and sharing good fellowship. His father had run the Hare and Hounds in Lowton and Jonathan decided that the hotel business was the best arena in which to deploy his talents. Parting from the theatre was a big wrench, but he recognised that the times were changing. Many old friends and colleagues had died – Osmond Tearle in 1901, Wilson Barrett and Frank Scudamore in 1904, and Henry Irving, knighted in 1895, in 1905.

So it was that, having considered the market, he found what he wanted in Chorley and, in September 1906, he and Fanny moved into the Royal Oak Hotel, the town's largest hotel, in a prime position in Market Street opposite the town hall. The Royal Oak was a substantial three-storey coaching inn. When it was previously sold in 1887 the *Chorley Guardian* described it as having 'spacious cellars, commercial and other rooms on the ground floor, assembly room and billiard room and numerous bedrooms; five stables with stallage for 24 horses; loose box, coach-houses, saddle room, ostler's house and taproom, and vacant land for future requirements'. Jonathan had regained his old enthusiasm. His advertisement in the *Chorley Guardian* reflected the fact that by 1906 the motor car had become at least as important as the horse and a wide range of whiskies was a major attraction!

ROYAL OAK HOTEL
MARKET STREET, CHORLEY
MR JONATHAN DEWHURST
has pleasure in announcing that he has taken over the
above OLD ESTABLISHED COMMERCIAL AND FAMILY
HOTEL, where he will be pleased to welcome old and
new friends
WINES AND SPIRITS OF THE BEST BRANDS
AND QUALITIES
Ask for what you want in Scotch or Irish and you will
get it
John Dewar, Black and White, Red Seal, Glenlivet,
Teacher, Dunville, Roderick Dhu, Annie Rooney,
John Jameson, &c., always to be had for the asking
ORDINARY DAILY at 1-0 o'clock
Luncheons, Teas, &c., provided as required
TONG'S NOTED ALES (Mild & Bitter) in splendid
condition; second to none. Try it!

BASS AND GUINESS STOUT IN BOTTLE
TENNANT'S LAGER BEER
MOTOR GARAGE and large STABLING
ACCOMMODATION in the yard of the Hotel
BILLIARDS
Telephone 0124

He was already well-known in Chorley and soon settled successfully into his new life. As ever, Fanny was completely supportive. The following year, in their series entitled 'Our Portrait Gallery', a reporter from one of Wigan's newspapers interviewed him:

'The subject of our sketch will hardly require an introduction to our readers. As far back as the sixties Mr Jonathan Dewhurst has declared his position on the English stage, and has maintained all the loftiest traditions of his profession during an association which dates as far back as 1845, when he made his first appearance in the Old Theatre Royal, Wigan. The other day, in a chat, I found the veteran actor as hearty as ever, and brimful of reminiscences of his early days, enjoined with sympathetic references to the joy with which the boys of another day entered into the spirit of triumph upon his success as an actor. "Many of those generous-hearted men are asleep," he observed tenderly, "but I preserve the memory of them as amidst my most sacred treasures".'

42   Allan Wilkie, whose company supported Dewhurst in his final stage appearance –
Richelieu at the Theatre Royal, Wigan, in 1909.

He still found the energy to give occasional performances, usually *A Night With The Poets*, but in 1907, at the age of 70, he returned to the stage to present *Richelieu* at the Chorley Grand Theatre, followed a few months later by a solo recital of *Hamlet*. To mark his 71st birthday, he gave his solo recital of *Othello*, judged by the *Chorley Weekly News* as 'an astonishing feat'. On 20 August 1909, at the age of 73, Jonathan Dewhurst gave his final stage performance, appropriately in Wigan, where at the age of eight he had first appeared on the stage. And what more fitting than the performance should be as Richelieu, his favourite role. By special arrangement he was supported by the Allan Wilkie Repertoire Company and the farewell performance was attended by all the elite of Wigan and district. The *Wigan Observer* reported that:

'He had a most hearty reception from a large audience. He acted extremely well and showed that he had lost none of his old histrionic power. Such a performance for a man of his years must be accounted a very considerable feat. At the conclusion of the play Mr Dewhurst

175

43   Richelieu, his favourite role.

was called before the curtain and appeared to be much touched by the reception accorded to him. He expressed his sincere thanks to the audience and also to Mr Worswick and Mr Wilkie's company for allowing him to perform with them.'

So the curtain fell on his stage career, but it is probably no coincidence that the tradition was carried on by his three sons, Harold, William and Percy. All went into the theatre and remained active in it for the rest of their lives. Only Daisy failed to follow in her father's footsteps. However, although the boys were no doubt inspired by their father (and quite possibly in some awe of him), none of them matched his achievements, although William and Percy found success in their own fields.

In March 1911 Alfred Rivers was working in Manchester and was able to find time to visit his sister. He recorded the visit in his diary:

'Up in good time. Did a few little things then to the Victoria Station (L&Y) to take train to Chorley – to see my sister who I haven't seen now for quite three years. The last time I was here I hadn't time as I had the wife near – in Blackburn – so couldn't go over – and other visits I have always been so busy at the theatre with rehearsals or changes of bill. Well I found all those there very well – and doing well. The sister looking very handsome – very grey – but still young, her husband still hale in spite of his 74 years and rheumatism and gout – and my niece quite luscious but rather tired of the dull little town. It seems a busy place for its size – and fairly clean for Lancashire. We had long chats over the old folks and old times – and the new – I got back in time to go to the theatre.'

It was only seven months later, however, in April 1912, that tragedy struck again when Fanny died suddenly. Jonathan never recovered from the shock. They had been married for 26 years and it was with Fanny that he had found his soul mate and lasting happiness. His health declined but his sudden demise on Friday, 1 August 1913 came as a complete shock to everyone. We feel it appropriate to quote in full the report of his death in the *Leigh Chronicle*:

'Mr Jonathan Dewhurst, who was for 18 years lessee and manager of the Leigh Theatre Royal, but has latterly been the licensee of the Royal Oak Hotel, one of the chief business places in Chorley, died unexpectedly at his residence on Friday night, shortly before eleven o'clock. Two Leigh gentlemen were in the hotel at three o' clock on Friday afternoon and his condition then was not such as to give rise to any anxiety. He was sitting in his chair upstairs, one of his daughters looking after the house. In the evening he had a relapse and died as stated. The shock of losing his wife about 18 months ago had a weakening effect on his strong constitution and he never thoroughly rallied. He was married four times and leaves three sons – Harold, Percy and William – and two daughters.

'Born in Stonecross Lane, Lowton, on April 28th 1837, he was in the 77th year of his age. Early in his youth he conceived a great liking for the stage and his ambition was soon gratified. He became associated with the famous actor, the late Mr Chas. Calvert at the Prince's Theatre, Manchester, and subsequently performed with success at the various London and provincial theatres. As a Shakespearean actor he had a great reputation. Many in this district will recall him as Shylock in *The Merchant of Venice*. This was one of his finest impersonations and in this he ran the whole gamut of human passion and gave a display which stamped him as one of the leading tragedians of the day.

'Another character that suited him very well was Macbeth. He played this with a dramatic fire and energy that absolutely thrilled his hearers and his elocution was beyond reproach. Indeed when Mr Dewhurst appeared in a Shakespearean character it was a case of Eclipse first and the rest nowhere. Equally fine was he as King Lear, whilst other characters he excelled in were Hamlet and Louis XI. Some of his friends held the opinion that the latter was one of his masterpieces as it was that of Sir Henry Irving for he had to simulate the feelings of a hypocrite, a murderer, a scheming king, a statesman and a decrepit old man. Othello was another great part in which he excelled, and he could also play Iago. *The Stranger* and *Belphegor the Mountebank* were also pieces in which Mr Dewhurst made his mark. He had a commanding personality. Tall, broad-shouldered and dignified, he brought his physical advantages to the assistance of his mental energies and always produced a great impression upon the audience.

'In 1881 he went to Australia and played in all the principal cities, and received many valuable gifts, especially at Melbourne. He also played at several of the theatres in India. After his return to this country from Australia he gave a few performances in the Assembly Rooms, Leigh, where he was very well-received. On August 6th 1888 he leased the Leigh Theatre Royal from Mr J.W. Cragg and for 18 years – up to April 1906 – he was lessee and manager. He introduced many improvements and secured some excellent companies. On one occasion his friend the late Mr Wilson Barrett came to Leigh to give a matinee and drew a crowded house.

'Whilst in this district he was in great demand as an elocutionist at various entertainments and festivals. He was a member of the Leigh Literary Society and on several occasions gave *A Night With The Poets*, and for upwards of two hours held his audience spell-bound. His recital of Edgar Allan Poe's "The Bells" has probably never been excelled in this district, and how he managed to reproduce the wonderful tones of a bell puzzled his auditors considerably. He could also recite many Lancashire pieces, including "Owd Pinder", "Eawr Folk", "Owd Bodle" and "Come whoam to thi childer and me". Dramatic pieces like "Shamus O'Brien", "The Dream of Eugene Aram" and "The Story of Horatius" were child's play to him. In short he was an all-round elocutionist and was a master of tragedy, comedy and farce. He had wonderful facial expression, could change his tone in a remarkable manner and his memory was never at fault. He could recite whole plays of Shakespeare without making a slip and change his voice for each character. He was a born elocutionist. Occasionally, whilst lessee of the Leigh Theatre Royal, he was induced to go and play for his old friend, Mr Wilson Barrett and, as The Holy Clement in *Claudian*, he made a great impression in Manchester. He was also associated with the late Mr Augustus Harris of Drury Lane fame. He retained his memory almost to the last, and when he had attained the age of 70 years he gave a remarkable performance of *Richelieu*, one of his favourite characters, at the Chorley Grand Theatre.

'Ill-fortune assailed him during his last years at Leigh and it was a big wrench to him to have to sever his connection with the theatre and the town. He finished at the Leigh Theatre in April 1906 and a few weeks later was the recipient of a presentation from his numerous friends. He went to Blackpool for about seven weeks to recuperate and then became lessee of the Royal Oak Hotel, probably the biggest hotel in Chorley, where he lived for the last seven years.

'His sons have some of their father's histrionic ability and are doing well on the stage. Mr Dewhurst, who was a Freemason and a Conservative, had a large circle of friends. He will be much missed, not only in Chorley, but in this district. Imperious, fond of command and always striving to preserve the dignity of his profession, he was a good friend and splendid storyteller. He could keep his friends in a roar when telling them some of his humorous experiences. He lived an eventful life, and as Shakespeare says, "he was a man of infinite jest", and it is long before we shall look on his like again. He was a man who in his time played many parts, and played them all well, and in the annals of the British stage he leaves behind an honoured name.'

He was buried with Fanny at Chorley Cemetery. The local press reported:

'The funeral took place on Monday morning at the Chorley Cemetery. The principal mourners were Mr W. Dewhurst (son) and Miss Dewhurst (daughter), Mr J.R. Smith (nephew), Mr James Wilcock (nephew), Mr W. Taylor (nephew), Mr P. Collier, Mr Unsworth, Mr Roberts, Mr Ball, Mr Hall and Miss Kay. Among those also present were Alderman Tong (Bolton), Messrs J. Thompson and A. Leach, and at the graveside Councillors H.W. Hitchin and J. Turner, and Mr McCormack. The service was conducted by the Rev F. Jackson M.A.

44   The gravestone in Chorley cemetery which bears the tribute from Wilson Barrett.

The funeral cortege was headed by a number of members of the Chorley Licensed Victuallers Association.'

It is interesting to note that of his children only William and Daisy were present at the funeral. It may well be that in view of the short notice Harold and Percy were unable to attend because of their theatrical commitments. Among the floral tributes there was one from all four children. The report of his death refers incorrectly to four marriages – he was married three times only. The report also refers to two daughters, but this, too, was incorrect.

Jonathan Dewhurst's will, dated 30 November 1912, was proved by his executors, Coaker Whiteway (Bank Manager) and John Thompson (Schoolmaster) on 28 August 1913. The gross estate was £328.17s.9d. Under the terms of the will, the executors each received a gold ring. Harold was bequeathed 'my gold watch and Australian chain and a diamond stud'; William, 'my Indian diamond ring, my tiger claw and a diamond stud'; Percy, 'my gold curb chain, my silver cigar case, my ten dollar hanger and a diamond stud'. Daisy was bequeathed her mother's 'jewellery, trinkets, personal ornaments and theatrical wearing apparel'. The residue passed equally to the four children. In 1936 the Royal Oak was demolished as part of a road-widening scheme and replaced by a new and not very attractive public house standing some 30 feet to the rear of the old frontage.

When we visited Chorley to locate the grave we were given the plot number, but told that there was no headstone. Our delight knew no bounds when we found that not only was this not so, but that the stone was an impressive black marble edifice which, as well as names and dates, was inscribed with the words of Wilson Barrett's tribute:

'True Artist, Good Fellow and Honest Gentleman.'

We feel that Jonathan would rest happy with these words as his epitaph.

17

The Rivers and the Dewhursts

Before passing on to the Dewhurst children it is appropriate to say a few words about the three sons of Henry and Fanny Rivers. Little is known of Charles, the eldest of their sons. He and his brothers were on the stage as children and our earliest record is of Charles and Robert appearing as spiders in a pantomime at the Alhambra Theatre, Leicester Square, in 1871/72. In 1876 Charles and Alfred appeared with their father in *Medea* at the Haymarket Theatre. In May 1878 Gilbert and Sullivan's *HMS Pinafore* opened and such was its success that in December the following year a *Pinafore* company was formed entirely of children, performing in London and subsequently touring the provinces. Alfred and one of his brothers were in the company, but whether it was Charles or Robert we do not know. In recording events Alfred had the unfortunate habit of referring to 'my brother' or 'my friend' without any further identification. In 1947, at a party given by friends to mark his 80th birthday, Alfred recalled the Children's *Pinafore*:

'In 1880 my brother and I were in the Children's *Pinafore*, that is the first ever children's company to tour with an opera. I recall many pleasant and some unpleasant times with that company and many exciting events. Also many dirty tricks were played on me and my brother by the other boys in the company. My brother and I were old stagers for we were then quite old hands at the business. I had been six years on the stage and my brother a little longer. I recall the visit to Brighton towards the end of the first tour and we were there in December. The old theatre was very different from the present one. I remember a Green Room just off the stage. It went down a step and was quite a large place with chairs and tables and seats along the sides with a very handsome gold clock hanging on the wall with pictures round. There is one pleasant recollection that will always remain in my memory. It was seeing Miss Nye Chart, the manageress, a very nice handsome lady with golden curly hair on the matinee day serving tea off a large silver tray in the Green Room to us children. She was like the fairy god-mother to us. I wonder what happened to some of the boys and girls who were in the show with me. Some of them became quite famous but many just drifted away.'

Charles's career was dogged by ill-health. In January 1889, when touring America with the Rosina Vokes Company, he took a turn for the worse and, despite 'the best medical advice and careful nursing that could be procured', he died of consumption.

Robert was a little younger than Charles. We have not traced his death, but he was still acting in 1933 when he would have been in his late 60s. An early photograph of Robert shows him to be slim and good-looking, but with the passage of time he put on a little weight and in middle age his appearance was not unlike that of his nephew William. Robert had a successful career and a high reputation as a character actor. Although he

45   Robert Rivers in a character role – no longer the slim young man.

occasionally played in the provinces, he spent the major part of his career on the London stage.

Alfred, Henry's youngest son, acted occasionally and 'filled in' when necessary, but his serious approach and meticulous attention to detail made him the ideal stage-manager. A newspaper report on the occasion of his 88th birthday described his introduction to the stage:

'Back in 1873 the producer at the Haymarket thundered, "I want a little girl!" "But I have only got a little boy", replied a leading lady, wife of the stage-manager Mr Henry Rivers. "He'll do", grunted the producer and on went six-year-old Alfred Rivers dressed as a little girl. That was the beginning of the career of actor/stage-manager Mr Alfred Rivers.'

The producer was John S. Clarke and the play was *Among the Breakers*. Alfred played as 'Miss River' for over a year before graduating to boys' roles. He stage-managed for some notable actors – Wilson Barrett for 18 years, John Martin-Harvey for 13 years and Julia Neilson and Fred Terry for 12 years. He toured America, Australia, New Zealand, South Africa and Canada. The tour of Canada with Laurence Irving might well have been his last. He recalled later:

'I should not have had any birthdays after May 1914 if Mr Laurence Irving, Sir Henry Irving's son, and his actress wife had not at the last moment cancelled their company's passages including my own on the liner *Empress of Ireland* from Canada and booked us at a cheaper rate in the *Teutonic* which brought us safely home. The *Empress of Ireland* met with disaster and poor Laurence and his wife were among many who perished. They went down clasped in each other's arms. I was the last person to shake hands with Irving before the *Empress* sailed.'

From the papers he left, Alfred comes across as a serious, rather humourless figure and something of a hypochondriac. He was keen on cricket, but watched rather than played and occasionally he seemed to resent the way in which he felt he was treated by some of those for whom he worked. The following comments from his diary (9 August 1895) relate to Wilson Barrett:

'I don't know what has come over WB lately. Nothing we do is right and he is always finding fault. Things that we have done for years are suddenly wrong and tonight when the curtain fell he went on and

184

called us idiots and fools and the usual nonsense he can talk. For a man who thinks himself a clever man he talks some of the biggest nonsense and tells the greatest lies I have ever heard. He thinks nobody knows or can do anything but himself. If you do or say anything good he says it is all nonsense – couldn't be done etc. Then a few days after proposes the same thing as one of his own ideas. He can never do anything wrong. You are wrong – he is always right and he will not argue with you. I have put up with it for a good time now but even the worm will turn and I don't think I shall stand much more of it. It will either end in a row or an understanding or I shall give in my notice and try my luck elsewhere – I felt like it tonight. After serious thought I made up my mind to do my very best and to keep myself right in the eyes of others and the world and bear with it a little longer.'

He stayed with Wilson Barrett for another eight years!

In 1901 Alfred married Maud Twamley, an attractive young actress who played leading roles in John Martin-Harvey's company. After some initial enthusiasm, Alfred makes little mention of Maud in his diaries and presum-

46   Maud Rivers and John Martin-Harvey in *Boy O'Carroll*.

ably they followed their own careers, spending comparatively little time together. Maud, who was living in Birmingham at the time, died in 1954 after 53 years of marriage and left her modest estate to Alfred, who was still living in London. Alfred died a year later at the age of 88 – not a bad age to reach considering his lifestyle and his concerns about his health.

★ ★ ★

The photograph we have of the Dewhurst children shows them posed in an attractive family group. All four wear serious expressions, but that was expected on a visit to the photographer's studio in the late Victorian Era. William, Percy Jonathan (later known as Jonty) and Daisy are dressed in the sailor suits so fashionable at the time, with the two boys holding appropriate sailing vessels. Somewhat incongruously, a golf club leans nonchalantly against the balustrade, presumably placed there for the eminently sensible purpose of balancing the composition of the picture. Harold, sadly, appears to be the odd one out. Dressed in a dark, adult-style jacket he was, perhaps,

47   The Dewhurst children in 1895, from left to right:
William, Percy Jonathan, Harold, Daisy.

considered too old for the sailor suit, but it is not only the clothing that sets him apart. All the children look serious but there is more than that in Harold's face. Is our imagination suggesting too much or is there a lonely, haunted quality in his expression – a reflection, perhaps, of the somewhat sad and lonely figure we are told he became in later life? With such a successful, relatively famous and dominant figure as Jonathan for a father, it would have been understandable if his children had eschewed the theatre completely or, inspired by him, had decided that the stage was their future. It is not really surprising that they chose the theatre, as, quite apart from their father, it was very much in their blood. Their mother Fanny Rivers was an actress; her parents Henry Rivers and Fanny Morelli were actors, as were her brothers Alfred, Robert and Charles. Fanny Morelli's father was Charles Morelli, actor and clown, who as a boy had appeared with Joe Grimaldi.

Of the three boys Harold is the one about whom we have the least information. We know that as a child in 1894 he appeared with his father in *Much Ado About Nothing*, using the name 'H.Brotherton' and seven years later he acted with him again as Lorenzo in *The Merchant of Venice*. No doubt there were many other occasions when he made similar appearances. The next 'appearance' we have traced was in 1908, when the 21-year-old Harold was touring with H.F. Maltby's London Company. Harold is listed as the Advance Manager and there is no mention of him as a member of the cast.

When the Great War started Harold and his two brothers were of conscription age. By the end of 1916 every able-bodied actor of conscription age was in the armed forces and, as it would be too much of a coincidence to suppose that all three boys were medically unfit, one or more of them had presumably joined up. By the end of 1917, the Entertainment Branch of the NACB had been formed under the control of Basil Dean and it is quite possible that they were involved with Forces' entertainment, but we have found no concrete evidence of such service, nor was the war mentioned by Harold or Jonty to those of their fellow actors whom we have met. In the 1920s and 1930s our only references to Harold involve London theatres, *Oedipus at Colonus* at the Scala in 1926 with Ralph Richardson and John Laurie in the cast; *Hamlet* at the Court in 1930 with Esme Percy as Hamlet, and *Othello* at the Savoy in 1930 with Paul Robeson as Othello and Peggy Ashcroft as Desdemona. Unfortunately Harold, by now 40 years of age, was 'a guard' in one play and an extra in the others. It is some consolation to find that in *Othello* the extras also numbered Alastair Sim.

By now it would have been evident to Harold that he was not to achieve the success of his father, nor to command leading roles. He was a very competent provincial rep actor and was to spend the rest of his professional life in the provinces. He was with Harry Hanson's Court Players in 1940 and in 1942 joined the Fortescue Players at the Wigan Hippodrome, playing a variety of character and supporting roles and receiving due commendation from the local press. The actor Colin Bean, who was at school in Wigan at the time and who published his autobiography recently, has vague recollections of Harold, but by the time that Colin had joined the Hippodrome in 1944 for his first professional engagement, Harold had moved on. From working for Frank Fortescue, Harold returned to Harry Hanson's Court Players at Worcester and Westcliff-on-Sea.

Raymond Graham, who sadly died in 1999, remembered him well. Raymond at the time was playing the leading roles at Westcliff, where Harold continued with character and supporting roles – butlers, vicars, policemen and, in *The Chinese Bungalow*, a Chinese servant. Raymond told us that Harold was of medium height – 5'8" or so – fairly well built and with a likeness to William. Harold and Jonty, whom Raymond also knew, were good, versatile actors of the period.

Wyn Calvin met Harold in 1946 at Redcar, where they were with the

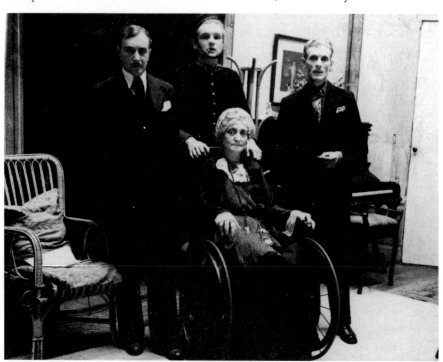

48   Harold Dewhurst (first on left) in *Night Must Fall*, June 1943.

188

Fortescue Victory Players. He remembered him as a very experienced character actor, who excelled in comedy roles, and also as a very lonely and rather sad man whose sadness was not expressed but emerged nevertheless. Wyn could still picture Harold walking up and down the prom at Redcar learning his lines for the next play. A couple with whom Harold became very friendly at Redcar were Harold and Veronica Twidle. Harold Twidle was not in the theatre, but his wife, the actress Veronica Lumley, still appears on television. She was considerably younger than Harold Dewhurst, but recalls that he would visit them and have lengthy discussions with her husband. Unfortunately Harold Twidle died a few years ago and, as Veronica said, he would undoubtedly have been able to provide us with much more background detail about Harold. Veronica confirmed that Harold was of stocky build and had a good voice. He was not a smart dresser, habitually wearing an old Burberry mac with a silk scarf, brown trousers and no hat.

As we heard later, his appearance was quite different from that of his brother Jonty, who was smart, dapper and who always wore a soft brown trilby. As it is Harold remains a rather shadowy figure. There was no mention by him of his parents, his brother William, or his theatrical background. He was however proud of his successful brother Jonty, but seemed to resent the fact that when he was in poor financial circumstances Jonty had declined to help him. Wyn Calvin told us that Harold was semi-settled in the Cleveland area during the Second World War and seems to have remained there subsequently. The last positive appearance we have for him is in February 1948 at the New Pavilion, Redcar, where he was appearing in *Rope*.

But the biggest mystery of all is that surrounding the death of Harold. His Equity subscription was paid up to and including 1965. Veronica Twidle recalls seeing his obituary and is sure that he died in the Middlesbrough area. The indications are that he died within a few years of 1965. We have searched the St. Catherine's House Index from 1950 to 1980 and have found no entry where the name, description and age correspond with the known facts, or even approximate to them. We have also searched the burial and cremation records at the Middlesbrough Crematorium and again have found nothing. Of course he died, and of course his death must have been registered here unless he died abroad. But indications are that he was in very poor circumstances in his later life: he would almost certainly not have been able to go abroad. A sad thought occurs to us that possibly his circumstances were so poor that when he died no one knew who he was, and that consequently an incorrect name and occupation might have been used. We continue to look, but wonder whether we will ever find the answer to the mystery of the fate of Harold B. Dewhurst.

★　★　★

Jonty Dewhurst, or P. Jonty Dewhurst as he sometimes styled himself, was, like his brother Harold, a very competent provincial rep actor and his obituary in the *Stage* referred to him as 'a distinguished character actor'. He also evidently excelled in comedy roles. Hubert Warren, who in 1947 was with Harry Hanson's Court Players at Hastings, remembers Jonty, at the time a member of the Westcliff company. Hubert told us that Jonty, as well as being a character actor, was something of a character himself. He was 'rather eccentric and prone to drying up – not averse to sticking his head up the chimney and asking the prompter what was next'. In 1944 Peter Green and Nicholas Brent joined the Court Players at the Prince's Theatre, Bradford, where they met Jonty and his wife, Vera, both of whom were established members of the company.

The Players then moved to the Lyceum, Sheffield, and in 1945 Peter and

49　P. Jonty Dewhurst with Harry Hanson's Court Players.

Nicholas joined the Forces. Peter recalls that he and Nicholas shared a dressing room with Jonty. He remembers Jonty as 'a lovely man [who] was extremely helpful to me, as at that time I was only sixteen years old. He had a fund of theatrical stories, lots of good humour and taught me the secrets of character make-up. He was a quiet man, very dapper and so gentle in demeanour'. Nicholas Brent recalls Jonty as 'small in build, not someone of striking appearance, although dapper and a smart dresser'. Vera Dewhurst is remembered as quiet, appearing in small or non-speaking roles and often involved as assistant stage-manager.

Neither Nicholas nor Peter remembers any mention of children or involvement in the First World War, although it is quite probable that Jonty was conscripted, and we have found no mention of theatrical activity during the war years. Jonty however was more broadly talented than his brother Harold. He was a gifted amateur artist and the author, either by himself or in collaboration, of seven plays, all of which were professionally produced. His first play *Mrs 'Arris* was written in 1927 and was followed two years later by *The House on the Moor* (originally *The Snatcher*), an example of the haunted house type of comedy thriller popular at the time and possibly influenced by the 1927 film *The Cat and the Canary*. Other plays such as *Boy Wanted* and *No Home of Their Own* sought to address social issues, though not with marked success.

Jonty's obituary gives his date of death as 17 February 1955. We obtained a copy of his death certificate, which showed that he was at the time living in Uppingham, Rutland, and his death was registered by his widow, Vera. Our visit to Uppingham proved fruitful on two counts. We were delighted to find Jonty's grave almost immediately, but were then faced with another mystery. The inscription on the stone read:

'In Loving Memory of
P. Jonty Dewhurst
Died 17th February 1955
Aged 65
Till We Meet Again
Loved By Us All.'

We understood he had no children, so who were 'Us All' who loved him? And, more exciting still, daffodils had been placed on the grave – and they were still quite fresh. Our attempts to solve this latest mystery continued over a 16-month period, involving articles in the local church magazine and the press, appeals through Radio Leicester, notes left on the

191

grave requesting anyone leaving flowers to contact us and speaking with any inhabitants of Uppingham who might have some information. All to no avail. After 16 months of fascinating though time-consuming enquiry, we reluctantly came to the conclusion that 'Loved By Us All' referred to Vera and the Court Players at Westcliff, of which Jonty had been a popular member. And the flowers? That some kind person with more than enough for their own needs had put a few on a nearby grave which had none.

Our second stroke of luck involved a visit to the local pharmacy in Uppingham (part of our door-knocking and questioning), where we met the pharmacist, Mr John Steward, who remembered Jonty and more particularly his wife Vera. They had moved to Uppingham in 1954 and Jonty had died within a year. Their house in Orange Street was next door to Mr Steward's aunt, and she and Vera became firm friends. Unfortunately both ladies died some time previously so again the trail went cold. However Mr Steward told us that Jonty had been a talented artist and said that he had a painting which Vera had given to his aunt. He had no great desire to keep it and on our next visit to Uppingham we were delighted to purchase it from him. Re-framed, signed by P. Jonty Dewhurst in 1934, it is now one of our prized Dewhurst possessions. We wonder whether we will ever find any more of his pictures. The Probate Registry has no record of a will or any application for probate or letters of administration for either Jonty or Vera. It was also evident from the small house in Orange Street that Jonty had not made much money from his acting or the performance of his plays. Although Harold might well have been disappointed that his brother offered him no practical help, it was probable that he was unable to do so.

* * *

Daisy, Jonathan's youngest child, did not make the stage her career. My father's cousin, Eric Wilcock, remembers that she used to visit his mother fairly regularly in the 1940s and 1950s, but Eric was either abroad in the Forces or at work and saw little of her himself. He believes she was married twice, had children and moved from Leigh to the Preston area in the early 1950s. Our researches show that she had a daughter, Daisy Frances, and possibly a son, Jack, but we have tried without success to trace them or any of their descendants. As Jonathan's three sons appear to have left no issue we seem to have come to the end of the road. There is however one matter about which we are very grateful to Daisy. In 1955, when her uncle Alfred Rivers died, she dealt with the administration of his estate. He had a considerable amount of material relating to his stage career and she passed this, together with a few items relating to her parents, to the Victoria and Albert Museum, where it is now safely kept in twelve boxes as the 'Alfred Rivers Collection'.

* * *

William Henry Bostock Dewhurst made his first stage appearance at the age of three and for all his adult life appears to have been fully employed in his theatrical career. The information we have obtained suggests that as an actor he was more naturally talented than his brothers and generally he mixed in more elevated company, spending most of his stage years in London. None of the three boys followed their father into Shakespearian or other strong dramatic roles, and William, like Harold and Jonty, was principally a character actor. His obituary in the *Stage* recorded that 'he was much in demand for character parts, for which he was admirably suited'. Jonathan Dewhurst regretted the fact that he did not pursue his career in London and no doubt voiced this thought to his sons. Both Harold and Jonty spent some time in

50   William and his wife Beatrice on tour in *Hindle Wakes* in 1913.

London, but soon migrated to the provinces. William on the other hand went to London early in his career and became mainly involved with London theatres and provincial tours. Like his brothers he was of medium height and by the time he reached his 40s was of portly physique and almost bald.

One of the most popular and successful plays of 1912 was *Hindle Wakes* by Stanley Houghton, who had accepted £100 from Annie Horniman of the Gaiety Theatre, Manchester for the sole rights. The play was presented at the Gaiety and by the Horniman company in London. In July 1912 Miss Horniman's business manager Edwin T. Heys married and Miss Horniman gave him the touring rights to the play as a wedding present. It was so successful that Heys left the Gaiety to take charge of his several touring companies. In November 1913 one of the companies came to the Theatre Royal, Leigh. The cast included William Dewhurst and Beatrice Fielden-Kaye, who, as Beatrice Maud Woods, had married William the year before. The *Leigh Chronicle* reported that William had been connected with six of Heys's companies and had played the part of Christopher Hawthorn over 300 times! These details bear testimony to the popularity of the play and also to William's ability as a character actor. At the age of 24 he was playing the part of a middle-aged weaver and must have been doing so for virtually the entire period that Heys had been touring the play. The *Chronicle* commented:

'An interesting fact to local play-goers is that the part of the old slasher, Christopher Hawthorn, is played in a remarkably effective manner by Mr Wm. H. Dewhurst, son of the late Mr Jonathan Dewhurst, who was for about 14 years lessee and manager of the Leigh Theatre Royal. The mantle of the father has apparently fallen upon the son, for young Mr Dewhurst plays the part of the phlegmatic, though tender-hearted slasher to the life. His quiet dignified style is in keeping with the character and he uses his fine resonant voice to great advantage. His wife (Miss Beatrice Fielden-Kaye) plays the part of his wife in the drama and shows a wonderful conception of a typical old Lancashire weaver with a raucous, shrill voice and a keen eye to the main chance. Only a Lancashire woman could do this part justice, for it requires a thorough acquaintance with Lancashire life to reproduce it.'

We have no details of any theatrical activity by William during the years of the First World War, but in 1914 a son, Paul, was born to William and his wife.

51   Dorothy Dewhurst aged 27.

It was at this point that we were faced with another of our Dewhurst mysteries. As we mentioned in the previous chapter, the report in the *Leigh Chronicle* of the death of Jonathan referred to 'one of his daughters looking after the house'. But we had found reference to only one living daughter, Daisy, who was the Miss Dewhurst present at the funeral. We assumed that the implied reference to two daughters was merely a journalistic error, but then we read William's obituary. The *Stage* (28 October 1937) commented that 'He [William] was the brother of Dorothy Dewhurst, the actress, with whom he lived' and the same comment was made in *The Times*. This came as a complete bombshell. Was Dorothy in fact Jonathan's daughter and if so was she a child of his marriage to Fanny – in which case was she older or younger than the four children of whom we were aware – or was she a child of an earlier marriage? Why was she not mentioned in the report of Jonathan's funeral? Could it have been that she had been born before he married Fanny? Might it be that she was not his child but had been adopted and raised as his daughter? Or could it be that she was not William's sister and the description was used to throw a cloak of respectability over an illicit relationship? William's obituary made no mention of his wife Beatrice.

195

Tracing details of Dorothy's acting career proved relatively easy – and more of that anon – but establishing precisely who she was proved to be far more difficult and, again, very time-consuming.

Beatrice did not appear to be acting with William in the early 1920s and by 1925 he and Dorothy were appearing in the same productions. William died in 1937 without leaving a will and his estate passed to his widow, Beatrice Maud Dewhurst, who was then living in Chelsea.

But to return to his acting career. Apart from a lengthy national tour of *The Jeffersons* with Wilfred E. Shine's company in 1920/21, we have nothing recorded until early 1925, when William and Dorothy were appearing in Manchester at the Rusholme Theatre. Later that year they were presenting a one-act play, *The Odd Trick*, as part of a variety show touring northern theatres. The only point of interest is the appearance of the young Robert Donat in the cast. For the next six years they remained in London. At the Everyman and Royalty theatres in 1926 William shared the role of 'Rummel' with Charles Laughton in Ibsen's *Pillars of Society* and his obituary refers to his appearance in one of the Fred Terry/Julia Neilson productions of *The Scarlet Pimpernel*, although we have so far been unable to find corroboration.

The Regent Theatre in King's Cross was the home of Martin Sabine's London Repertory Company and very convenient for the Dewhursts, who were then living in King's Cross. Dorothy was engaged by the Regent company in September 1926 and William joined her the following March. For the next four years, virtually without a break, they appeared in rep at the Regent: six nights a week, two performances each evening and a different play every week. During this period they appeared together in 171 productions with a further 36 for Dorothy alone. The plays presented were good standard repertory fare – comedy, farce, thriller, drama and melodrama. *The Silver King* was presented, as was *Hindle Wakes*, but this time William was promoted from the weaver of Chris Hawthorn to the mill-owner of Nathaniel Jeffcote. Dorothy played Mrs Hawthorn, the role taken in Leigh by Beatrice. When John Drinkwater's *Abraham Lincoln* was played, the part of Lincoln was taken by W.E. Holloway. For the special 1928 Christmas show Oscar Asche visited the Regent to produce his record breaking *Chu Chin Chow*, taking the leading role of Abu Hasan himself, with William playing the dual roles of Kasim Baba and Baba Mustafa, for which his singing of the Cobbler's Song was praised in the press. Asche is quoted as saying, 'Your Cobbler is the best I've ever had. It's always a treat to have an actor in one's company'. Serious drama during the period daringly included Coward's *The Vortex* and Brieux' *Damaged Goods*, the 'Astounding Scientific

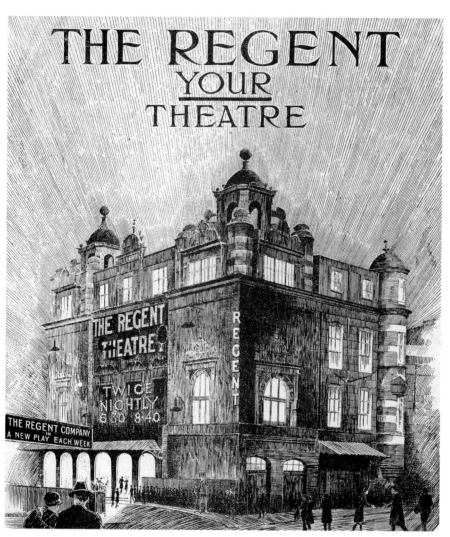

52   The Regent Theatre, London, where William and Dorothy were members of
Martin Sabine's London Repertory Company for several years.

53   Oscar Asche in *Chu Chin Chow*.

Play', which the publicity warned was 'For Adults Only'. It ran for two weeks to packed houses.

Apart from the occasional tour the Dewhursts were now established in the West End, although they were largely playing at different theatres. Film work was also becoming an increasingly important part of their acting careers. William appeared in 12 films between 1934 and 1937, and for Dorothy we have traced 23 films and two television productions (see Appendices 3 and 5). During this period William appeared in some notable stage productions. *Clive of India*, which included Leslie Banks, Gillian Lind, W.E. Holloway, Raymond Huntley and Leo Genn in the cast, had a run of 409 performances at Wyndham's Theatre followed by a lengthy season at the Savoy. In 1936 he played 'Garble' in *The Happy Hypocrite* which ran for 68 performances at His Majesty's Theatre with Ivor Novello, Vivien Leigh, Viola Tree and Isabel Jeans. Late that year William and Dorothy appeared in *Young Madame Conti* which ran for 50 performances at the Savoy. *The Times* commented:

'The presiding Judge is drawn with shrewd humanity by Mr William

54 Ivor Novello, Vivien Leigh and William Dewhurst in *The Happy Hypocrite* at His Majesty's Theatre, London, in 1936.

Dewhurst and the better drawn because the temptation to comic relief, in the narrow sense, is firmly resisted.'

When the play transferred to New York, however, the *New York Times* saw it only as a vehicle for Constance Cummings. The critic evidently did not like courtroom drama and commented that the scene was virtually a still life and:

'... it is further vexed by the monotonous and inaudible voices of some of the actors, notably the president of the court whose voice has the soothing tone of a slumber song.'

This perhaps reflected the different expectations of courtroom drama on the other side of the Atlantic. A minor point of interest is that hidden away among the jurymen, spectators and witnesses is the name Mary Martin – the same Mary Martin, we rather think, who 12 years later made such a hit in *South Pacific*. There were signs that the relentless pace of life in the theatre

199

was beginning to tell on William's health and it may be that this affected his performance in New York. On his return to England much of his time was taken up with filming. His last stage appearance that we have traced was in *The Man Who Meant Well* at the Arts Theatre in June 1937. Happily, we think, Dorothy was also in the cast. In March that year, William's son Paul joined the International Brigade to fight in the Spanish Civil War. He was killed almost immediately. William was not informed until August. He took the news very badly and never recovered. He died from heart failure on 26 October 1937, only three days after completing his role as the butler in the film *Sailing Along*.

Dorothy had been in the theatre all her adult life, appearing mainly in the North, including the Liverpool Rep, early in her career. In 1917 she married the actor George Bernard Copping, who was 15 years her senior. Bernard Copping was already a successful actor and the author of several plays when he met Dorothy. There is no record of the reason for their separation, but they each went their own way in the theatre. As well as provincial tours, Copping played seasons in London and was involved with Miss Horniman's Gaiety Theatre and the Liverpool Playhouse. He was an inspirational director of the Plymouth Rep from 1929 to 1934. He died in 1939, two years after William.

Dorothy Dewhurst was an actress who was always in demand. Capable, reliable and well-organised she was indispensable in a variety of supporting and character roles. Talented, with a wide range of dialects − *Spotlight* lists, 'North Country, West Country, Welsh and Irish' and in a later edition, 'all dialects' − she always gave 100 per cent and never provided less than a first-rate performance. We have amassed a considerable amount of detail about her career, far more than it is appropriate to include here, and we will therefore refer only to a few milestones.

Her film work stretched from 1936 to 1957 and included landmarks in film history such as *Wings of the Morning* (1937), Britain's first technicolour film with Henry Fonda, Annabella, Leslie Banks and John McCormack; *South Riding* (1938) with Ralph Richardson, Edmund Gwenn and John Clements, and *Pygmalion* (1938) with Leslie Howard and Wendy Hiller. There were also lighter offerings such as *Old Mother Riley Joins Up* (1939). Most of the plays in which she appeared had London runs with pre- or post-London tours, but real success came with *Little Women* in 1941, which visited 23 provincial theatres before a six-week run at the Westminster Theatre, London. Dorothy played Aunt March throughout, the *Stage* commenting that 'The querulous Aunt March finds an amusing exponent in Dorothy Dewhurst who is much applauded'. *Little Women* was one of Patrick

MacNee's first major roles, but unfortunately for the theatre he was called up shortly thereafter. He remembers Dorothy with affection as 'a famous actress and a dear lady', but as he says, 'at 19 one tended not to notice what anyone else did!' Their paths were not to cross again.

In 1943 John Steinbeck's *The Moon is Down* proved to be another success with a tour lasting from April to September, including 112 performances at the Whitehall Theatre, London. There was a second tour of ten weeks in 1944. Dorothy played the mayor's wife opposite Lewis Casson. Paul Scofield had a small part in the full run of the play and remembers Dorothy well. We have kept his comments until the end of the chapter. 1945 saw another great success, *The Cure for Love* by Walter Greenwood, which followed a provincial tour with 220 performances at the Westminster Theatre. The role of Jack Hardacre was initially played by Robert Donat and later taken over by Wilfred Pickles. Marjorie Rhodes was 'magnificent as his mother' and Dorothy was Mrs Jenkins, his would-be mother-in-law. Priestley's *Eden End* at the Duchess Theatre in 1948 provided Dorothy with the role of Sarah, 'an old servant ... cleverly of her time and place', which she was able to repeat in the television production.

In February 1953 the provincial tour of Graham Greene's first play *The Living Room* preceded a run of 307 performances at Wyndham's Theatre and a further run at the Q Theatre. It was an excellent, thought-provoking drama with a first-rate cast including Eric Portman, Violet Farebrother, Mary Jerrold and, in her first West End role, the young Dorothy Tutin. The week at the Alexandra, Birmingham, in March 1953, provided me, as a young man who had just completed his National Service, with an enthralling theatrical experience – I admired Eric Portman, fell in love with Dorothy Tutin and was completely unaware that Dorothy Dewhurst, who initially played 'Mary, the daily woman', was someone about whom I would be writing 47 years later. Shortly after the start of the London run Mary Jerrold left the cast and Dorothy took over the part of Miss Teresa Browne. Dorothy Tutin very kindly wrote to us with her memories of Dorothy Dewhurst and *The Living Room*:

'I remember Dorothy well – *The Living Room* was my first West End role and the whole process of rehearsals fairly fraught – the director didn't want me (but I didn't know that!) and I was trying so hard (having been told I had no temperament) in a scene with Dorothy where I had to be very angry with her – that I shouted and burst a blood vessel and had to be silent until we opened! She was so kind and supportive – and *such* a good actress. But I'm afraid I don't remember

201

anything very personal. She may have told me the story of her life on one of our long journeys on tour – but I don't think so. I think she was quite private.'

A tour of *Hedda Gabler* followed with 154 performances at the Westminster Theatre. *Theatre World* (October 1954) commented:

'Rarely can such enthusiasm have greeted a revival of this Ibsen play, but the occasion more than merited the tremendous ovation which has followed each performance at the Lyric, Hammersmith.'

The company included Peggy Ashcroft, George Devine and Rachel Kempson, with Dorothy as Bertha the housekeeper, later in the run taking over the role of Miss Julia Tesman. *The Potting Shed* which toured in 1958, with three months at the Globe Theatre, was described by the *Stage* as Graham Greene's best play. John Gielgud had 'never been so good in a modern part'. All the major roles provided 'flawless performances'. 'Dorothy Dewhurst, as the gardener's wife, and Redmond Phillips, as the priest, have

55   *The Potting Shed* with (left to right) Sarah Long, John Gielgud, Dorothy Dewhurst and Gwen Frangcon-Davies toured with great success in 1958.

only one relatively short scene each. But these are vital and both artists are brilliant in them.'

Our search for Dorothy's death certificate was eventually rewarded. The certificate described her as 'Dorothy Dewhurst, otherwise Dorothy Irene de Singleton Copping, widow of George Bernard Copping, Actor'. She died in 1959 aged 73 and from this information we were then able to trace her birth certificate. Her parents were Edward Peel Dewhurst and Emily, née Heap. Edward Peel Dewhurst was born in 1852 and from his birth certificate we found that his parents were Edward Dewhurst and Elizabeth, née Davidson. The family came from Lancashire and Cheshire, as did 'our' Dewhursts, but Dewhurst was a very common name in that part of the North of England. We were therefore forced to the conclusion that if William and Dorothy were indeed related, it was a more distant relationship and we decided that no more time should at present be spent on that line of enquiry.

We know nothing of the nature of William and Dorothy's relationship. They evidently enjoyed very busy acting careers, which were closely linked, and frequently appeared in the same productions. They were obviously happy together and derived mutual support from the arrangement. From everything we have discovered it is clear that they were well-liked and respected, both professionally and personally. The reader may well ask why we mention Dorothy at all, in that she was not related (or closely related) to the family. There are two reasons why we feel it appropriate. Firstly, she may well have been a distant blood relation – we do not know. Secondly, she was certainly an integral part of William's life and career, as much as, if not more than, if she had been married to him and her place in our story is as relevant as if she had been a close blood relation.

The very kind letter we received from Paul Scofield is, we feel, the best tribute to her that we can provide:

'I remember Dorothy Dewhurst so well. She played the mayor's wife opposite Lewis Casson in *The Moon is Down*, a John Steinbeck story of a Nazi-occupied town in Norway during the 1939–45 war. I played a small part in it and my wife was also in the production. It was in fact during the run of that play that we were married. Dorothy was the sweetest woman I have ever worked with, as an actress she represented comely middle age with enormous grace and modesty. She was perhaps somewhat self-effacing with a completely *un*egotistic and totally professional attitude to her work. She was pretty, with dark (if greying) hair taken back into a soft bun, her eyes were large and bright and dark

brown, she had a neat body and was always charmingly and conserva-
tively dressed. She had a lisp and when she spoke to Joy and me of
her treasured collection of pot dogs, we always relished her calling
them "pot dogth". She was one of the type of experienced actresses of
her time who was entirely self-sufficient – we toured for many months
and Dorothy was always on time, quietly fulfilling her professional
duties and then disappearing back to her lodgings – always alone but
obviously never lonely. We both loved her. I fear that this is not much
help to you, but at least I can express my devotion to her.'

18

A Final Word

The driving force in Dewhurst's life had been the theatre. He saw it as a great educational and civilising force, at least equal in importance to the influence of the church. His mission was to present good drama and the highest standards of production to as many people as possible – to spread his message as much to the workers in the Australian outback as to the audiences in the palatial theatres of Melbourne or Sydney, to the provincial audiences of industrial Lancashire and the sophisticated play-goers of Drury Lane.

The spotlight of public attention has, in the past, focused more on the managers of London theatres than on their provincial cousins. However, the contributions of provincial managers of the Victorian Era are now, perhaps, receiving greater recognition – men such as Edward Saker at Liverpool, Charles Calvert at Manchester, James Rodgers at Birmingham and Wilson Barrett at Hull and Leeds.

The following article from a Liverpool weekly was reproduced in the *Leigh Chronicle* on 16 March 1894. It reported an interview with an actor who had known Dewhurst since his early days on the stage and includes interesting comment on his management of the Leigh Theatre Royal. We have so far been unable to identify the weekly or the actor:

'I knew Jonty before I was born – histrionically I mean. I knew him as a stock actor with the late Charles Calvert in Manchester. I remember when in '69 or '70 he came like a good soul from the Theatre Royal, Sheffield, then under the management of the genial William Gomersall, where he was playing leading business, to appear for a friend's benefit at the Theatre Royal, Oldham, playing Romeo to an excellent cast. Oh yes, I was in it, so it must have been good – that goes without saying. I have seen him in the entire round of the legitimate and have witnessed his performance of the Ghost at the Princess's, London, to Wilson Barrett's Hamlet. I also saw his splendid performance of the Holy Clement and have always watched his career with keen interest and admired the motto he chose:

> "What merit to be dropped on fortune's hill?
> The honour is to mount it." (*Hunchback*)

'I wished him God speed a few days prior to his departure for Australia some years ago, where I was pleased to learn he was received with open arms, as any and every artiste is always received by those warm-hearted Colonials. I have known him in Calcutta, where he achieved a great triumph, despite his inadequate support, I was *not* in the cast then, hem! The honoured guest of the leading European residents, the officers of the different regiments stationed there, at whose mess he was always welcomed when opportunity afforded, and particularly so by the ex-King of Oude, whose *paradisical* residence it is impossible to describe, or to be appreciated by anyone unacquainted with Eastern splendour. I have not time to tell you of the oft-repeated story of my escape from Calcutta. I am simply going to tell you of my experience of Jonty's Theatre in Leigh.

'No, you rascal, it is not of colossal proportions, it is not even a pretentious theatre with a magnificent façade and porticos, but it is a theatre where the comforts of the travelling artistes are considered. It is a theatre where you might say, "lower out that cut-wood, I have a sandwich in my pocket, and let us imagine we are having a picnic". You could spread your humble fare upon the bare stage, being perfectly certain that it would not be contaminated by any dirt or filth.

'Why is this, and why should it be relegated to this particular Lancashire playhouse that comfort, cleanliness and consideration should be studied? Simply because, as I take it, Jonty is an actor and a gentleman. In considering his own interests he does not neglect his contributors. Art with him is not a secondary principle, for he does not sacrifice it to Mammon. You hear a modest knock at your dressing room door. "Who's there?" you enquire. "It is I, are you comfortable, gentlemen?" "Yes, thank you." "Anything you want, please ask for." It has often been said that Shakespeare spells bankruptcy! I disagree with that statement and here you have a proof. Jonty Dewhurst produced *King Lear* and ran it a week in such a small town as this, and so successful was his venture that he is producing *Much Ado About Nothing* for the present Easter, another Shakespearean revival, also to run a week.

'Now, you shoddy managers with palatial residences, magnificent theatres, fully mortgaged and a working staff of one half man and boy, and who never come near the theatre except at night, and to draw more than your share, take a lesson from Jonty, a sound, honest, conscientious, typical "Lancashire lad", who scorns to prostitute his art for £ s.d.'

Dewhurst lived for the theatre and in the end it disappointed him. Not the theatre as such, nor those who worked in it, but the changes which inevitably were taking place – variety and the infant cinema – and the influence was perhaps greater in the provinces than in London. For every actor about whom much is written and recorded, there must be at least 100 over whom the waters of time have closed without trace, but without whose contribution the theatre would not exist. To them also we raise our glass as we salute

Jonathan Dewhurst – the Lancashire Tragedian.

APPENDIX 1

Productions traced in which Jonathan Dewhurst appeared and, where known, the roles he played

c.1845 (Age 8) Amateur performance at Theatre Royal, Wigan.

Pre-April 1865 Appeared at Southport 'as a very young man' reciting selections from the poets. His first appearance was at the Saturday evening concerts given by James Turvey in the Town Hall before the Cambridge Hall was built.

1865 **MANCHESTER – Prince's Theatre**
25 April 1865 – Manager – Charles Calvert
24 May 1866 Company included Charles and Adelaide Calvert,
  Henry Irving, Fred Maccabe, J.L. Toole, Henry Haynes, J.L. Cathcart,
  J. Hudspeth, Florence Haydon, Teresa Furtado and Maria B. Jones

Arrah-na-Pogue	Major Coffin; Patsy
Aunt Charlotte's Maid	Mayor Volley
Betsy Baker	Mr Crumney
Billing and Cooing	Sir Thomas Turtle
Birthplace of Podgers	
Chimney Corner, The	
Daughter of the Regiment, The	
Extremes	Mr Cunningham
Hamlet	The Ghost
Heir-at-Law, The	Kenrick
Hunchback, The	Master Wilford
Ingomar the Barbarian	
King Lear	Earl of Gloster
Lady of Lyons, The	Mons Deschappelles
Little Bo-Peep	Opoponax
Louis XI	Philip de Cominie
Macbeth	Rosse
Maid with the Milking Pail, The	Lord Philander
Merchant of Venice, The	Duke of Venice
Midsummer Night's Dream, A	Egeus
Money	Capt Dudley Smooth
Much Ado About Nothing	Friar
Othello	Lodovico
Our Clerks	
Parish Clerk, The	
Richelieu	Baradas
Rip Van Winkle	Hendrick Vedder
Robert Macaire	Germeuil
Steeple Chase	Buzzard
Tempest, The	Gonzalo

Through Fire and Water	
Two Foscari, The	Chief of the Ten
Weavers, The	
Wife, The	Antonio

1867
12 August –
9 October 1867

OXFORD – Victoria Theatre
Clifford Cooper's company
Company included G.F. Sinclair, Edmund Phelps, Jane Rignold and
Mrs Cooper

Bartons of Barton Wold	
Belphegor, the Mountebank	Lavarennes
Bowl'd Out	
East Lynne	Mr Carlyle
Fraud and Its Victims	Mr Warrington
Hamlet	Hamlet
Hunchback, The	Master Walter
Ill-Treated Il Trovatore	
Isle of St Tropez, The	Antoine
Katherine & Petruchio	
Kiss In The Dark, A	
Lady Audley's Secret	
Lady of Lyons, The	Claude Melnotte
Leah	
Macbeth	Rosse; Macbeth
Married Daughters and Young Husbands	
Married Life	
Masks and Faces	
Meg's Diversion	
Merchant of Venice, The	Antonio
New Way to Pay Old Debts, A	Sir Giles Overreach
Not a Bad Judge	
Othello (Act III)	
Plot and Passion	
Richelieu	Baradas
Rob Roy	
Rough Diamond, The	
School for Scandal, The	
Sheep in Wolf's Clothing, A	
Spoiled Child, The	
Still Waters Run Deep	John Mildmay
Stranger, The	The Stranger
Ticket-of-Leave Man, The	Mr Gibson
Unfinished Gentleman, The	

1868

NEWCASTLE – Theatre Royal
Manager – E.D. Davies
Dewhurst joined the company and recorded that he played all the heavy parts
for the entire season

9–10 March 1868

MANCHESTER – Prince's Theatre
Manager – Henry Haynes
Company included Henry Haynes and Maria B. Jones

Othello	Othello
King O'Scots	Lord Dalgarno

MANCHESTER – Free Trade Hall
and elsewhere including

	OLDHAM	recital
	CARLISLE – (Summer season)	
	OXFORD – Victoria Theatre	
1869 20 January 1869	**OLDHAM – Town Hall**	recital
30 January 1869	**OLDHAM – Theatre Royal** *Jack Long of Texas*	
8 February 1869	**OLDHAM – Town Hall**	recital
24–28 July 1869	**OLDHAM – Theatre Royal** *Capitola* *Corsican Brothers, The* *Duke's Motto, The* *Othello*	Othello
October 1869	**SHEFFIELD – Theatre Royal** Manager – W. Gomersal *Turn of the Tide, The*	Philip Earnscliffe
18–20 December 1869	**OLDHAM – Theatre Royal** *Othello* *Romeo & Juliet* *Rose of Ettrick Vale, The* *Taming the Shrew* [sic]	Othello Romeo
1869/1870 (4 weeks) (4 weeks) (6 weeks)	**OLDHAM – Theatre Royal** *Faust & Marguerite* *Macbeth* *Richard III* *Tempest, The*	Mephistopheles Macbeth Richard Prospero
	ROCHDALE – Prince of Wales Manager – George Warde A 'short season' of plays	
	MANCHESTER – Prince's Theatre Manager – Charles Calvert *King of Scots* [sic]	
	SHEFFIELD – Cutlers' Hall	recital
	BRADFORD – Theatre Royal Manager – Charles Rice	lead roles
1871 March 1871	**LIVERPOOL – Alexandra Theatre** Manager – Edward Saker *Amy Robsart*	Varney
8–21 April 1871	**BIRMINGHAM – Prince of Wales** Manager – James Rodgers *Amy Robsart*	Varney

9 May 1871	**SHEFFIELD – Theatre Royal** Manager W. Gomersal *Amy Robsart*	Varney
29 May 1871 (12 nights)	**BIRMINGHAM – Prince of Wales** *Amy Robsart*	Varney
	NEWCASTLE – Theatre Royal *Lady of the Lake, The*	Fitzjames
14–30 August 1871	**GLASGOW – Theatre Royal** *Lady of the Lake, The*	Fitzjames
23 September– 9 December 1871	**DRURY LANE – Theatre Royal** *Rebecca*	Sir Brian de Bois Guilbert
25 November 1871	**DRURY LANE – Theatre Royal** Special Farewell Benefit for Harry Boleno Scene from *Othello*	Othello
18 December 1871– 24 February 1872	**WIGAN – Weston's New Royal Amphitheatre** Pitney Weston Company *Black-Eyed Susan* *Don Caesar de Bazan* *Hamlet* *Katherine & Petruchio* *Macbeth* *Merchant of Venice, The* *Othello* *Richard III*	 William Don Caesar Hamlet Petruchio Macbeth Shylock Othello Richard
1872	**BOLTON – Theatre Royal** Pitney Weston Company	
26 February 1872	*Othello*	Othello
27 February 1872	*Macbeth*	Macbeth
1 April 1872	**BIRMINGHAM – Prince of Wales** *Rebecca*	Sir Brian de Bois Guilbert
21 September– 19 December 1872	**DRURY LANE – Theatre Royal** Manager – F.B. Chatterton *Lady of the Lake, The*	 Douglas
1873	**HAYMARKET – Theatre Royal**	
9 June 1873 (12 nights)	**BIRMINGHAM – Theatre Royal** With Mlle Beatrice's Company *Nos Intimes*	Dr Tholosan
June onwards	**Tour** with Mlle Beatrice's Company	
	CHORLEY – Charles Duval's Theatre in 'a round of Shakespeare's plays'	

1874	**WIGAN – Theatre Royal**	
15–20 June 1874	*Hamlet*	Hamlet
	Macbeth	Macbeth
	Merchant of Venice, The	Shylock
	Othello	Othello

Provincial Tour with the Australian actress Mrs Gladstane's company

28–30 September 1874	**BIRMINGHAM – Theatre Royal**	
16–18 November 1874	With Mrs Gladstane's company	
	East Lynne	Mr Carlyle
	Elizabeth	Earl of Essex
	Frou Frou	

SHOREDITCH – National Standard Theatre
Manager – John Douglass
Rank and Fame

1875	**SHOREDITCH – National Standard Theatre**	
	With Mrs Gladstane's company	
	Elizabeth	Earl of Essex

SOUTHPORT
Various benefit performances and a production of:
Antigone   Creon

1876	**NEWCASTLE – Theatre Royal**	
21 February–	Company included Phyllis Glover and Kate Compton	
18 March 1876	*Antigone*	Creon
	Lady of the Lake, The	Fitzjames
	Macbeth	Macduff; Macbeth

4 September–	**LIVERPOOL – Alexandra**	
4 December 1876	Manager – Edward Saker	
	Rob Roy	Rob Roy
	Winter's Tale, The	Leontes

| 1878 | **LONDON –** | |
| August 1878 | *Richelieu* | Richelieu |

20 December 1878	**LIVERPOOL – Liverpool Dramatic Lodge, 1609**	
	A special performance in aid of Masonic Hall Fund	
	Still Waters Run Deep	John Mildmay

1880	**LEIGH – Assembly Rooms**	
19–24 January 1880	Supported by his own 'powerful legitimate company' including	
	Edmund Tearle, F.A. Scudamore, Leonard Calvert and Kate Clinton	
	Hamlet	Hamlet
	Intrigue	
	Lady of Lyons, The	Claude Melnotte
	Lottery Ticket, The	
	Merchant of Venice, The	Shylock
	Othello	Othello
	Richard III	Richard
	Still Waters Run Deep	John Mildmay
	Taming of the Shrew, The	Petruchio

Tour with his 'specially selected company':

29 March– 3 April 1880	**OLDHAM – Theatre Royal**	
	Don Caesar de Bazan	Don Caesar
	Hamlet	Hamlet
	Lady of Lyons, The	Claude Melnotte
	Merchant of Venice, The	Shylock
	Othello	Othello
	Richard III	Richard
	Richelieu	Richelieu
	Robert Macaire	Robert Macaire
	Taming of the Shrew, The	Petruchio
	BLACKPOOL	
	Much Ado About Nothing	Benedick
	SOUTHPORT	
	Much Ado About Nothing	Benedick
8–13 November 1880	**LEIGH – Assembly Rooms**	
	Hamlet	Hamlet
	Intrigue	
	Katherine & Petruchio	Petruchio
	Lady of Lyons, The	Claude Melnotte
	Merchant of Venice, The	Shylock
	Much Ado About Nothing	Benedick
	Richard III	Richard
	Richelieu	Richelieu
	Robert Macaire	Robert Macaire
	Truth Versus Fiction	
9 December 1880	**MANCHESTER –**	
	Much Ado About Nothing	Benedick
1881	**Farewell Tour** including:	
4 April 1881 (6 nights)	**BURNLEY – Theatre Royal**	

TOUR OF AUSTRALIA

16 July–12 August 1881	**MELBOURNE – Theatre Royal and Athenæum**	
	Company included Charles Holloway, Bland Holt and Flora Anstead	
	Don Caesar de Bazan	Don Caesar
	Hamlet	Hamlet
	Katherine & Petruchio	Petruchio
	Lady of Lyons, The	Claude Melnotte
	Merchant of Venice, The	Shylock
	Much Ado About Nothing	Benedick
	Othello	Othello
	Richard III	Richard
	Richelieu	Richelieu
	Still Waters Run Deep	John Mildmay
	Taming of the Shrew, The	Petruchio

213

20 August–September 1881 (6 weeks)	**SYDNEY – Queen's Theatre** Company included Newton Griffiths, J.B. Steele, George Melville and Marion Willis

Hamlet	Hamlet
Othello	Othello; Iago
Richelieu	Richelieu

10 October– 14 November 1881	**BRISBANE – Theatre Royal** Company included Miss Julia Featherstone

Don Caesar de Bazan	Don Caesar
Faint Heart Never Won Fair Lady	Ruy Gomez
Hamlet	Hamlet
Katherine & Petruchio	Petruchio
Lady of Lyons, The	Claude Melnotte
Louis XI	Louis XI
Macbeth	Macbeth
Much Ado About Nothing	Benedick
Othello	Othello
Richard III	Richard
Richelieu	Richelieu
Romeo & Juliet	Romeo
Still Waters Run Deep	John Mildmay

21–25 November 1881	**BRISBANE – Ipswich School of Arts** With Theatre Royal Company

Don Caesar de Bazan	Don Caesar
Hamlet	Hamlet

Appearances in **TOOWAMBA, GATTON** and **LAIDLEY**

1882 16–21 January 1882	**BENDIGO (SANDHURST) – Royal Princess's Theatre**

Hamlet	Hamlet
Katherine & Petruchio	Petruchio
Merchant of Venice, The	Shylock
Othello	Othello
Richelieu	Richelieu

23 January– 4 February 1882	**BALLARAT – Academy of Music** Supported by W.J. Holloway's company Company included W.J. Holloway, Charles Holloway, W.H. Metcalfe, Essie Jenyns and Annie Mayor

Faint Heart Never Won Fair Lady	Ruy Gomez
Hamlet	Hamlet
Katherine & Petruchio	Petruchio
Lady of Lyons, The	Claude Melnotte
Louis XI	Louis XI
Macbeth	Macbeth
Merchant of Venice, The	Shylock
Othello	Othello; Iago
Richard III	Richard
Richelieu	Richelieu

20 February– 4 March 1882	**HOBART – Theatre Royal** Company included Miss Carry George, H.N. Douglas and Walter Reynolds	
	Don Caesar de Bazan	Don Caesar
	Faint Heart Never Won Fair Lady	Ruy Gomez
	Katherine & Petruchio	Petruchio
	Louis XI	Louis XI
	Macbeth	Macbeth
	Merchant of Venice, The	Shylock
	Othello	Othello
	Richard III	Richard
	Richelieu	Richelieu
	Romeo & Juliet	Romeo
	Still Waters Run Deep	John Mildmay
8–9 March 1882	**HOBART – Town Hall** *A Night With The Poets*	recitals
10–13 March 1882	**LAUNCESTON – Mechanics' Institute** *A Night With The Poets*	recitals
10–15 April 1882	**BENDIGO – Royal Princess's Theatre**	
	Hamlet	Hamlet
	Katherine & Petruchio	Petruchio
	Louis XI	Louis XI
	Othello	Othello
	Richard III	Richard
	Richelieu	Richelieu
24 May 1882	**BENDIGO – Masonic Hall** For Queen Victoria's Birthday *A Night With The Poets*	recital
	SYDNEY – Theatre Royal Company included George Rignold, J.R. Greville and J.F. Cathcart	
8 July– 31 August 1882	*Youth*	The Vicar
4 August– 6 October 1882	*Lights O' London, The*	Seth Preene

TOUR OF INDIA

1883 1 January– 17 March 1883	**CALCUTTA – Corinthian Theatre** With the Pomeroy Dramatic Combination Company included Louise Pomeroy and Arthur Elliott	
	As You Like It	
	Cymbeline	Leonatus Posthumous
	Diplomacy	
	East Lynne	Mr Carlyle
	Hamlet	Claudius
	Hunchback, The	
	Ingomar, The Barbarian	Ingomar
	Katherine & Petruchio	Petruchio
	Lady Clancarty	Donagh Macarthy, Earl of Clancarty
	Lady of Lyons, The	Claude Melnotte
	Led Astray	Count Rudolph Chandoce

215

London Assurance	
Macbeth	Macbeth
Masks and Faces	Sir Charles Pomander
Much Ado About Nothing	Benedick
Pique	Mathew Standish
Pygmalion & Galatea	Pygmalion
Richelieu	Richelieu
Romeo & Juliet	Mercutio
School For Scandal, The	Charles Surface
Still Waters Run Deep	John Mildmay
Taming of the Shrew, The	Petruchio

18 March 1883 onwards

CALCUTTA – Theatre Royal
With the Gaiety Company
Company included Lizzie Gordon

Don Caesar de Bazan	Don Caesar
Faint Heart Never Won Fair Lady	Ruy Gomez
Hamlet	Hamlet
Louis XI	Louis XI
Merchant of Venice, The	Shylock
Othello	Othello
Stranger, The	The Stranger

CALCUTTA – Dalhousie Institute   recitals

SIMLA and 'up country'

RETURN TO ENGLAND

SOUTHPORT – Pavilion Theatre at Winter Gardens

30 July–
4 August 1883

WIGAN – Theatre Royal
Manager – George Warde
JD's company included Edmund Tearle and Adelaide Calvert

Hamlet	Hamlet
Louis XI	Louis XI
Macbeth	Macbeth
Much Ado About Nothing	Benedick
Richelieu	Richelieu
School for Scandal, The	Charles Surface

13 August 1883 onwards

OLDHAM – Theatre Royal
Manager – Lindo Courtenay
Company as for Wigan

Hamlet	Hamlet
Louis XI	Louis XI
Macbeth	Macbeth
Much Ado About Nothing	Benedick
Othello	Othello
Richelieu	Richelieu

1884
22 April 1884

MANCHESTER – Prince's Theatre
For Ben Brierley's Testimonial Fund

Richelieu (4th Act)	Richelieu

	Tour of *Claudian* with Wilson Barrett's company:	
	Company included Leonard Boyne	
	Claudian	The Holy Clement
15–27 September 1884	**BRADFORD – Theatre Royal**	
29 September– 4 October 1884	**NOTTINGHAM – Theatre Royal**	
16 October 1884– 21 March 1885	**LONDON – Princess's Theatre**	
	With Wilson Barrett's company	
	Hamlet	The Ghost
1885	*Claudian* tour continued:	The Holy Clement
30 March–4 April 1885	**NOTTINGHAM – Theatre Royal**	
27 April–2 May 1885	**BRADFORD – Theatre Royal**	
	Tour of *A Night With The Poets*	recitals
10–15 August 1885	**LEIGH – Theatre Royal**	
	JD's company included Rose Murray	
	Hamlet	Hamlet
	Lady of Lyons, The	Claude Melnotte
	Louis XI	Louis XI
	Macbeth	Macbeth
	Othello	Othello
	Richelieu	Richelieu
23–28 November 1885	**LEIGH – Theatre Royal**	
	JD's company included Fanny Rivers and Kate Varley	
	Faint Heart Never Won Fair Lady	Ruy Gomez
	Merchant of Venice, The	Shylock
	Much Ado About Nothing	Benedick
	Richard III	Richard
	Romeo & Juliet	Romeo
	School for Scandal, The (Screen Scene)	Charles Surface
	Stranger, The	The Stranger
	Taming of the Shrew, The	Petruchio

Tour with his own company presenting a selection of plays from their repertoire as noted above with the addition of *Carpio*, a new play by John Finnamore in which Dewhurst played Bernardo Del Carpio:

December 1885	**SCARBOROUGH – Londesborough Theatre**
1886 February 1886	**WARRINGTON – Public Hall**
	BOOTLE – Beaconsfield Hall
March 1886	**BURNLEY – Theatre Royal**
	SALFORD – Prince of Wales
	WAKEFIELD – Theatre Royal
	ST HELENS – Theatre Royal
April 1886	**WIDNES – Theatre Royal**
May 1886	**DONCASTER – Theatre Royal**
	BRADFORD – Prince's Theatre
June 1886	**SHEFFIELD – Theatre Royal**

July 1886	**SOUTHPORT – The Hall**	
	With Fanny Rivers	recital
July–August 1886	**CHORLEY** and other venues	recitals
August 1886	**LEICESTER – Theatre Royal**	
	Macbeth	Macbeth
	LONDON – Olympic Theatre	
	Manager – Mrs Anna Conover	
2–17 September 1886	*Macbeth*	Banquo
18–27 September 1886	*Macbeth*	Macbeth
1 November–	**Tour** with Augustus Harris's '*Run of Luck*'	
20 December 1886	company:	
	Run of Luck, A	Squire Selby
	SHEFFIELD – Theatre Royal	
	NEWCASTLE – Tyne Theatre	
	BRADFORD – Prince's Theatre	
	GLASGOW – Theatre Royal	
	EDINBURGH – Theatre Royal	
	LIVERPOOL – Court Theatre	
	Tour of *A Night With The Poets*	recitals
1887	**MANCHESTER – Theatre Royal**	
	With Mrs Dewhurst (Fanny Rivers)	
	Duke's Motto, The	Henry of Navarre
29 June 1887	**LEIGH – Theatre Royal**	
	A Night With The Poets	recital
19 December 1887	**MANCHESTER – Prince's Theatre**	
	Still Waters Run Deep	Claude Melnotte
1888	**LIVERPOOL – Alexandra Theatre**	
26 March–	Manager – Mrs Saker	
14 April 1888	*London Assurance*	Harkaway
	Perfect Love	The Caliph
	Pygmalion & Galatea	Leucippe
	('under the superintendance of Mr W.S. Gilbert')	
July 1888	**MANCHESTER –**	
	Merchant of Venice, The	Shylock
August 1888	**LEIGH – Theatre Royal Lessee/Manager**	
3–8 December 1888	*Hamlet*	Hamlet
	Macbeth	Macbeth
	Merchant of Venice, The	Shylock
	Richard III	Richard
	Stranger, The	The Stranger
1889	**LEIGH – Literary Society**	
8 April 1889	*An Hour With The Poets*	recital
1890		
31 March 1890	**LEIGH – Literary Society**	recital

218

Tour with H.C. Arnold's 'Lights O' London' company:

	Lights O' London, The	Seth Preene
Week commencing:		
7 April	**BLACKPOOL – Prince of Wales**	
14 April	**DEWSBURY – Theatre Royal**	
21 April	**WAKEFIELD – Royal Opera House**	
28 April	**ACCRINGTON – Princess's Theatre**	
5 May	**PRESTON – Prince's Theatre**	
12 May	**STOCKPORT – New Theatre Royal**	
19 May	**YORK – Theatre Royal**	
26 May	**NEWCASTLE – Tyne Theatre**	
2 June	**JARROW – Theatre Royal**	
9 June	**BIRKENHEAD – Theatre Royal**	
27 October–	**LEIGH – Theatre Royal**	
1 November 1890	*King Lear*	Lear
1891	**MANCHESTER – Arts Club**	
15 January 1891	*A Night With The Poets*	recital
19 June 1891	**LEIGH – Assembly Rooms**	
	A Night With The Poets	recital

Tour with Wilson Barrett, acting as his understudy for main parts and also doing special secondary parts. Rehearsals prior to the tour took place at the Olympic Theatre, London
Company included Wilson Barrett, Maud Jeffries, Alfred Rivers
Selection of plays included:
Acrobat, The
Ben-my-Chree
Claudian
Hamlet
Lights O' London, The
Miser, The
Othello
Silver King, The

Week commencing:	
20 July	**PLYMOUTH – Theatre Royal**
27 July	**CROYDON – Theatre Royal**
3 & 10 August	**ISLINGTON – Grand Theatre**
17 August	**BRIGHTON – Theatre Royal**
24 August	**RAMSGATE – Amphitheatre**
31 August	**PORTSMOUTH – Theatre Royal**
7 September	**LEEDS – Grand Theatre**
14 September	**NOTTINGHAM – Theatre Royal**
21 September	**HANLEY – Theatre Royal**
28 September	**CARDIFF – Theatre Royal**
5 October	**BIRMINGHAM – Theatre Royal**
12 October	**ST HELENS –**
19 October	**LIVERPOOL – Court Theatre**
26 October	**BRADFORD – Theatre Royal**
2 November	**MANCHESTER – Theatre Royal**
9 November	**BLACKBURN – Theatre Royal**
16 November	**HULL – Theatre Royal**
23 November	**SHEFFIELD – Alexandra**

	Tour with Mrs Dewhurst, included:	
7 December 1891	**WIGAN – Royal Court Theatre**	
(1 week)	*Lady of Lyons, The*	Claude Melnotte
	Louis XI	Louis XI
	Richelieu	Richelieu
1892	**LEIGH – Literary Society**	
24 October 1892	*A Night With The Poets*	recital
1893	**LEIGH – Theatre Royal**	
	Supported by J.F. Preston's company	
18 April 1893	*Merchant of Venice, The*	Shylock
21 April 1893	*Othello*	Othello
26 June 1893	**MANCHESTER – Queen's Theatre**	
	Belphegor the Mountebank	Belphegor
1894	**LEIGH – Theatre Royal**	
26 March 1894	*Much Ado About Nothing*	Benedick
31 March 1894	*Hamlet*	Hamlet
1895		
9 April 1895	*A Night With The Poets*	recital
1896	Supported by F.A. Scudamore's company	
22 December 1896	*Richelieu*	Richelieu
1897		
21 December 1897	*Othello*	Othello
1898		
18 July 1898	*Macbeth* (Dagger Scene)	Macbeth
14 November 1898	**LEIGH – Literary Society**	
	Hamlet	recital
20 December 1898	**LEIGH – Theatre Royal**	
	Stranger, The	The Stranger
	Katherine & Petruchio	Petruchio
1899	**LEIGH – Literary Society**	
11 December 1899	*Hamlet*	recital
19 December 1899	**LEIGH – Theatre Royal**	
	Supported by Mr & Mrs Giffard's company	
	Richelieu	Richelieu
1900		
November 1900	**MANCHESTER –**	
	Othello	recital
3 December 1900	**LEIGH – Literary Society**	
	Othello	recital
	WIGAN – Workhouse	recital

1901 18–19 June 1901	**LEIGH – Theatre Royal** *Merchant of Venice, The*	Shylock
	MANCHESTER – Comedy Theatre For Osmond Tearle *Richard III* *Othello*	Richard Othello
4 November 1901	**LEIGH – Literary Society** *A Night With The Poets*	recital
1902 August 1902	**SOUTHPORT –** **Convalescent Hospital**	recital
17 November 1902	**LEIGH – St Joseph's Lecture Hall** *A Night With The Poets*	recital
1903 26 January 1903	**LEIGH – Literary Society** Selections from Shakespeare	recital
1906 5 February 1906	**LEIGH – Literary Society** Selections from Shakespeare	recital
	LEIGH – Theatre Royal Supported by Ian Maclaren's Shakesperian & Classical Repertoire Co., including B. Iden Payne and Frank Cellier	
16 April 1906 20 April 1906	*Othello* *Merchant of Venice, The*	Othello Shylock
1907	**CHORLEY – Grand Theatre** *Richelieu*	Richelieu
May 1907	**CHORLEY** *Hamlet*	recital
1908 April 1908	**CHORLEY** *Othello*	recital
1909 20 August 1909	**WIGAN – Royal Court Theatre** Supported by the Allan Wilkie Rep Co. His final stage performance. *Richelieu*	 Richelieu

APPENDIX 2

Jonathan Dewhurst – Theatrical Roles

Acrobat, The	Duke of Montblazon
Amy Robsart	Varney
Antigone	Creon
Arrah-na-Pogue	Major Coffin; Patsy
Aunt Charlotte's Maid	Mayor Volley
As You Like It	(*)
Bartons of Barton Wold	(*)
Belphegor, the Mountebank	Lavarennes; Belphegor
Ben-my-Chree	(*)
Betsy Baker	Mr Crumney
Billing and Cooing	Sir Thomas Turtle
Birthplace of Podgers	(*)
Black-Eyed Susan	William
Bowl'd Out	(*)
Capitola	(*)
Carpio	Bernardo del Carpio
Chimney Corner, The	(*)
Claudian	The Holy Clement
Corsican Brothers, The	(*)
Cymbeline	Leonatus Posthumous
Daughter of the Regiment, The	(*)
Diplomacy	(*)
Don Caesar de Bazan	Don Caesar
Duke's Motto, The	Henry of Navarre
East Lynne	Mr Carlyle
Elizabeth	Earl of Essex
Extremes	Mr Cunningham
Faint Heart Never Won Fair Lady	Ruy Gomez
Faust and Marguerite	Mephistopheles
Fraud and Its Victims	Mr Warrington
Frou Frou	(*)
Hamlet	The Ghost; Hamlet; Claudius
Heir-at-Law, The	Kenrick
Hunchback, The	Master Wilford; Master Walter
Ill-Treated Il Trovatore	(*)

222

Ingomar the Barbarian	Ingomar
Intrigue	(*)
Isle of St Tropez, The	Antoine
Jack Long of Texas	(*)
Katherine and Petruchio	Petruchio
King Lear	Earl of Gloster; Lear
King O' Scots	Lord Dalgarno
Kiss In The Dark, A	(*)
Lady Audley's Secret	(*)
Lady Clancarty	Donagh Macarthy, Earl of Clancarty
Lady of Lyons, The	Mons Deschappelles; Claude Melnotte
Lady of the Lake, The	Fitzjames; Douglas
Leah	(*)
Led Astray	Count Rudolph Chandoce
Lights O' London, The	Seth Preene
Little Bo-Peep	Opoponax
London Assurance	Harkaway
Lottery Ticket, The	(*)
Louis XI (W.R. Markwell)	Philip de Cominie
Louis XI (Boucicault)	Louis XI
Macbeth	Rosse; Macbeth; Macduff; Banquo
Maid With The Milking Pail, The	Lord Philander
Married Daughters and Young Husbands	(*)
Married Life	(*)
Masks and Faces	Sir Charles Pomander
Meg's Diversion	(*)
Merchant of Venice, The	Duke of Venice; Antonio; Shylock
Midsummer Night's Dream, A	Egeus
Miser, The	(*)
Money	Capt Dudley Smooth
Much Ado About Nothing	Friar; Benedick
New Way to Pay Old Debts, A	Sir Giles Overreach
Nos Intimes	Dr Tholosan
Not a Bad Judge	(*)
Othello	Lodovico; Iago; Othello
Our Clerks	(*)
Parish Clerk, The	(*)
Perfect Love	The Caliph
Pique	Mathew Standish
Plot and Passion	(*)
Pygmalion and Galatea	Pygmalion; Leucippe
Rank and Fame	(*)
Rebecca	Sir Brian de Bois Guilbert
Richard III	Richard
Richelieu	Baradas; Richelieu
Rip Van Winkle	Hendrick Vedder
Robert Macaire	Germeuil; Robert Macaire
Rob Roy	Rob Roy
Romeo and Juliet	Romeo; Mercutio

Rose of Ettrick Vale, The	(*)
Rough Diamond, The	(*)
Run Of Luck, A	Squire Selby
School for Scandal, The	Charles Surface
Sheep in Wolf's Clothing, A	(*)
Silver King, The	(*)
Spoiled Child, The	(*)
Steeple Chase	Buzzard
Still Waters Run Deep	John Mildmay
Stranger, The	The Stranger
Taming of the Shrew, The	Petruchio
Taming the Shrew [sic]	Petruchio
Tempest, The	Gonzalo; Prospero
Through Fire and Water	(*)
Ticket of Leave Man, The	Mr Gibson
Truth Versus Fiction	(*)
Turn of the Tide, The	Philip Earnscliffe
Two Foscari, The	Chief of the Ten
Unfinished Gentleman, The	(*)
Weavers, The	(*)
Wife, The	Antonio
Winter's Tale, The	Leontes
Youth	The Vicar

Notes:

1. The above roles represent all we have managed to trace, but inevitably in a career as long as Dewhurst's he must have played many other roles.
2. The above list includes plays in which we know he took part, but where we have not been able to establish the character played. These are indicated with a (*).

APPENDIX 3

William Dewhurst – Film Appearances

Title	Starring	WD's Role	Year Released
Blossom Time	Richard Tauber	An opera singer	1934
Sabotage	John Loder, Sylvia Sidney, Oscar Homolka	The Professor	1936
Second Bureau			1936
Bulldog Drummond at Bay	John Lodge, Victor Jory	Reginald Portside	1937
Dark Journey	Conrad Veidt, Vivien Leigh Ursula Jeans, Cecil Parker	Killer	1937
Dinner at the Ritz	Annabella, David Niven, Francis L. Sullivan	Devine	1937
Non-Stop New York	John Loder, Anna Lee, Francis L. Sullivan	Mortimer	1937
Toilers of the Sea		Landois	1937
Victoria the Great	Anna Neagle, Anton Walbrook	John Bright (a cameo)	1937
The Windmill	John Laurie, Hugh Williams	Mons Asticot	1937
Sailing Along	Jessie Matthews, Roland Young, Alastair Sim	Winton	1938
Twenty-One Days	Vivien Leigh, Laurence Olivier, Leslie Banks, Francis L. Sullivan	Lord Chief Justice	1940

APPENDIX 4

Plays Written By P. Jonty Dewhurst

1927	*Mrs 'Arris*	(in collaboration with Gilbert Payne)
1929	*The Snatcher*	(later re-titled *The House on the Moor*)
1936	*Dying to Live*	(in collaboration with Mary Stafford)
1946	*Families Supplied*	
1948	*Have Twins And Like It*	
1952	*The Cosh And The Woman*	(later retitled *Boy Wanted*)
1956	*No Home Of Their Own*	(in collaboration with P. Jones-Blakey)

APPENDIX 5

Dorothy Dewhurst – Film Appearances

Title	Starring	DD's Role	Year Released
Full Speed Ahead			1936
Grand Finale		Miss Pittaway	1936
Love at Sea	(featured Beatrix Fielden-Kaye, William Dewhurst's wife)	Mrs Hackworth Pratt	1936
Two on a Doorstep	Kay Hammond	Mrs Beamish	1936
Behind Your Back	Dinah Sheridan		1937
London Melody	Anna Neagle, Robert Douglas		1937
Passenger to London			1937
Wings of the Morning	Henry Fonda, Annabella, Leslie Banks, John McCormack	Gypsy fortune-teller	1937
East of Ludgate Hill			pre-1938
Mr Smith Carries On	Edward Rigby, H.F. Maltby		pre-1938
Bedtime Story		Lady Blundell	1938
Father O' Nine			1938
Pygmalion	Leslie Howard, Wendy Hiller, Wilfrid Lawson	Mrs Birchwood, the vicar's wife	1938
South Riding	Ralph Richardson, Edmund Gwenn Ann Todd, John Clements		1938
The Mind of Mr Reeder (released in 1940 in America as The Mysterious Mr Reeder)	Will Fyffe, Kay Walsh, George Curzon		1939
Old Mother Riley Joins Up	Arthur Lucan, Kitty McShane Martita Hunt, H.F. Maltby	Mrs Rayful	1939
A Stolen Life	Michael Redgrave, Elisabeth Bergner, Wilfrid Lawson		1939
Facing the Music	Chili Bouchier, H.F. Maltby, Wally Patch		1941
A Place of One's Own	James Mason, Dennis Price, Margaret Lockwood	(voice only)	1944

Stranger at My Door			1950
The Lark Still Sings			1954
Raising a Riot	Kenneth More, Ronald Squire, Shelagh Fraser, Mandy Miller, Olga Lindo, Michael Bentine	Mother	1955

Television

Pride and Prejudice	Mrs Reynolds
Eden End	Sarah

Note: We have been unable to identify some of Dorothy Dewhurst's specific film roles or details of several of the films.

FAMILY TREE (SIMPLIFIED) OF DEWHURST, RIVERS, MORELLI FAMILIES

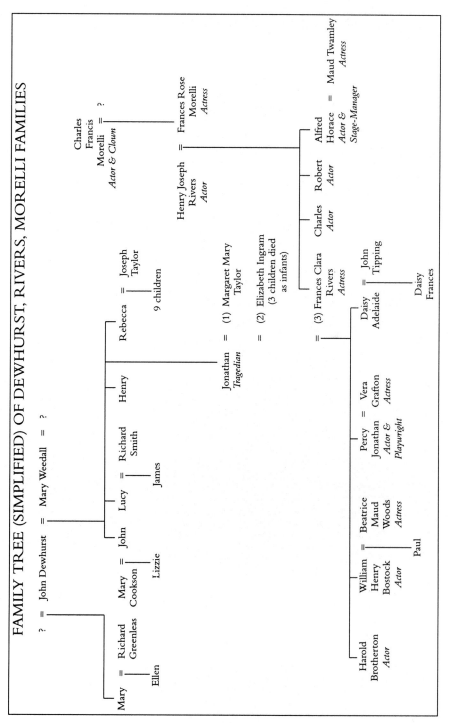

LIST OF SOURCES

Primary Sources
Playbills, programmes and photographs. Our principal source of information has been contemporary newspaper reports and these have been quoted liberally throughout the text.

Books
Baker, Michael, *The Rise of the Victorian Actor* (London 1978)
Banham, Martin (ed.), *The Cambridge Guide to the Theatre* (Cambridge 1992)
Best, Geoffrey, *Mid-Victorian Britain 1851–1875* (London 1971)
Bingham, Madeleine, *Henry Irving and the Victorian Theatre* (London 1978)
Booth, Michael R., *Theatre in the Victorian Age* (Cambridge 1991)
Brooks, Phillips, *Letters of Travel* (New York 1895)
Calvert, Mrs Charles, *Sixty-Eight Years on the Stage* (London 1911)
Dean, Basil, *Seven Ages* (London 1970)
Foulkes, Richard, *The Calverts – Actors of Some Importance* (London 1992)
Gooddie, Sheila, *Annie Horniman, a Pioneer in the Theatre* (London 1990)
Greenhill and Giffard, *Travelling by Sea in the Nineteenth Century* (London 1972)
Harrison, J.F.C., *Early Victorian Britain 1832–1851* (London 1988)
Hartnoll, Phyllis (ed), *The Oxford Companion to the Theatre* 4th Ed. (Oxford 1983)
Holloway, David, *Playing the Empire* (London 1979)
Holloway, Laura C., *Adelaide Neilson – A Souvenir* (New York 1885)
Huk, David, *Ben Brierley 1825–1896* (Manchester 1995)
Irving, Laurence, *Henry Irving – The Actor and his World* (London 1951)
Jerrams, Richard, *Weekly Rep* (Droitwich, Worcs. 1991)
Lunn, John, *A History of Leigh* (Runcorn, Cheshire 1958)
Mander, Raymond and Mitchenson, Joe, *The Theatres of London* (London 1975)
McGuire, Paul (with Betty Arnott and Frances M. McGuire), *The Australian Theatre* (Melbourne 1948)
Marston, John Westland, *Our Recent Actors* (London 1888)
Mullin, Donald (compiled and edited by), *Victorian Actors and Actresses in Review* (Westport, Connecticut 1983)
Nicoll, Allardyce, *A History of Late Nineteenth Century Drama 1850–1900* (Cambridge 1946)
Palmer, Scott, *British Film Actors' Credits* (London 1988)
Payne, B. Iden, *A Life in a Wooden O: Memoirs of the Theatre* (New Haven, 1977)
Redgrave, Michael, *In My Mind's Eye* (London 1983)
Rowell, George, *The Victorian Theatre: a Survey* (Oxford 1956)
Scott, Clement, *The Drama of Yesterday and Today* (London 1899)
Southern, Richard, *The Victorian Theatre: a Pictorial Survey* (Newton Abbot 1970)
Tammita-Delgoda, Sinharajah, *A Traveller's History of India* (Moreton-in-the-Marsh 1994)
Taylor, George, *Players and Performances in the Victorian Era* (Manchester 1989)
Towse, J.R., *Sixty Years of the Theater* (New York 1916)
Trewin, J.C., *The Edwardian Theatre* (Oxford 1976)
Trewin, J.C., *The Theatre Since 1900* (London 1951)
Wardle, Arthur C., *Steam Conquers the Pacific* (London 1940)
Wyke, Terry and Rudyard, Nigel *Manchester Theatres* (Manchester 1994)

Newspapers and Journals

Birmingham Post
Chorley Weekly News
Court Circular
Daily Gazette
Daily Telegraph
Echo
Era
Era Almanack
Evening Standard
Glasgow Herald
Illustrated London News
Illustrated Sporting and Dramatic News
Jackson's Oxford Journal
Leigh Chronicle
Leigh Journal
Leigh Observer
Manchester City News

Manchester Courier
Manchester Examiner and Times
Manchester Guardian
Manchester Weekly Times
Midland Counties Herald
Newcastle Daily Journal
Observer
Oldham Chronicle
Porcupine
Sheffield and Rotherham Independent
Sheffield Daily Telegraph
Southport Visitor
Stage
Standard
Theatre World
The Times
Wigan Observer

Australia

Age
Ballarat Courier
Bendigo Advertiser
Brisbane Courier
Launceston Examiner
Mercury
Melbourne Bulletin
Melbourne Weekly Times
Queensland Times
Sydney Bulletin
Sydney Morning Herald
Tasmanian Mail

India

Indian Daily News

Other

The Theatre in Leigh – a paper by
   Stephen Hampson, 1973 –
   copy held in local history
   archives of Leigh Library.

INDEX

Newspapers, magazines and periodicals, and Theatres are shown together under these headings.

Holloway, Charles 74, 91
Holloway, David, *Playing the Empire* 90, 91
Holloway, George 91
Holloway Theatre Company 90
Holloway, W.E. 90, 198
Holloway, W.J.: background 90; other 74, 91, 93, 95
Holmes, C.B. 9
Holt, Bland 71
Horniman, Annie 168, 194
Houghton, Stanley 194
Howard, J.B. 43, 45
Hudspeth, Jane 30
Hudspeth, John 20, 28
Huntley, Raymond 198

India 100–105
Ingram, Elizabeth (see Dewhurst, Elizabeth)
Ireland, G.R. 88
Irving, (later Sir) Henry: background 20–23; exposure of Davenport Brothers 20–24; other 57, 84, 102, 116, 123, 172, 173
Irving, Laurence 184
Irwin, Miss 42

Jeaffreson, J.C. 123
Jeans, Isabel 198
Jeffries, Maud 129, 148
Jenyns, Essie 91
Jerrold, Mary 201
Jones, H.A. and Herman, H. 115
Jones, Maria B. 27, 46, 47

Kean, Charles 35, 54, 74, 123
Kean, Edmund 123
Kemble, Charles 123
Kemble, John Philip 123
Kempson, Rachel 202
Kendal, Mr and Mrs 51
King, Claude 158
Kipling, Rudyard 102, 105
Kitts, James 95
Knowles, John 19–20, 24
Kotzebue, August 143

Lane, Sarah 35
Laughton, Charles 116, 196
Laurie, John 187
Leigh, Lancs: Assembly Rooms 57, 130, 139; history of theatre in 139–140; 'death' of the theatre 171
Leigh Literary Society 146
Leigh, Vivien 198
Leighton, Margaret 121, 125
Limerick, Mona 168
Lind, Gillian 198
Loraine, H. 40–42
Lunn, Dr John 139, 145
Lytton, Edward George Bulwer, 1st Baron 24, 27, 33, 56, 61, 70, 77, 81

Maccabe, Frederick 23, 24, 96
McIntyre, Mr 44
Macklin, Charles 123
Maclaren, Ian (and company) 166, 168–169
MacNee, Patrick 201
McNeill, A.D. 53
Macready, William 35, 57, 111, 123
Maltby, H.F. 187
Markwell, W.R. 24
Marquis of Lorne Lodge 151
Marriott, Alice 35
Marston, John Westland 46
Martin, Mary 199
Martin-Harvey, (later Sir) John 184, 185
Massey, Rose 27, 28
Mayor, Annie 91
Medway, Marion 78
Melford, Austin: tribute to JD 158–161; other 152
Melville, George 77
Melville, Miss 75
Mendelssohn, Felix 27, 52
Merritt, Paul 99
Montgomery, Walter 74
Morelli, Charles Francis 129, 187
Morelli, Frances Rose (see Rivers, Frances Rose)
Murray, Rose 130